Care

The Highest Stage of Capitalism

Premilla Nadasen

Haymarket Books
Chicago, IL

Published in 2023 by
Haymarket Books
P.O. Box 180165
Chicago, IL 60618
773-583-7884
www.haymarketbooks.org
info@haymarketbooks.org

ISBN: 978-1-64259-966-4

Distributed to the trade in the US through Consortium Book Sales
and Distribution (www.cbsd.com) and internationally through Ingram
Publisher Services International (www.ingramcontent.com).

This book was published with the generous support of Lannan Foundation, Wallace Action Fund, and Marguerite Casey Foundation.

Special discounts are available for bulk purchases by organizations and institutions. Please email info@haymarketbooks.org for more information.

Cover design by Anna Morrison.

Printed in Canada by union labor.

Library of Congress Cataloging-in-Publication data is available.

10 9 8 7 6 5 4 3 2 1

Praise for *Care: The Highest Stage of Capitalism*

"Nadasen takes a deep and discouraging dive into current practices of care as they have been shaped by historical precedents and capitalist greed. Her research illuminates generations of resistance by recipients and uncovers creative approaches to collective care that promise effective solutions to poverty, housing, and the well-being of the ill, the unhoused, children, and the elderly. I hope everyone who wants to understand what is perhaps our greatest contemporary concern will read this book."

—**Alice Kessler-Harris**, author of *In Pursuit of Equity: Women, Men, and the Quest for Economic Citizenship in Twentieth-Century America*

"With this book, Premilla Nadasen has made an invaluable contribution to the ongoing debates around care and capitalism. In clear and concise prose, she takes apart the care-industrial complex that has emerged, like the military- and prison-industrial complexes before it, to wring the last drops of profit from the lives and deaths of working people. An absolutely necessary intervention in the most important political debate of our times."

—**Sarah Jaffe**, author of *Work Won't Love You Back*

"If you think the 'care economy' sounds like a socialist nirvana, think again. Premilla Nadasen reveals how the exploitation and commodification of reproductive labor has enriched corporations, compensated for a shrinking welfare state, and pauperized the very workers responsible for the sustenance, health, and well-being of others. The consequences of a gendered racial capitalist 'care economy' are deepening inequality, more broken people, and a culture of sacrifice that only serves to mask misery and low wages. Once you read this highly original, incisive, and unsettling book, you will no longer honor nurses by banging pots together but by joining a picket line instead."

—**Robin D. G. Kelley**, author of *Freedom Dreams*

"Premilla Nadasen is a pathbreaking scholar of Black women's labor and welfare organizing, as well as a radical feminist activist in her own right. She has a passion and a powerful talent for telling the complicated truths that define working-class women of color's lives. In *Care: The Highest Stage of Capitalism*, Nadasen offers a brilliant interrogation of the exploitative and profit-driven care system in the United States. To fully understand racial capitalism in the twenty-first century, you have to read this book."

—**Barbara Ransby**, professor and director of the Social Justice Initiative, University of Illinois at Chicago, and author of the award-winning *Ella Baker and the Black Freedom Movement*

"Premilla Nadasen's *Care* is a clear, useful tool for thinking about both the brutal exploitation of capitalist care relations and the transformative power of grassroots collective care projects. Nadasen deftly weaves insights from labor resistance, Black feminism, anticolonial struggles, disability justice, and other radical traditions into a cohesive analysis of reproductive labor that will be a readable primer for classroom and community use as much as it is a visionary inquiry into what new social relations we need to be building right now. This book is a generous contribution to the most urgent conversations happening in social movements and embattled communities right now."

—**Dean Spade**, author of *Mutual Aid: Building Solidarity During This Crisis (and the Next)*

For all the organizers, low-wage workers, and grassroots community advocates who are practicing and fighting for care as a site of joy and radical possibility

Contents

Introduction

The Labors of Life

The notion of care seems simple enough. Care is about nurturing, feeding, nursing, assisting, and loving human beings. It is "the work that makes all other work possible"—a slogan first used in the early 2000s by the New York City–based advocacy group Domestic Workers United and later adopted by the National Domestic Workers Alliance. Although it is historically unpaid or underpaid and unaccounted for in gross domestic product (GDP) and other economic measures, without care work, things would simply shut down. Yet, while care is essential to our survival, care as a politics, as discourse, as policy, and as labor is complicated, nuanced, and contradictory.

Our reliance on care work became abundantly clear when the COVID-19 pandemic hit the US in March 2020. Support systems suddenly disappeared, and families grappled with who would take care of the kids, clean the house, and walk the dog. Over 2 million women left the workforce, family relationships were strained, and, while some children managed, others suffered. Some employers expected domestic workers to live in because they were fearful that, otherwise, those workers would bring disease into their homes. Parents realized that, without childcare assistance, it was difficult—if not impossible—to do their jobs; employers had to acknowledge the critical need for childcare for their employees and for the functioning of their workplaces.

1

The shutdown of schools and day cares and the strain on hospitals and nursing homes made essential labor, which includes care but also extends beyond it, more visible. Teachers did double duty, Zooming with students and minding their own children. As hospitals overflowed, people employed in health care worked grueling and dangerous shifts, often forgoing sleep and putting their own well-being, and that of their families, at risk. Supermarket workers stocked shelves or packaged Instacart orders. Truck drivers transported necessary goods, including food and medical equipment. And public transit workers were crucial in enabling essential workers to travel to and from their places of employment. This essential labor falls disproportionately on immigrants, people of color, and white women.

Although the pandemic propelled care to the forefront of the liberal and progressive agenda, care policy has been debated for decades. Feminist economists, policy researchers, the nonprofit sector, and grassroots activists embraced a care agenda in part to push back on neoliberal free-market principles and revive a liberal agenda, often understood as a robust welfare state. For them, investing in care is the most sensible way to create support structures for families and to remake social policy. Care as a policy goal is especially appealing because it connects us all. Everyone needs care. The collective commitment to care and a belief in mutual interdependency have been the basis of many policy proposals over the past few years. This was crystallized during the pandemic with the expansion of the childcare tax credit, assistance for the childcare industry, and funding for low-income childcare programs such as Head Start and the Child Care and Development Block Grant Program.

As promising as a renewed care politics might seem, *care* has become a catchall term that substitutes for rigorous analysis: what a comprehensive care policy looks like, who is left out of care programs, and who benefits from the care economy are all inadequately addressed. The care crisis, for example, is often framed in terms of the "work/family balance," the double burden on working women, and families that lost access to childcare during the pandemic. But how is our analysis of care deepened when we shift our gaze, for example, to disabled people who are also care workers? Or care workers who have to leave their own children to care for someone else's, just to put food on the table? Or people outside the labor market? How is that analysis complicated when we consider the companies profiting from the care crisis?

I wrote this book with two main strategies. First, I draw attention to the inequity of care and how care for some people is built on the backs of other, more vulnerable people. I look at who has care and who doesn't, who benefits from the privatized care economy and who pays the price, and, equally important, why this dysfunctional care system continues to expand, despite the perpetual and recurring care crisis. Although care is framed as universal, much of the mainstream care agenda, labor policy, and government programs benefit the middle class. The poor and working class are usually considered important to the degree that they can meet the needs of middle- and upper-class Americans. The welfare system is rarely brought up as part of the care discourse, even though it can be one of the most important sources of support for the care work of poor families. On top of that, poor single mothers, people who are disconnected from the labor market, many gig workers, and undocumented immigrants are shut out of employment-based benefits such as childcare tax credits or the Family Medical Leave Act. As the remnants of the welfare state have become even more punitive, the poorest families must try to survive without reliable childcare, quality education, health care, and economic security. The discourse of care privileges the care of some people over others.

Second, I shed light on the care economy and how capitalist profit accrues from our basic human need to care for ourselves and our communities. Both the public and private sectors are increasingly finding ways to benefit financially from the care industry. Capitalism has always caused pain, whether through dispossession, forced labor, or environmental destruction. This is not new. But under free-market neoliberal policies, investment in "people as profit" has expanded and accelerated. In this new stage of capitalism, the care economy parasitically feeds off pain; that is, some people's pain translates into other people's profit. This is distinct from what we might call collateral casualties of, for example, communities that were displaced for the purpose of extractive mining or the pain and suffering associated with the exploitation of colonial labor. Now, pain and suffering are lucrative rather than unintended effects. If someone feels pain, Big Pharma will quickly market a pill to alleviate it—but only for the right price and the right person. Companies that aim to meet "care" needs and "help" people adopt mottos like "doing well by doing good."[1] Stock prices are an indication that they are indeed doing well, but it's not altogether clear that they are doing good.

The sanitized discourse of "care work" as mutually beneficial and an alternative to neoliberalism, has, in fact, been deployed in service of neoliberalism. By masking unequal racial and economic access to care and the drive for profit underpinning the care economy, the care discourse transforms the paid and unpaid labor necessary to maintain and reproduce life—what Marxist feminists have called *social reproduction*—into a category disconnected from its larger economic and political significance.

Care work has always served an economic purpose. Because people are both workers and consumers, the state and capital are invested in supporting life and the labor necessary to maintain and reproduce life. The New Deal welfare state—although uneven, hierarchical, and exclusionary—provided some support for care work for white families, elderly and disabled people, and temporarily unemployed workers. In the middle of the twentieth century, high wages for mostly male industrial workers subsidized the unpaid labor of white middle-class housewives, thus ensuring the reproduction of the labor force.

Since the 1970s, the US has transitioned from an industrial economy that economically supported many Americans through government programs or high wages to a neoliberal economy that embraces free-market principles. The closing of factories, along with devastating shifts in state policy, have shredded the economic safety net, reduced wages, weakened the power of the working class, and diminished public services. As more household members enter the workforce to make ends meet, families and households have found it harder to provide and care for themselves and their loved ones. The ensuing crisis has fueled the care economy. Obtaining quality care for loved ones propels people to spend more in this area than ever before, by hiring care workers and purchasing products and services. Those who can have turned to the market, relying on for-profit companies or hiring poorer women to assist them in ensuring their care needs are met. These poorer women then struggle to find care for their own children, which is especially difficult because of their low wages. This reliance on market solutions to solve the care crisis has both widened the class divide and proven to be a boon for capital. In this moment of capitalism, social reproduction is a growing source of profit.

The care economy has benefited ideologically as well as monetarily from the evisceration of the public sector. First, the dismantling of the welfare state sends a message of personal responsibility by criminalizing and stigmatizing people on public assistance.

This, in turn, releases the state from any responsibility to provide for the poor and creates a rationale for and reliance on the market for care needs. Second, diminished services and resources for middle-class families have made life more difficult for them. The state has disinvested in public schools and hospitals and redirected resources to the private sector. Middle-class families increasingly rely on private schools, private hospitals, and buying books on Amazon rather than visiting public libraries. Third, the shredded safety net creates a pool of low-income workers to fuel the growth of a privatized care system in which poor women have little choice but to labor as nannies, home care aides, and in similar occupations, or in work that caters to the needs of the better-off. The expansion of service-sector employment has furthered the class and race divides. These low-paying, exploitative jobs don't provide the pay or benefits to ensure that the workers or their families are cared for or compensated properly. Last, because welfare reform loosened constraints on how states can spend antipoverty funds, tax dollars have been funneled into the private sector. For-profit and nonprofit companies have found it advantageous to partner with state agencies to fill the void left by the state. State-funded programs for the poor are not benefiting the people most in need. Instead, profit is extracted from the poorest of the poor because the carceral state, the child welfare system, the nonprofit sector, and finance companies have all spawned new profit-making mechanisms.

Capitalism's seeming disregard for the well-being of people, families, and communities could signal the demise of the economic system—because, without workers and consumers, capitalism will not survive. Instead, capitalism is remaking itself by turning to forms of accumulation that are rooted in the very crises it has created. Contemporary capitalists earn profit from producing and sustaining humans, sometimes for their labor power but increasingly because they need care. The profits of care accrue from providing market-based services, managing state programs, or financing people's efforts to combat poverty and misery. Look at Care.com, for instance: an online platform for people who want to hire or work as caregivers. It calls itself "the world's largest online destination for care." The website helps families fill the gap between their household care needs and their available time and capacity, which has widened for middle-class families as increasing numbers of women enter the workforce. It has grown exponentially because people need jobs or need care and have nowhere else to turn. But Care.com is not a public service. The company makes a hefty profit as a care marketplace. And, in February 2020, it was bought by a US public holding company, Interactive Corp, for $500 million and made private.[2]

Contrary to predictions that the crisis of social reproduction would undercut capital's ability to produce profit because it would no longer have the labor power to make commodities, the crisis has served instead as a basis for new wealth. During the pandemic, when it seemed that the care crisis had bottomed out, the stock market soared to new heights. Some companies, such as Pfizer and Quest Diagnostics, used the emergency to get rich quick: Quest's net revenue in the last quarter of 2020 was up 56 percent over the same period the previous year and shares were up 127 percent.[3] Pfizer, which also saw a massive increase in earnings, reported that vaccine revenue rose from $1.7 billion in 2019 to $14.6 billion in 2020, accounting for 60 percent of the company's sales.[4] As with so many other neoliberal disasters, capitalism—or what Naomi Klein calls "disaster capitalism"—found ways during the COVID-19 pandemic to adapt and thrive, turning crises into opportunities.[5]

The larger claim this book makes is about the value of a racialized, gendered analysis of social reproduction to understand the character and evolution of capitalism. This book, then, is not about "women's work" but about how capitalism functions. I find the repeated calls to "engender capitalism" somewhat tiring, not because the people calling for it are wrong, but because so many studies of capitalism are *still* written without an analysis of gender or race. Indeed, scholars of race and gender have already racialized and gendered capitalism. We just need to read their work.

Social reproduction theorists argue that the labor of social reproduction is a precondition for capitalist profit because of the labor power it produces.[6] Under nineteenth- and twentieth-century industrial capitalism, profit flowed from the production of goods, which requires land and raw materials as well as people to work in the factories. Tithi Bhattacharya, for example, has explained that social reproduction is important because it produces the workers who produce the products. Without the paid and unpaid labor of cooking, cleaning, health care, education, birthing, and child-rearing, there would be no workers on the assembly line. Capital relies on the labor of social reproduction in order to create labor power, which is then used in the production of commodities. For these Marxist feminists, social reproduction is necessary for capitalist profit but does not create profit itself.

Social reproduction theorists also argue that there is a contradiction between social reproduction and capital accumulation. The more money capital allocates to workers' well-being (which has been the basis of worker organizing), the less money it hands out to shareholders. Therefore, capital has consistently sought to reduce the costs of social reproduction in order to maximize profit. With the dismantling of the welfare state and the rise of neoliberal free-market policies, the disinvestment in worker well-being accelerated to such a degree that it has generated a crisis of care. This crisis of care, Marxist feminist theorist Nancy Fraser argues, will ultimately destabilize capitalism because the crisis is destroying the very thing capital requires to produce profit: labor power.[7]

These Marxist feminist arguments—that the crisis of care is inextricably tied to capitalism and much bigger than the struggle of individual families—are crucial. However, the assertion of commodity production as the only or central profit-making strategy of capitalism results from a limited analysis. Yes, capital produced and earned profit from commodities. But capital also relied on other profit-making schemes, including slavery, finance, and, now, the care economy. And with the decline of commodity production in places like the US, capital has less need to produce workers strictly for assembly lines.

A gendered, racialized perspective, which understands capitalism as inextricably tied to structures of race and gender, shows us that social reproduction is not solely a precondition for capitalist profit but has been a source of capitalist profit for quite some time. Capitalism has long extracted profit from the social reproduction of people of color through slavery and the slave trade. Thus, capital benefited from the labor exploitation of the poorest people (mostly people of color) *and* earned profit from social reproduction, most clearly through the sale of human bodies. Economic extraction from life itself, not only from labor power, has been ongoing for much of the history of capitalism, although it was masked by a racial ideology that naturalized such extraction. If profit is earned from social reproduction, then we can agree that there is no inherent contradiction between capital accumulation and social reproduction as argued by social reproduction theorists.

But even when capital did rely on labor power, it did not invest in the social reproduction of all workers equally. Even before the dismantling of the welfare state, the labor of social reproduction of families of color was rarely supported because they were shut out of state benefits. Instead, women of color were deemed unfit mothers and expected to work. The economic insecurity and care crisis that many middle- and working-class white Americans are facing for the first time has been a reality for most people of color for generations.

Thus, although capital accumulation from social reproduction is operating on a new scale, it is not altogether new. Neither the pandemic nor even neoliberalism created this system of deriving profit from human bodies. When we shift our gaze to the lives of people of color, racial capitalism illuminates the long history of profit extracted from social reproduction. The neoliberal "turn" is less a turn than a speedup—yet this higher gear is important. Today, the public and private sectors are making money off the care economy to an unprecedented degree.

Given capitalists' exploitation of social reproduction, we need to interrogate the belief that a care agenda and more public investment in care—without the necessary oversight—is a viable strategy for addressing the crisis of care and helping the people who need it most. It is crucial to understand care as a site of economic extraction, the role of the state in the care economy, and how the discourse around care obscures what's at stake, because a lack of attention to these issues has hindered our ability to address the care crisis and to develop effective solutions for a more just economy.

For a long time, I believed that leveraging the state could be a building block for a better world by bringing us closer to the goal of economic transformation. The state can be a check on unbridled capitalism; it can provide services and resources to people in need; it can also generate political engagement. As people fight for basic needs, they may develop a deeper structural analysis. Demands for higher monthly welfare payments and housing assistance, for example, offer an economic cushion and create an opening for activism by ordinary people.

I have a framed poster in my living room with a quote from Brazilian Archbishop Hélder Pessoa Câmara that reads: "When I give food to the poor, they call me a saint. When I ask why they are poor, they call me a Communist." This is what happened with programs such as the New Deal in the 1930s and the War on Poverty in the 1960s. People (including poor people), often with federal dollars, started by making reforms in their own communities and ended by asking why inequality existed. But, as the character of the state changed, its carceral functions ballooned and welfare functions shrank. State resources became a grab bag for the political elite, and the potential for ordinary people to use state resources for radical transformation diminished.

Even during the best of times, liberal reforms were paired with new forms of structural inequality. The regulatory apparatus and labor legislation of the New Deal put a brake on radicalism and created new economic and political hierarchies because some workers benefited more than others. The removal of immigration quotas in 1965 was coupled with a new surveillance system on the southwest border.[8] And president Lyndon Johnson's War on Poverty contained the seeds that flourished into an expanded carceral state, as historian Elizabeth Hinton argues in *From the War on Poverty to the War on Crime*, through federal funding that facilitated the militarization of local police departments and co-operation between social service agencies and law enforcement.[9] There is a perpetual tension between the good and the harm done by liberal reforms. It is not altogether clear whether the benefit of state programs in the current moment is outweighed by the damage they cause.

Over the past half century, and particularly during the pandemic, the state has been instrumental in the growth of the care economy and deepening economic inequality. A close analysis of the care economy today shows us that the public policies that many of us on the left championed have only widened the existing class and race divisions. The care economy is an example of patterns of profit-making from the lives and labors of the marginalized and needy by the state and corporate sector, or what Keeanga-Yamahtta Taylor refers to as "predatory inclusion" in her deeply insightful book *Race for Profit*.[10] People are hurting because of, not in spite of, state programs. As I discuss later in the book, the Mississippi welfare program has served for several years as a feeding trough for politicians and their friends, with money doled out for university sports stadiums and inflated speaking fees for appearances that have little to do with assisting the poor. All the while, applicants are subject to greater scrutiny and surveillance. It is one indication of how public resources earmarked for the poor are being distributed to the wealthy.

This pattern is evident on the national level as well. I was alarmed by how few of the trillions of public dollars spent on COVID relief actually ended up in the hands of people who needed it. Pandemic relief was allocated in the name of addressing an unparalleled health-care crisis and presumably to ensure the health and well-being of the American people. Some of that money went into the pockets of American families, but the amount they received paled in comparison to what the corporate sector walked away with. The rich got richer and the poor were left behind.

The pandemic laid bare that the current iteration of capitalism is less about the reproduction of a system of production and more about the reproduction of the care economy. There is mounting evidence as to how profit is being extracted from poverty, inequality, disability, and need. Capital has always assessed value in human bodies, but the formula for determining that value has shifted. For instance, under industrial capitalism, racialized and gendered ideas about people who were presumably deemed able to work longer and harder were more highly prized. Under the care economy, more vulnerable people who need care—children and neurodiverse, elderly, formerly incarcerated, ill, disabled, and unhoused people—are often "worth" more to care industries that accumulate capital because of their care needs. The production and sustenance of human beings, simply for their existence or to be serviced in another way, is an enormous and flourishing site of capital accumulation. As the public and private care economy has expanded, social reproduction has become a source of, rather than a precondition for, capitalist profit.

Despite the warranted skepticism about the state, faith in state action has been a driving force behind campaigns to implement better and more robust care policies as an antidote to the care crisis. Most legislative proposals for a care infrastructure, including those from progressives, are tied to the profit-making care economy. The care crisis, we are told, can be ameliorated with more state funding, expansion of the nonprofit sector, or a better managed or more responsive corporate sector. Proponents assume that greater financial investment or holding the corporate sector accountable will improve the lives of the needy. However, as this book demonstrates, the care industry, which often relies on state resources, is instead exacerbating the crisis and feeding off misery.

In place of liberal social reform, we need radical social transformation. Although there are many models of transformative justice, the one I turn to is rooted in radical Black feminism that posits that an analytical focus on Black women as subjects of study offers insight into the structures of power and thus is also a site of liberatory potential. Radical Black feminists addressed the lived experiences of Black women and simultaneously worked for long-term change. Claudia Jones, a journalist with the Communist Party USA's newspaper the *Daily Worker*, argued in a 1949 article, "An End to the Neglect of the Problems of the Negro Woman!," that because African American women experienced "super-exploitation" they exhibited the revolutionary and leadership potential necessary for political organizing. Linda Burnham refers to a "wellspring" of Black feminist theory emerging from activism that has crafted a liberatory agenda and is about imagining possibilities for transformation.[11] The Combahee River Collective, for example, is a radical Black feminist organization that initially formed in response to the murders of Black women in Boston. In their powerful statement written in 1977, Combahee articulated why Black women were best positioned to develop a transformative politics: "We might use our position at the bottom . . . to make a clear leap into revolutionary action. If black women were free, it would mean that everyone else would have to be free since our freedom would necessitate the destruction of all the systems of oppression."[12] In short, the most marginalized communities have the potential for the most radical praxis because they have the most to gain from a truly liberated and just society.

I still have faith in the political engagement of ordinary people, but I believe it has to flow from the emancipatory vision of people on the ground. Over thirty years of academic research and collaborations with activist groups have taught me that poor and working-class women of color speaking from a marginalized position have deep insight into political organizing and social change. In writing this book, I set my sights not on abstract theory, but on how the care economy functions—what Cindi Katz calls the "messy, fleshy" components of social reproduction. I uplift the work and voices of grassroots organizers and people on the front lines of the care crisis to illuminate how the care economy has not only failed to deliver assistance but also has damaged and, in some cases, destroyed communities. People on the ground doing the work have enormous insight into how the care economy functions. They also offer a vision for how we can move forward.

Domestic workers, for example, have developed innovative labor organizing strategies. They are the original precarious workers: that is, workers without job security or benefits. They relied on public spaces as organizing sites, collectively mobilized to demand state benefits, reached out to documented and undocumented workers, and leveraged individual employers. Situated outside the boundaries of legitimate labor and outside the realm of mainstream organizing, they had to develop new labor formations. They foreshadowed how a growing number of contingent workers in the economy, writ large, can mobilize to wield power.

Radical Black and women of color feminists have also incubated oppositional practices of radical care grounded in support, community, equity, and care, and provide a model of collective political change. Mutual aid in communities of color dates back at least to the nineteenth century and has been tied to an explicit critique of racial capitalism since the 1960s. So, the mutual aid that has been so visible lately, important as it is, has a longer history among poor people of color. Many of the examples I uplift in the final chapter feature women of color who have been organizing for years and are skeptical of relying on the state or corporate sector to meet their needs. In particular, I have been deeply inspired by the practices and theorizations of radical care emerging from the Movement for Black Lives and Indigenous organizing, which are even more relevant in the context of neoliberalism.

In this book, I chronicle the multiple ways that care is discussed, theorized, implemented as policy, and practiced. I distinguish between the care discourse, the care economy, and radical care. I offer a critique of the discourse of care, but I am less interested in semantics than in the analysis that emerges from how care is talked about; that is, how a universalizing discourse masks inequality and exploitation. The *care economy* is an institutionalized, hierarchical, profit-oriented system in which wealth is accumulated by the for-profit sector, the state, nonprofits, and individual families and households. *Radical care*, on the other hand, is defined by alternative and transformative care practices emerging from and connected to social movement organizing. Thus, I do not reject the language of care, but I try to use the terms *care, care work, care policy, care economy*, and *radical care* as appropriate. I also believe that a praxis of care can and should be a part of any movement for social transformation.

Following the lead of Marxist feminists, I also rely on the term *social reproduction* because it is more expansive. My understanding of social reproduction is drawn from the large body of Marxist feminist scholarship, which includes—but is not limited to—social reproduction theorists for whom the term refers to a specific capitalist relationship. I discuss some of these differences later in the book. Marxist feminist understanding of social reproduction differs from that of sociologists, who use the term to refer to the reproduction of social class structure. For feminists, social reproduction involves both paid and unpaid labor in the public and private spheres associated with the reproduction and maintenance of human life and labor power.[13] It includes the services purchased or provided by the state, household consumer goods that ease this work, and the labor inside and outside the home. Unlike "care," social reproduction makes visible the economic relationship and the essential role of this labor in the functioning of capitalism, situating it in the context of financial accumulation, labor relations, and power. The term *social reproduction* is particularly useful to push back against how *care* and *care work* have been deployed in mainstream feminist discourse over the past few decades and most evidently during the pandemic to foreground the needs of middle-class families.

This book's title, *Care: The Highest Stage of Capitalism*, is a reference to Lenin's *Imperialism: The Highest Stage of Capitalism*, in which he chronicled a transition in the evolution of capitalism. Capitalism is always undergoing transition, but its current phase offers a different understanding of capital's relationship to social reproduction. The question of whether or not care is *the* highest stage is certainly up for debate. Manufacturing, agriculture, and finance still remain important in the US and globally. But care work is increasingly a hallmark of the US economy—perhaps as much as $6 trillion and comprising 60 percent of the GDP—according to an estimate by the Boston Consulting Group, with unpaid labor counting as more than half.[14] This estimate, although surprisingly large, includes only labor, not services and products that assist people in sustaining themselves and their families. If these were also taken into account, the care economy would be much larger.

Measuring the care economy is not easy—it is diverse, complex, and hard to track, encompassing many different and intertwined sectors, both public and private. A nonprofit antipoverty agency may get both public and private support. And state programs sometimes outsource areas of work to both the profit and nonprofit sectors. On top of all that, a great deal of the care economy is informal. A comprehensive assessment of profit accrued from the care economy that includes paid and unpaid labor, products, services, nonprofit agencies, for-profit companies, and government support requires more labor and skill than I have and would best be gathered by economists or statisticians. Careful accounting of the proportion of labor, profit, services, and goods that derive from the care economy is needed to verify its precise significance for capitalism.

My aim with this title is to show—and I *can* say this with certainty—that capitalism's relationship to the politics of social reproduction has led to new forms of profit-making, and this transition is rooted in the history of racial capitalism. I have focused my discussion on the US in part because the trends are so visible there, and because an analysis of state policy, the labor market, and grassroots organizing is more tangible on a smaller geographical scale. I suspect that some of these patterns may be evident in other places as well. At the very least, I hope this book will lead to new lines of inquiry.

*

Care work is deeply personal for me, as it is for most people. I am a mother of two, the daughter of an elder, and someone who tries to extend care (not always successfully) to people within my larger community. As an activist, I have worked intentionally to care for others who are in my political circles because I know we all need to be cared for in order to engage in social transformation. As an able-bodied woman with some physical limitations, I need less and/or different care than other people. As a well-paid, full-time worker with benefits, I have the privilege of turning to the market for some of my care needs. But like many other middle-class people, I, too, struggle to manage the unpaid care work I do with other responsibilities, including paid work.

I also have insight into the paid labor of social reproduction. For a brief period in high school, I cleaned our neighbor's home for pay, and prior to that did my share of babysitting. Perhaps more important than my fleeting time doing this work was the experience of my mother, who dropped out of school in the eighth grade to care for her younger siblings and wash clothes for white families so she could pay her brothers' school fees in apartheid South Africa. She spoke to me often about the physically taxing nature of the work, such as carrying large buckets of water on her head, and the emotional pain of not being able to attend school. My grandmother was a domestic worker in South Africa prior to getting married. I know little about her early experience except that she was the daughter of indentured servants, worked out of necessity, and had little choice about the type of employment to take up.

In an unexpected turn, my nineteen-year-old daughter has recently become a home health-care aide. She was taken aback by the level of forced intimacy expected of her with people she hadn't previously met, having to change diapers and help them shower, and shocked by a client's unexpected life-threatening emergency and the weight of responsibility she bore for their well-being. She found that she had earned more as a restaurant server than as a health-care aide, where people's lives were in her hands. At the same time, she grew very fond of some of her clients, bringing them gifts and baking banana bread with them. She learned both the joys and pain of this kind of low-wage work.

I am a firm believer that much of what we know about the world comes from our family, our community, and our daily interactions and experiences with other people. My thinking around care has also been shaped by the grassroots activists I have worked with for many years and who have taught me so much. I interviewed several of them for this book—their words and stories are powerful testaments to why we need to revamp both our care and our economic systems. Alongside these activists are the women of color I have learned about through my archival research—welfare recipients who demanded the right to care for their own families, as well as people who were locked into domestic work serving others but who did not receive much care themselves. They rarely talked about this work as care, although they may have cared for or cared about their employers. They were quicker to mention exploitation, instances of abuse, and the drudgery of the labor.

This book is organized thematically to illustrate the multiple meanings, diverse practices, and competing theorizations of care and social reproduction. I begin with the feminist care discourse as it has unfolded over the past thirty years. That discourse has attempted to uplift and revalue care work by pointing to its long-standing association with women's work and subsequent historic devaluation. I argue that the discourse has often mischaracterized care work, cast it as exceptional and distinct from other kinds of labor, and made a case for protecting and rewarding care workers because of their labor contributions to middle-class households.

In chapter 2, I bring into the conversation Marxist feminist theories of social reproduction, which reject the language of love and emotion and seek to understand this labor as essential for the functioning of capitalism. I trace how the history of social reproduction has intersected with the politics of race and class and has privileged the lives and reproduction of some people over others. I argue that, under neoliberalism, capital is increasingly finding social reproduction a source of capital accumulation rather than a precondition for capitalist profit.

Chapter 3 examines how care work has historically been a form of coercion. The state and corporate sectors have relied on multiple strategies to force people to do this work, including slavery, immigration policy, labor contracting, marital laws, and carceral policies. Chapter 4 chronicles the history of resistance and organizing around social reproduction, from day-to-day resistance to union formation, from strikes and work stoppages to demands for state support for household subsistence. I argue that the innovative struggles around social reproduction offer a different model of organizing that is relevant for a neoliberal economy and an increasingly diverse employer class.

In chapter 5, I discuss the divergence between care for the poor and care for the better-off. The dismantling of welfare, implementation of work requirements and other punitive demands on the poor, rise of the carceral state, and declining wages have led to greater economic, racial, and gender inequality. At the same time, some well-off Americans have access to flexible work schedules, accommodating workplaces, and family leave options, and are able to take advantage of federal tax policies that provide some support for caregiving.

Chapter 6 examines how care has become a source of profit for businesses, nonprofits, and the state. From the health and hospital industries to the guardianship system to the welfare system to food rescue programs, the corporate sector, the wealthy, and many middle-class people benefit materially from the poverty industry. Chapter 7 uplifts models of grassroots radical care that are collective, egalitarian, nonhierarchical, and committed to social transformation. The examples in this chapter embody alternative ways to imagine what a caring society can look like.

In a moment of growing economic inequality and worker disempowerment, it is imperative that we consider the rampant exploitation in the industry and create pathways for worker and community empowerment to move toward developing a collective liberatory politics. In that vein, I give space to ordinary grassroots activists in their struggle for justice. I am deeply inspired by the models of radical care, both historical and contemporary, in which people have utilized what they have at their disposal to create loving and caring communities.

In writing this book, I grappled a lot with what has to be done. How do grassroots models help chart a path forward in addition to being a future to which we can aspire? How do we get to a place where just, egalitarian, and collective models are the dominant mode of care? Do we have to abolish the old system to make way for a new one? The prison abolition movement offers both a vision and a strategy—a world where prisons are replaced with restorative justice, education, and training, where money is diverted from the carceral state to housing, food, and social services. Calling for the abolition of the care economy, however, raises complicated questions. Folks in need of care couldn't be "released," as is the case for people who are incarcerated. What would happen to the sick, children, the elderly and disabled people? How would people cope?

In the long run, the care economy needs to be abolished. However, it can only be abolished as part of a broader shift away from a profit-oriented system of racial capitalism. Perhaps the dismantling must be piecemeal until more wholesale transformation can take place. Either way, because care is fundamental to human survival, we must always create new forms of caring alongside efforts to transform old ones. Although I do not present a blueprint, I invite you to join me in thinking through how, given the challenges before us, we can create a caring world as part of a radical future.

Chapter 1

"Part of the Family"

Gender, Labor, and
the Care Work Discourse

Carolyn Reed was a labor organizer in New York in the 1970s. Before dedicating her life to activism, she worked as a live-in domestic for a wealthy family in Scarsdale, just north of New York City. Although her employers referred to her as "part of the family," she worked from seven in the morning until midnight and never got a raise, received Social Security, or had a vacation, even after five years of employment. After a particularly galling incident that exposed the fiction of familiarity, she had an epiphany that prompted her to organize:

> One night, the woman of the house—who had been having an affair and was very, very nervous—began to scream at me for not having done something she thought I should have done.... As she screamed I realized I wasn't real to her. I mean, I wasn't a person to her.... She had no respect for me, for what I did... I was a servant to her, maybe even a slave. I remember while she was screaming I began saying, "I don't work for you anymore." ... And that was it. I packed my bags in the middle of the night;

my husband, who was then my boyfriend, came and got me, and we took off.[1]

This incident illustrates how proximity and distance shaped the occupation of domestic work. Reed, like other household workers, labored in the intimate space of the home, was privy to some of the most personal details of the family's life, and was expected to be a confidant and nurturer. Yet, as an African American household worker, she was invisible and dehumanized, a process made possible through racial othering, exposing how she was anything but family.

The pretense that a care worker is "part of the family," embraced by many employers, conflated paid and unpaid labor and reflected the presumed bonds of affection and mutual love that informed the labor. Employers sometimes assumed that workers had an emotional attachment to them, just as they may have had an emotional connection to their workers. It did not mean that workers ate dinner with the family or inherited Grandma's china. What it did mean was that employers could ask them to go above and beyond the call of duty—to stay late, give up holidays, or listen to their employer's woes—because they were presumed to love those for whom they worked.

Domestic workers, however, categorically rejected and debunked their mythological status as "part of the family." Reed eventually came to head the Household Technicians of America (HTA), the first national organization representing domestic workers. The domestic workers' rights movement mobilized thousands of domestic workers around the country to fight for adequate pay, professionalism, and labor rights. They refused the language of family, love and care, and demanded rights and respect. As Reed once said, defiantly and succinctly, "I don't want a family. I need a job."[2] They believed that constructing domestic work in terms of "care" and "family" enabled employers to flout the law and create informal and unpredictable work situations. It became a way to mask the power dynamic in the relationship. Another HTA organizer, Geraldine Roberts, of Cleveland, explained: "I was not in the family will," and, if she got sick, "I was not a part of that family anymore."[3] In this way, the politics of love and care eclipsed the labor relationship at the heart of paid domestic work and undercut the struggle for rights.

Today, the term *care* is often used to describe the work, but that was not always the case. The domestic workers' rights movement reflects the dominant analytical framework from the 1960s until the 1980s that saw household labor as labor, rather than as primarily about caregiving or emotions. Activists and scholars in this period, including the wages for housework movement that I discuss in chapter 4, used terms such as *housework, household labor, domestic work,* and *social reproduction.* A vibrant feminist movement and robust body of scholarship insisted that household labor be treated the same as all other forms of work. Demands for emotional investment, they believed, were an indication of exploitation rather than cause for celebration. Sociologist Arlie Hochschild's landmark book *The Managed Heart,* for example, referred to the expectation that workers care for the people they are serving as "emotional labor." For Hochschild, emotional labor signified an unacknowledged form of capitalist exploitation: the production and management of human feeling for pay. This was especially important because of the growth of the service sector, where profits depend on the quality of service. That is, servers who project happiness and concern lead to satisfied customers and a more profitable business. She argued that emotional extraction, which was prevalent in but not confined to women's occupations, led workers to become alienated and detached from their labor.[4] This structural analysis was eclipsed in the 1990s by the care discourse.

This chapter will examine how the discourse of care has muddled our understanding of this labor. The term *care work*, as it has been used over the past three decades, refers to domestic work, and elder-, disability-, and childcare, and sometimes extends to institutionalized labor in hospitals, schools, and nursing homes. In the current political discourse, care work is treated as unlike other kinds of work—as even *more* important—because it requires an emotional investment and is critical for human well-being. This understanding of care work emphasizes the affective qualities and the social importance of the work, and the need to value, uphold, and properly compensate care workers. The expectations of care, then, become something not to attenuate or eliminate but to elevate. Advocates who want to uplift care work contend that paying workers enough and treating them well will alleviate the care crisis and lead workers to "love" the people for whom they work. Better care policies and higher wages will ensure that both "our" loved ones and those who tend to "our" loved ones are well cared for. The logical extension of this campaign to uplift care work is the valorization of care rather than empowering workers or rethinking whether or not workers *should* care.

The scholarship on care work is expansive, but there are several common threads that cut across much of it. First, it often frames care work narrowly in terms of "women's work," unpaid labor in the home, and the gendered division of labor. Care work is erroneously associated with female-dominated occupations because of assumptions about white, middle-class gender norms of nurture and tenderness. Second, much of the writing about care work valorizes the presumed connection between paid care and emotional investment, thus transferring employers' hopes and expectations onto the work. In this way, the language of care caters to the needs of employers, while employees are valued only to the degree that they serve their employers. Finally, the language of care and emotion erases the inequality and power dynamics inherent in the employer–employee relationship. Although care work is an exploitative occupation, the language of love has embedded within it an ethical imperative to do the work regardless of working conditions. In this way, the discourse of emotional investment and mutual interdependence inhibits organizing.[5]

I argue that the care discourse obscures the race and class relations that underpin both care work and care policy. Examining care work through an intersectional lens foregrounds the exploitation that is central to the labor of social reproduction, the unequal allocation of care, and the profit motive that undergirds the care economy.

The term *care work*, perhaps unwittingly, has become a depoliticized way of understanding a labor relationship. In the 1990s, feminist scholars and policy makers identified a growing care crisis—a crisis generated by white middle-class women's increasing employment outside the home and limited public support for care work. They wrote papers, organized conferences, and produced reports that examined how women are burdened by working inside and outside the home and how families struggle to find affordable household, childcare, and elder assistance. Feminist scholars were clear about one thing: the care crisis is the result of the social and economic devaluation of care work and domestic work—both paid and unpaid. They have pushed for recognition, higher wages for care workers, and an agenda to make care a cornerstone of public policy.

Organizers and activists have also taken up the mantle of care. The National Domestic Workers Alliance (NDWA), an advocacy organization that represents private household workers, asserts: "Domestic workers do the work most precious to us: caring for our homes and loved ones. But they don't have the basic rights and dignity they deserve."[6] In 2011, NDWA launched the Caring Across Generations campaign. Developed in conjunction with employers, the campaign aims to unite caregivers and the growing number of elder care receivers around a mutual commitment to care. NDWA has proposed encouraging migration from abroad, boosting worker pay, and giving workers legal status to simultaneously solve the care crisis and bring value to this occupation. Although a number of worker-led, grassroots groups have shied away from the language of care, NDWA's campaign has been influential in shaping the national discourse around care work.

The laudable intention in turning to moral arguments about care is to ensure the needy are cared for, make claims about the value of this labor, and ensure gender equity. Unpaid household labor is not acknowledged either in terms of wages (since people don't get paid for it) or national productivity (since it is not counted as part of the GDP). Feminists have long maintained that the many hours of unpaid labor in the home should be included in official measures of economic value.[7] Recognizing unpaid household labor would enable us to recalibrate metrics of economic worth, broaden the definition of labor, and incorporate human well-being into rankings of national well-being. It is also a rationale for more public support for this work, whether in the form of expanded welfare programs or workplaces that accommodate employees' household and family responsibilities.

Care scholars argue that our mutual dependency is a powerful rationale for a new civic culture and social policy around the politics of care, with the aim of recognizing our shared investment in a care infrastructure. There is value in rethinking democracy and considering care as a basis for a new system of ethics, as political scientist Joan Tronto has argued.[8] Such an approach would be a game changer for how we imagine political priorities and the responsibility of the government. A robust care agenda also undercuts the individualism inherent in neoliberalism—the idea of equating success with self-regulation, self-reliance, and discipline—as well as the assumption that care work is less valuable than other kinds of labor.

As important as this intervention is, the current care discourse also marks a troublesome linguistic and analytical shift, from the domestic workers' rights movement's analysis of social reproduction as a site of exploitation to the middle-class crisis of care, with a focus on the people receiving care. Workers became important to the degree that they provided a solution to what Arlie Hochschild named the "care deficit" or families' unmet care needs.[9] Although many feminist scholars intend to shift the conversation to a systemic framework, the use of the term *care* redirects to the needs of employers and foregrounds the emotional investment by workers. The *care crisis* is really a crisis of paid and unpaid labor—or a "time/wages/reproductive labor crisis," as described by women, gender, and sexuality studies professor Laura Briggs.[10] The question is: Who is going to care for dependents? Who is going to prepare meals and clean the house, especially if able-bodied adults in the household are employed full-time?

The calls for collective politics around care and mutual interdependence obscure the class divisions and disguise how the very definition of the care crisis is rooted in the experiences of white, middle-class families, the burdens of professional women, the work/family balance, and problems finding "good help." When advocates of a new care agenda propose raising wages and giving care workers more comprehensive legal protections, they premise care for workers as dependent on their care for their employers.[11] Workers' well-being matters because their labor serves others. This is consistent with productivist politics and the neoliberal tendency to attribute value to human bodies based on differential scales of worth: one must earn access to rights, labor protections, and ade-

quate pay. NDWA endorsed the congressional Domestic Workers
Bill of Rights because, as they explain: "Domestic workers who
work in individual homes free up the time and attention of millions of working families by caring for our children, our aging
parents, our loved ones living with disabilities, and our homes."
NDWA's campaign, as sociologists Mary Romero and Nancy Pérez
argue, "demonstrate[s] one's deservingness to legal personhood via
a national, dominant narrative of hard work and merit, justifies
and reestablishes a systematic gendered racism that profoundly produces detrimental consequences... and undermines the very struggles for fair wages, labor regulation, and protections."[12]

Part of the problem with the care discourse and why we landed
where we are is the conflation of paid and unpaid household labor.
Too often, feminist scholars and policy makers discuss paid and
unpaid labor without making distinctions. They assume that the
paid labor of social reproduction, like the unpaid household labor
of white middle-class women, is rooted in gendered norms of
nurture and care.[13] Although paid and unpaid household labor are
both devalued, the trajectory of the paid labor of social reproduction is tied to slavery, colonialism, immigration, and forced labor.
In addition, framing care work primarily as "women's labor" fails
to account for the growing number of men employed as nurses,
restaurant workers, and teachers and misrepresents the work that
women do. Thus, intersecting analyses of race, class, and gender
must be central to our understanding of this work.

The conflation of women's work with "caring occupations"
deters us from analyzing whether the work is about care—that
is, whether care as praxis, affect, or emotion describes the labor.[14] Not all women's work is care work and not everything that
falls under the rubric of "care work" actually involves caring for
anyone. Occupations are included in or excluded from the category of caring labor with little regard for whether care—as emo-

tional labor or as a practice—takes place. Nursing, education, and domestic work, as examples, are considered caring occupations. But research nurses don't interact with patients. And labeling the work of nurses who do interact with patients as *care* downplays their medical training and skills, and encourages people to evaluate them on their personality rather than expertise. Perhaps domestic work is the occupation that is most closely associated with care work. Domestic workers engage in a number of tasks, from caring for children to preparing meals to running errands. Some of these tasks involve the direct care of another human being, but others, such as laundry or cleaning, do not. The term *social reproduction* better encompasses the range of occupations and tasks that are obfuscated by the language of *care*.

Care work is structured along racial lines. In order to understand who is doing the care labor, we have to look closely at the racial inequalities and divisions within the broad category of care work. Women of color are less likely to do work that involves care and more likely to do the "back room" cleaning, according to sociologist Evelyn Nakano Glenn, who writes about "the social organization of care" and the "racial division of reproductive labor." Law professor Dorothy Roberts argues similarly that "spiritual" and "nurturing" care work is dominated by white women, who tend to be better educated and higher paid, while the "menial" work (like cleaning) is performed by women of color. Although there are jobs where workers do both, the racial division within the labor of social reproduction suggests that "care work" is the domain of white women, while other kinds of social reproductive labor is relegated to women of color.[15] Thus, collapsing everything under the term *care work* falsely universalizes the experiences of white women.

There may be useful ways to invoke the term *care* as applied to some kinds of work. It should not, however, refer to an en-

tire sector of work, such as health care or education. There are
multiple and vastly different occupations in these sectors, such as
nurses' aides, janitors, cafeteria workers, and bill collectors, some
well-paid, some not, some that involve working directly with patients, and some that don't. Instead, considering the practice of
care enables us to think more carefully about who is a care worker
and what constitutes care. We might consider how professors and
preschool teachers presumably practice care. Doormen who help
carry groceries and inquire about a resident's day could also be
included in the category of care workers. Therapists, personal
trainers, nutritionists, and doctors, who have direct contact with
and provide care for other humans, might fall in the care work
category. Where these occupations land is up for debate, but redirecting to the practice of care offers a more concrete way to
analyze different kinds of work.

Besides associating care with whole sectors of work, sometimes care work is associated with labor that takes place in the
home. If so, should we consider plumbers care workers? Men's
labor in the home is not necessarily devalued and is not usually
called care work. Moreover, the paid and unpaid labor of women
of color was devalued whether it took place in the home or in
public or institutional spaces. Clearly, the geographical space of
the home is not a plausible explanation for the devaluation of
paid labor. The racialized images and ideologies of the "Mammy"
stereotype, long associated with Black women's domestic service
work, accompanied Black women as their jobs moved from the
private home to low-wage service settings such as hospitals and
schools, as anthropologist Dána-Ain Davis has argued.[16] In the
end, Black women were underpaid whether they worked in the
household or as janitors, nurses, or clerical workers. The devaluation of their labor cannot be explained by the domestic sphere
or gender alone; their labor was and is devalued because of both

race *and* gender.

The association of care work with female-dominated occupations and women's nurturing capacities has led many people to believe that care work is always carried out by women. This excludes male-dominated occupations that entail care, such as athletic coaches who mentor young people or even financial advisers who discuss people's life goals and aspirations, expressing interest in their long-term well-being. We rarely call this care work because of the term's common association with women's work. At the same time, the men employed in typical care work occupations are obscured. Although women are still disproportionately responsible for care work in the home, more and more men are taking on unpaid household labor and childcare. In addition, men have always been employed as household workers. African American men worked as drivers, cooks, valets, yard workers, and butlers both during and after slavery. From the middle of the nineteenth until the early twentieth centuries, Chinese men served as bonded household workers in the US, as historian Andrew Urban has shown. In a context of anti-Chinese sentiment, employers cast male Chinese workers as submissive and nonthreatening, making them ideal servants in the private domestic sphere alongside female employers and an exception to the prevailing stereotypes about Chinese people as dangerous.[17]

Today, a growing number of male workers, especially men of color, labor in the field of social reproduction. At the beginning of the twenty-first century, most cleaning jobs were outside private homes, and a many were filled by men.[18] Nonnurturing care occupations—laundry, food preparation, and cleaning—that have the highest concentrations of women of color also employ the most men, even if women are still in the majority, according to care work researcher Mignon Duffy.[19] This means that nonnurturing care work is largely done by people of color, both men and women.

Both a drawback and benefit of the care work discourse is its centering of gender. The burden of unpaid household labor and care work is unquestionably a barrier to women's economic success. Across the globe, social expectations about women's responsibility for unpaid care for the household and family have profound implications for women's economic and psychological well-being and how women fare in the political sphere.[20] Women earn lower wages, sometimes need to drop out of the workforce, or have a harder time keeping jobs or advancing occupationally because of care responsibilities. Single mothers are six times more likely to be poor than are two-parent families, in part because of care demands, and twice as likely to be poor compared to families headed by a single father because of women's lower wages.[21] Gender equality and women's progress depend to a large degree on alleviating the burden of household responsibility. The lack of recognition and policy solutions around unpaid care work speaks to a broader failure to provide systemic support for the labor of social reproduction.

The gendered assumptions that inform unpaid care work, however, cannot be mapped onto paid care work. Paid care work is primarily associated with women and vice versa, in part because of misguided assumptions that women are naturally caring and nurturing.[22] Scholars attribute the devaluation of paid care work to gendered norms and expectations and the historically constructed public/private distinction between home and workplace. But that simply does not apply. As I discuss further in chapter 3, the paid labor of social reproduction emerges from a very different historical trajectory.

The language of care presumes a worker's emotional attachment to their labor or suggests that an emotional connection undergirds the employment relationship. In 2000, in a departure from her earlier work on emotional labor, Arlie Hochschild developed the concept of "global care chains," which she described as "a series of personal links between people across the globe based on the paid or unpaid work of caring" where migrant care workers "transfer" their feelings about their own children onto their employer's children.[23] Hochschild argues that the migration of care workers is a form of "emotional imperialism" or a "global heart transplant."[24] Hochschild is just one example of how scholars have grappled with the emotional impact on children, workers, and parents when a mother hires someone to care for her children.[25] The association of care work with emotional investment is rooted in employers' desire to hire someone who will care for their loved ones the same way they would. Feminist economist Nancy Folbre, for example, has written extensively about the commodification of care and argues that there is no inherent tension between love and money, and that it is possible for workers to be motivated by both.[26] Within this framing, however, there is no question of whether these workers *should* care.

Characterizing these workers as inherently caring resonates with long-standing popular images of women of color as deeply emotional and ideal domestic workers. The discourse of care and love conjured up the "Mammy" stereotype that cast Black women as devoted servants to white families during the late nineteenth and early twentieth centuries, a period of racialized violence and few job opportunities for African Americans. The "Mammy" stereotype romanticized the slave past and dominated popular culture. Margaret Mitchell's novel and the blockbuster film *Gone with the Wind* famously brought the character of Mammy, a "happy servant," to the big screen in the late 1930s. Mammy's presumed loyalty, love, and care for her employer, a white slaveholding family, erased her own agency, desire, and family ties. Throughout much of the twentieth century, this stereotype defined day-to-day employer–employee interactions between Black employees and white employers.[27] It turned domestic workers into servants. The nature of this servitude is one in which the employer not only controls the products of a workers' labor but also retains complete bodily ownership of the worker, including emotional control.[28]

The perspective of emotionally invested workers is a kind of cultural hegemony that applies to migrant workers from the Global South as well. The Philippines, a primary provider of care and domestic workers globally, has transformed its citizens into commodities on the world market, as Asian studies scholar Anna Guevarra has examined. Governed by a cultural logic and a gendered moral economy, Filipino migrant workers, Guevarra argues, are considered prized workers with "added export value." That is, a process of racial branding constructs Filipinos as ideal hardworking, compassionate, well-trained, and docile workers, making them more valuable in the global economy.[29]

The research on both African American domestic workers and Filipino migrant workers that emerges from a labor perspective challenges the romanticized understanding of mothering that Hochschild, Folbre, and others impose onto paid care workers. Hochschild's assumption that workers love the people they are caring for may or may not be the case, but it is highly unlikely that they transfer their feelings from their children onto their employers' children. Sociologist Valerie Francisco-Menchavez has written about how Filipino migrant workers stay connected to and forge intimacy with their own family members at home through new forms of telecommunication, while simultaneously building "communities of care" with other Filipinos in host countries.[30] The issue of family separation for migrant workers is a heartbreaking one, but it does not mean that workers stop loving their children or transfer that love onto their employers' children. Nor is the pain of family separation a gender issue specific to domestic work. Undoubtedly male migrants and migrant workers who are not domestic workers feel similarly. Hochschild's perspective erases male Filipino care worker and fails to acknowledge migrant workers as desiring and pleasure-seeking subjects, as American Studies professor Martin Manalansan argues.[31]

When I write that an occupation should not be defined by emotion, my intention is not to discount the dedication of workers. Many domestic workers are emotionally invested in their work: they are committed to improving someone else's life, and they go above and beyond, making physical and emotional sacrifices. Rather, my point is that workers should not be *expected* to invest emotionally, nor should the conversation about emotion eclipse the rights of the worker or determine what tasks they should do. Although household workers have reported that they love their work and the people for whom they worked, few see it as a labor of love or even as care work. They may love doing the work, but they don't do the work because of love. Regardless, most employers want care workers to invest emotionally—that is, they want them to work for both "love and money." And advocates and policy makers who insist on recognition and rewards for workers because of their emotional investment reify the imagined emotional component of the labor and obscure the fact that care workers are, first and foremost, workers. But do these workers really care? *Should* they?

Folbre's assertion that paid workers labor for both love and money is premised on the commodification of care. I take issue with the notion that *care* is commodified—that assumption mischaracterizes the labor relationship. Care is not commodified; rather, the *practice* of care is commodified. Consider perfume companies as a metaphor: they sell their products as an avenue to intimacy, but do not actually sell intimacy—they sell perfume, and the buyer hopes to achieve intimacy through their purchase. So, while we might hope that receivers of care feel cared for, the workers who express care in a labor relationship do not necessarily care. The expectation that they do may more accurately be called the *coercion of compassion*. Rather than expect that workers care, it might be more fitting to know if they are carrying out their responsibilities, to focus on the tasks or practice of taking care rather than the emotional performance of caring. Do they put a Band-Aid on a child's scraped knee? Are they giving a blanket to an elderly person who is chilly? What's important is that they are doing the work of care. The question of felt emotion is irrelevant.[32]

Conflating the emotion of care with the practice of care blurs the fact that one might engage in caring acts without an emotional attachment. Workers can be responsible and attentive care givers without actually caring about the individual. By valorizing paid care as emotional labor, scholars and activists essentially transfer employers' expectations for an emotional investment and "familial love" onto the worker and fail to recognize how those demands are exploitative. An internalized or externalized expectation of care can also inhibit resistance. Heather Berg documents how care workers (including teachers) who feel an ethical responsibility to those they serve are constrained from challenging the terms of their labor—how either the language of care or actual feelings of love inhibit labor actions.[33] Why would anyone go on strike or demand higher wages if they are doing this work out of love? The perspective of care-as-emotion erases the inequality and power inherent in the relationship between the work, the worker, and the recipient by redirecting the conversation into a realm of emotional bonds and mutual responsibility.

Examining the labor of social reproduction from the perspective of women of color illustrates the problems with a language of care and demands of the occupation. The story of Carolyn Reed and her allies in the domestic workers' rights movement of the 1960s and 1970s offers insight into employer expectations of and worker resistance to love in the occupation.

Dorothy Bolden, a household worker who began employment at the age of nine, lived not far from Martin Luther King Jr. in the Vine City neighborhood of Atlanta. She was a community leader who was deeply involved with the civil rights movement. In 1968, with King's encouragement, she formed the Atlanta-based National Domestic Workers Union of America (NDWUA). With the intention of bringing recognition to the occupation, Bolden initiated an annual Maid's Honor Day in Atlanta in 1970.[34] A wonderful collection of primary source documents at Georgia State University contains letters written by employers nominating their household workers for "Maid of the Year." The letters illuminate the value employers placed on the occupation and the specific qualities they cherished in their employees. For employers, love and self-sacrifice, despite meager pay, were the hallmarks of what they believed was an ideal domestic worker. For example, employer Anne Winston nominated Rosie Powell, who, she said, "swooped in like Mary Poppins" and saved the family from being broken apart, all while accepting a "very low salary." Moreover, according to Anne, Rosie "sustained third-degree burns of her forearm when she risked her life to put out a kitchen fire which endangered my baby. When she returned from the hospital with her arm wrapped in bandages, she insisted on serving supper to the family rather than leaving the chores to me after I had been at school all day."[35]

In 1976, Johnnie Saulsberry won the honor of Maid of the Year. According to her employer, Johnnie was deserving because she bathed and cared for the employer's seventy-five-year-old mother, entertained the mother's friends for afternoon tea, took care of a dog, cleaned a ten-room house, did the laundry, tended fifty plants, cooked fabulous meals, never complained about unexpectedly having three or four guests or large numbers of extended family for dinner, and often stayed late if her employer was delayed returning home. One supporter wrote that Johnnie was "cheerful, bright-eyed, and remarkably pleasant." Another letter writer described Johnnie as "unselfish" in giving extra time, implying that a refusal to work additional hours would have been viewed as selfish and uncaring. We see this in Jeanette Everhart's nomination for Atlanta's Maid's Honor Day as well, when her employer claimed that "numerous times she has neglected [her] family and come to my rescue."[36]

The implicit, or perhaps explicit, message from employers was that the worthiest household workers operated from a place of love and selflessness. Employers repeatedly uplifted workers' sacrifice, devotion, and willingness to give more than what was asked, implying that the best employees were not interested in compensation but simply cared about the people for whom they worked—sometimes more than their own families. The demands for and glorification of care emanated from employers' concerns, hopes, and desires. Employers entrusted their homes and dependents to another individual. In order for that situation to be viable, they had to believe that the domestic worker was uninterested in money, or even in being with her own family, and was instead motivated by care and love.

Domestic worker activists in the 1960s and 1970s, however, repeatedly testified that emotional demands were the most taxing part of their job. Reed explained succinctly: "Household workers have not been selling their services; they have been selling their souls."[37] African American domestic workers and their allies vehemently rejected the "Mammy" caricature and sought to dislodge the culture of servitude that underpinned the occupation. Edith Barksdale-Sloan, director of the National Committee on Household Employment, which facilitated the organizing of household workers and the formation of the HTA, proclaimed in a rousing speech before a gathering of household workers in Washington, DC, in 1971: "We refuse to be your mammies, nannies, aunties, uncles, girls, handmaidens any longer."[38] Workers emotional investment or perceived emotional investment, was a politics of performance that did not necessarily reflect inner feelings, perhaps akin to what Paul Laurence Dunbar referred to as "wearing the mask" or what Darlene Clark Hine called a culture of dissemblance, in which enslaved Black women strategically used silence to cope with and resist sexual exploitation.[39]

Many domestic worker activists today also reject the language of care and instead advocate a contractual relationship with specified rights and responsibilities, with no expectation to care. Rosa Navarro, who worked for the Latino Union of Chicago, said in an interview in 2021: "Our union was much more interested in building worker power than in care or developing alliances with middle-class constituents. We were certainly not interested in having to prove why we deserved labor rights."[40] Damayan Migrant Workers Association, a worker-led Filipino organization in New York City, also rejects the assumption that this labor is about care. Executive director Linda Oalican, a domestic worker for eighteen years, shared with me and my students recently, when we produced a report for Damayan: "The current discourse about the politics of care is reformist and will not fundamentally transform the status of caregivers. Equity and dignity for domestic workers and other excluded workers requires that the government and power holders in American society address structural racism, economic exploitation, and de facto discrimination."[41] The experiences of women of color illustrate that, rather than an occupation in which workers willingly invest emotion and care, the demand to care is viewed as a source of exploitation for most workers. A history of domestic worker organizing suggests that rather than elevating the caring relationship as the most important characteristic of the work, and a reason to reward people, a care agenda should refocus its efforts on rights, wages, and benefits for workers.

The paid labor of social reproduction is predicated on racialized and class power that is sutured to the legacy of slavery, immigration, settler colonialism, and imperialism. The language of care-as-emotion has no more place in discussions of paid domestic work than the language of affection has in studies of slavery. Of course, slave owners, like household employers, sometimes expressed fondness, care, or an emotional connection to those who worked for them, but this did not translate into an objective characterization of the labor and, in most cases, did not reflect the sentiments of the people who did the work. Paid household labor is not akin to slavery but may be understood as part of slavery's lineage. For paid household labor, race and gender determine power, compensation, rights, and the value of the work.

The care work discourse emerging in the 1990s overshadowed, and was a departure from, the analysis of housework and care work as a source of economic exploitation that was more prevalent in the 1970s and 1980s. With the rise of neoliberalism, workers of all occupational backgrounds are expected to invest emotionally in their jobs, to go above and beyond, to assume that one's employment is one's identity. This analysis is laid out in *Work Won't Love You Back,* in which journalist Sarah Jaffe examines how the demand to "love your work," historically derived from unpaid household labor, has created what she calls a "new tyranny of work." Where the demands of paid employment are endless, this tyranny that Jaffe identifies is a cover for the economic insecurity, coercion, and exploitation that is characteristic of neoliberalism.[42]

The discourse of care has functioned as code for the employer's interests: workers are valued to the degree that they meet employers' needs, and claims for worker protection often rest on the service they provide. It becomes egregious, for example, that those who care for "our" loved ones live in abject poverty or are subject to deportation. Although the care discourse and its policy outcomes provide much-needed support for some workers, it has created greater hurdles for worker justice more broadly. Justifying proper compensation for workers because of their "caring" labor implies that the worth of poor and working-class people of color is important to the degree that they serve and care for the middle and upper classes. It makes a claim for workers' rights based on the kind of work that an individual performs and who benefits from it, rather than on employment status. In the neoliberal era, contributions to better-off households have become the basis for workers' political and economic rights.

Of course, this historically devalued labor should be valued. We should thank people who step up in times of crisis. We should account for this labor economically. We should give unpaid household workers the financial assistance they need. We should ensure that care workers and domestic workers are paid fairly and have the necessary labor protections and rights. But rewarding and valuing care workers because of their contributions to the well-being of the better-off creates distinctions and a hierarchy for who deserves rights. All people deserve adequate income, respect, and decent living and working conditions, regardless of the kind of work they do—or if they work at all. The allocation of rights premised on care work feeds into a dangerous neoliberal logic of valuing people because of productivity. The focus on productivity has the potential to perpetuate anti-Blackness, ableism, and carceral policies. If rights are distributed based on what people contribute, then people deemed less productive may be targeted for containment, elimination, or disposability, creating what anthropologist Miriam Ticktin calls the "casualties of care," in which some people are deemed worthy of care and others are not.[43]

Despite its good intentions, the care discourse feeds into a particular narrative—also present in some strains of the immigrants' rights movement—that affirms the worthiness of some individuals because their labor benefits those with power. The care discourse places worker rights on the scaffolding of employer needs and emotional investments in the labor. In this way, it premises the collective social good on the interests of the more privileged sectors of society while making the needs of the less privileged contingent on the well-being of the better-off.

Proponents of a new public policy based on care claim that care is a common denominator linking everyone. Unfortunately, the "we" and "us" of this collective liberal vision have distinct boundaries. The language of universality and mutual interdependence—like the language of love and family—masks the racial and economic inequality and the role of the care industry as an engine of exploitation and source of profit. Despite the universal claims, the care discourse is centered on how poor and working-class people of color can meet the needs, emotional and otherwise, of those with economic means. The expansion of this employment sector over the past forty years makes it imperative that we craft campaigns to ensure that household and service workers, and in fact all people, are equally valued and protected. One small step in this direction is to reject a politics of assessing human worth based on contributions and identify people who labor in the home not as carers but as *workers*.

Since the 1990s, the term *care work* has been deployed on behalf of neoliberalism to detach the paid labor of social reproduction from the history of racial capitalism and capitalist labor and profit. Academics and policy makers have analyzed care through a gendered lens and have sought to uplift and revalue caring labor, women's nurturing capacities, and the commitment to a caring society as a possible new formulation for a policy agenda around which we can all rally. The care discourse contributes to the logic of neoliberal capitalism, sanitizing and repackaging exploitative labor relations and unequal access to resources. Claims of collective care and mutual dependence, especially when articulated by people in power, mask the race and class character of care work, generate a politics in which workers rely on employers for empathy and validation, and create greater hurdles for building an oppositional politics. The care economy, which is rooted in a privatized, market-driven model of care, cannot be a solution to the crisis of social reproduction because it fuels inequality, as I discuss in chapter 6.

The pandemic vividly exposed the hollowness of the claim of universal care. At the start of the COVID-19 crisis, window banners, public service announcements, and free donuts attested to the public's gratitude to essential workers, and care workers were sometimes, though not always, included in that appreciation. Workers were hailed as heroes for their commitment, sacrifice, and care because of *whom* they cared for. A *Time* magazine cover story in April 2020 was headlined, "Heroes of the Front Line: Stories of the Courageous Workers Risking Their Own Lives to Save Ours." As important as this recognition is, it often did not come with the necessary material support and protection. According to a survey conducted by the American Federation of Teachers in August/September 2020, 86 percent of public school teachers purchased their own protective equipment.[44] Even as essential workers were tasked with ensuring the safety and health of others, their own health and safety were compromised.

Over the course of the pandemic, essential workers protested, went on strike, or organized to demand hazard pay or protective equipment. Emergency medical service workers in New York City boycotted the city's ticker-tape parade honoring essential workers, preferring pay over pats on the back. Union leaders and rank-and-file workers insisted that workers deserve adequate wages, respect, and support, not just applause. So, although the pandemic was universal (by definition) and there was a rhetoric of collective interests, the costs of the pandemic were not borne equally by all.

In the spring of 2021, I taught a course in partnership with Damayan, which helps people escape labor trafficking situations. My students interviewed members, including labor trafficking survivors, about their experiences during the pandemic: care workers who lost their jobs, who contracted COVID from their employers, and even one part-time worker whose employer demanded she live in but refused to pay more than her part-time salary. Many of these workers did not qualify for unemployment insurance or pandemic relief dollars because they were undocumented. Perhaps most important, however, and what Damayan made very clear, is that the trauma did not begin in March 2020 for them. Linda Oalican, executive director of Damayan and a brilliant organizer, explained: "This pandemic is severe... Its impact is global, but human trafficking, labor trafficking and modern-day slavery is a far worse problem... than COVID."[45]

The crisis of care has hit working-class and poor people of color the hardest, yet the care discourse has made little difference in their lives. Instead, policies that privilege the care needs of the well-off by bolstering a privatized system widens class divisions and leads to more demands on low-wage workers. Race and class inequality are being, and have been, recreated through so-called caring policies. It is time to move away from care as a justification for immigration, human worth, or labor rights. Every human being, whatever their citizenship status, should be valued, respected, and protected, and everyone deserves justice, regardless of whether they care for us or about us—and whether or not they work.

Chapter 2

What Is Social Reproduction
and Why Should I Care?

Johnnie Tillmon was born in Scott, Arkansas, in 1926 into a sharecropping family. She started work at the age of seven, washing clothes for a white man and picking cotton. She married, had six children, and later divorced. As an African American woman, well-paying work was hard for her to find, and she struggled to take care of her children as a single mother. She moved to Los Angeles in 1959 in search of better job opportunities. A few years later, while working at a commercial laundry, she became ill and applied for welfare assistance. She was appalled by the disrespectful and patronizing treatment she received from caseworkers, who inventoried her refrigerator and handed her a detailed welfare budget outlining how she should spend her money.[1]

When Tillmon applied for assistance, the Aid to Families with Dependent Children (AFDC) program for poor single parents was undergoing transition. Designed in the 1930s with white widows in mind, the program initially relied on multiple strategies to deny women of color assistance or deter them from applying for it. They were considered undeserving of assistance and were expected to work rather than stay home and care for their children. But in the 1950s and 1960s, because of migration to

47

urban areas and policy reforms intended to achieve greater equity in the program, women of color joined the welfare rolls in
greater numbers. In response to a growing outcry about women
of color receiving assistance, caseworkers surveilled recipients
more closely and the program became more punitive. In 1967,
for the first time, Congress enacted mandatory work rules that
required recipients to work, thus prioritizing their employment
over their caregiving. AFDC is one example of state policy that
privileged the social reproduction of white mothers over that of
women of color.[2f]

Shortly after enrolling in the program, Tillmon reached out
to fellow recipients in her public housing project to strategize,
and together they formed Aid to Needy Children: one of dozens of local groups that became part of a broader movement for
welfare rights. Made up primarily of African American women,
the welfare rights movement of the 1960s and 1970s demanded
resources and support from the state to help them care for their
families. They argued that mothering was valuable work and that
every mother should have the right to stay home and care for her
children. When local chapters coalesced in 1967 to form the National Welfare Rights Organization (NWRO), which eventually
represented thirty thousand welfare recipients across the country,
Tillmon was elected the first chairperson.

In chapter 1, I traced the emergence of the current care discourse and its distortion of our understanding of care, which is
rooted in part in the failure to incorporate the history of racial
capitalism. In this chapter, I examine more closely the nexus between social reproduction and racial capitalism by tracing the
history of social reproduction and the care economy, and how
the value attached to the social reproduction of white families
was distinct from the value attached to the social reproduction of
families of color. Racial capitalism shows, as I argue, that the state

and capitalists valued social reproduction for both the labor power it produced and the profit extracted from life itself.

A body of scholarship, known as social reproduction theory, argues that capital or the state supported this labor because women's labor of cooking, cleaning, and caring created the capacity for labor power needed by capital to generate profit through commodity production. Social reproduction, they suggest, was a precondition for capitalist profit but did not create profit itself. The argument that social reproduction was necessary for, but not a source of, profit is premised on a presumed distinction between social reproduction and production—what social reproduction theorists see as the separate yet connected spheres of producing goods and services and producing life. They maintain that, although capitalists depend on social reproduction for the production of labor power, there is a fundamental contradiction between support for social reproduction and the capital accumulation of profit because social reproduction sits outside of capital accumulation, and support for it directly cuts into profit margins.

An analysis of racial capitalism offers a different perspective, however. First, capital and the state provided much less support for the labor of social reproduction of people of color, even though they were an important source of labor power, thus calling into question whether reliance on labor power necessarily leads to support for social reproduction. In fact, keeping people of color in a perpetual state of crisis made them more controllable as workers.

Second, for many people of color, there was little distinction between production and social reproduction. Capital benefited from both their labor power and their life itself, as I show with the example of enslaved people, who were both workers and considered commodities. Historically, capitalism has reaped profit not only from human labor but also from human bodies. In the case of enslaved people, there was no contradiction between social reproduction and capitalist profit because social reproduction *was* a source of profit. This analysis enables us to better understand the current crisis of care. More specifically, I argue that the evisceration of state and capital support for social reproduction will not necessarily lead to a crisis of capitalism, as some Marxist feminists have predicted. Rather, the evidence shows us that capital has found new ways to profit from this crisis by expanding the care economy.

Owners of capital have always struggled with how to replenish labor power. Under industrial capitalism, people were needed to grow, harvest, and process raw materials; to manufacture goods; and to engage in a multitude of other tasks, including transportation, energy production, and sales. Industrialists strived for a balance between ensuring a steady labor supply and keeping costs low. High labor costs cut into profit margins, yet owners had to ensure that workers were fed, clothed, and housed, and that there would be another generation of workers available. Throughout the history of capitalism, securing labor power, recruiting workers, and allocating work broke down along racial and gender lines.

For nonimmigrant white families, the two-parent heterosexual household was one important site where labor power was replenished. The gender division of labor allocated unpaid household labor to women and wage-earning to men.[3] Women cooked, cleaned, and birthed and cared for children, sustaining the current generation of workers and raising the next. The presumption of a male breadwinner who would be the sole financial supporter of the family justified both women's unpaid labor in the home and women's lower wages in the workforce. Women's labor thus subsidized capital and served as an essential building block for capitalist profit: because wives did the work of social reproduction for free, employers could pay their employees less, since those workers didn't have to hire someone to cook their meals, clean their houses, and rear their children. In this regard, profit was extracted from both the bodies engaged in manufacturing and those engaged in the un- or underpaid labor of social reproduction that sustained those workers.[4]

The artificial separation of work from home, the rise of wage labor, and gendered ideas about family and household enabled the social organization of labor and the extraction of profit.[5] In the nineteenth century, waged labor became associated with the so-called public sphere, masculinity, profit-making, politics, and economic competition. Home, in contrast, was associated with the female or so-called private domestic sphere and designated a site of leisure, love, sexuality, purity, and cleanliness. The private sphere was devalued in part because the work that took place in the home did not have monetary value attached to it. Thus, wages, or lack of, masked the real economic contributions of different kinds of work. Industrial labor was overvalued, and household labor was undervalued. In fact, it was believed that household labor wasn't work at all but was presumed to be carried out because of women's love, care, and their supposed natural capacities.[6] The organization of the household and women's unpaid and underpaid labor of social reproduction, then, sustained the economic system and served as a backbone of capitalist profit.

The two-parent heterosexual family, with a mother leading a life of "leisure" and a breadwinning father, was a normative ideology that served to discipline women, men, and families. Most families—particularly families of color, unconventional families, and working-class households—didn't conform to this middle-class ideal. For them, neither their labor nor their gender identities mapped easily onto dominant ideologies because they chose or had little option but to adopt alternative household and employment arrangements. Nonnormative families were considered deviant and a threat to the social and economic order. They were either marginalized or penalized by limited state support, low wages, or social stigma. Poor mothers were more likely to work outside the home and could rarely devote themselves full-time to their own domestic sphere. They managed, nevertheless, to combine the work of social reproduction and paid labor.

The gendered ideal of the domestic sphere as a site of leisure also obscured the physical strain and economic contributions of household labor. In the nineteenth century, this work included hauling water, washing clothes in a tub, carrying coal, slaughtering livestock, scrubbing floors, and emptying chamber pots. The gendered characteristics of nurture, leisure, and cleanliness that came to define nineteenth-century white middle-class womanhood were only possible when the most difficult and backbreaking household tasks, what historian Phyllis Palmer calls "dirty work," were outsourced to other women.[7] Because of labor market segregation, even white working-class families could hire Black domestic workers. Outsourcing this work both eased the labor and signaled a higher social status.

Women's household labor was not the only way capital reproduced its workforce. Slavery was another. During the transatlantic slave trade, systemic theft of human bodies from the African continent coupled with brutal violence enabled capitalists to enslave people to work in the booming sugar, rice, cotton, and tobacco industries.[8] Slavery was essential for the rise of an industrial economy. In addition to growing products destined for industry, enslaved people also worked in mining and manufacturing and in the homes of slave owners to care for children, clean, wash clothes, cook, and keep the fires going. Slave labor underpinned both production and social reproduction, boosting profits and—by doing much of the labor of social reproduction for white families—bolstering the ideology of white middle-class womanhood's purity and cleanliness.

Slave labor was replenished through both natural reproduction and an ongoing investment in the slave trade. Slave owners found it cheaper at certain moments during the slave trade to bring in newly enslaved people rather than to support the social reproduction of already enslaved people.[9] With the end of the trade in the early nineteenth century, slave owners began to invest more in reproduction of people held in bondage, encouraging or forcing enslaved women to have children. As historian Jennifer Morgan has shown, enslaved women's labor as reproducers was critical for the slave economy because the children they bore became their master's property.[10] In fact, encouraging reproduction for the purpose of selling enslaved people became a common strategy. In this way, the labor of social reproduction that enslaved people engaged in contributed directly to capitalist profit. Slavery established a pattern of racialized labor organization that continued well beyond its abolition: as both producers and reproducers, Black women were forced, as Sarah Haley puts it, "to labor on both sides of the gender divide." Thus, unlike for most white workers at this time, for enslaved people, there was no clear distinction between work and home, production and reproduction.[11]

Capitalists also replenished the labor force through immigration. Since before the nation's founding, immigrants had worked alongside African and Indigenous people to build railroads and cities, work in the mines, and labor in factories, fields, and homes.[12] At the turn of the twentieth century, immigrants from Europe, Asia, Mexico, and US territories filled the rapidly expanding industrial and agricultural sectors. At the peak, between 1900 and 1915, more than 15 million immigrants entered the country.

A chorus of voices—fearful about immigrant radicalism, labor organizing, or tainting the racial purity of Northern and Western Europeans—helped institute a number of restrictions on immigration in the late nineteenth and early twentieth centuries.[13]

With the stream of immigrants dwindling, industrialists increased their dependence on white and African American migrants from the US South and immigrants from south of the Rio Grande. When restrictions were eased in 1965 with the Hart-Celler Act, a growing number of documented and undocumented immigrants once again joined the workforce, many becoming a critical part of the service sector.

Both immigration and slavery were racialized labor systems that drastically reduced the cost of social reproduction.[14] For immigrants, the costs of social reproduction were borne by their countries of origin. In addition, by opening or closing the borders, employers controlled the flow of migration to ensure a steady supply of new workers during periods when US industry was booming. And because enslaved people were unpaid and given little beyond survival rations, the cost of labor and social reproduction was minimal. Social reproduction, then, was not located only among people birthing and raising babies in the household. It could also be found in a legal system that sentenced some people to bondage, sanctioned a trade in human bodies, and made their offspring property, as well as in the border politics that allowed in people whose labor was needed. Some of them may have been tired, poor, and hungry, but that alone was not reason enough to allow them to land on US shores.

Capitalism's continued reliance on a superexploited or bonded labor force was untenable, however, because working people did what they've always done: they resisted. Enslaved people rebelled, retaliated, and organized, ultimately putting an end to chattel slavery in the US.[15] After emancipation in the US South, freedpeople, and especially freedwomen, withdrew from wage labor and chose instead to care for family and community.[16] Waged workers, often led by immigrants, demanded higher pay and better working conditions, as well as the eight-hour workday, and greater control over social reproduction. Industrial workers who formed unions in the nineteenth century aimed for a "family wage"—that is, wages sufficient to support both themselves and their families. For many white working-class people, a male breadwinning family in which a wife did not have to work outside the home but engaged in the unpaid labor of social reproduction was a marker of economic success.[17] There were also radical elements within the labor movement that called for worker control of production and a whole new political and economic system. So, as capitalists tried to squeeze more and more out of workers, they bumped up against the heady reality of workers who wanted higher wages, space to define the terms of social reproduction for their families, and/or to seize the means of production.

Faced with the demands of the burgeoning labor movement, some capitalists and middle-class reformers anticipated political disruption. The widening class disparities and economic insecurity that stemmed from capitalism's unfettered economic expansion seemed to be a ticking time bomb. In order to stave this off, beginning in the 1920s, industrialists experimented with supporting and managing their workers' labor of social reproduction by piloting programs that historians have named "welfare capitalism." Henry Ford, for example, paid workers an unprecedented five dollars a day, provided home mortgages, and opened a social service division in order to assimilate and discipline workers—to teach them how to save money, show up to work on time, and avoid excessive alcohol use. Ford offered concessions to American-born workers in part because he wanted a more stable workforce and a consumer market. But he was also deeply xenophobic and antisemitic and hoped to curtail the tide of immigration through these efforts.[18] Ford's business model illustrates how immigration and support for social reproduction worked in tandem:

If capital supported social reproduction at home, the US could replenish its workforce internally; however, if it sought to maximize profits through low-paying jobs that could not sustain social reproduction, then it had to reproduce the workforce through some other means such as immigration.

Despite these meager, self-interested efforts, the time bomb exploded. After the Great Depression hit, in 1929, 25 percent of Americans were unemployed—bread lines snaked around city blocks, and makeshift homeless encampments were set up in public parks. Massive and unprecedented grassroots protest among a wide swath of Americans—tenants, autoworkers, sharecroppers, the unemployed, seniors, and veterans—pushed for both immediate economic assistance and structural reform. Activists deployed militant tactics such as anti-eviction campaigns and the sit-down strike—the physical takeover of workplaces—formed new labor federations, and joined groups such as the Communist Party. The political and economic crisis awakened politicians to the need for radical federal intervention. Eventually, politicians and business leaders came to believe that capitalism would function better if it was regulated and if Americans were assured a basic standard of living. In this context, the modern welfare state was born.

The welfare state supported social reproduction by providing old-age pensions, education and job training, monthly stipends for single mothers, unemployment and disability assistance, minimum wage, and housing assistance, all of which expanded people's ability to live. Although these programs may have cut into capital's short-term profitability because of higher wages or higher taxes, in the long run they tamped down on labor radicalism, fueled consumption, ensured a steady supply of labor power, and, by mitigating poverty, forestalled the possibility of another economic crisis. For many liberals and some conservatives, maintaining stability dovetailed with the goals of economic growth and ensuring profitability.[19]

Federal government policies around social reproduction were shaped by race, much like capital's strategy for securing labor. Not everyone was included in New Deal protections. The welfare state's racial and gendered logics determined who was worthy of assistance and what counted as "work." The most well-funded programs—Social Security, the contributory old-age pension program; the Fair Labor Standards Act, which guaranteed minimum wage and overtime pay; and the National Labor Relations Act, which gave workers the right to organize and bargain collectively—benefited long-term, full-time, mostly white, male workers. These programs reinforced the gender division of labor and white middle-class women's roles as mothers and housewives by giving women assistance based on their husband's employment, such as surviving wives who collected their husband's Social Security. In this way, Social Security supported the social reproduction of white women.

In contrast, Black and Brown people with less stable, part-time, or intermittent work histories received fewer benefits, even though they were some of the most economically marginal. Most New Deal programs excluded occupations such as agricultural and domestic work, where people of color were concentrated. And even when people of color qualified for benefits, administrators on the state and local levels routinely practiced discrimination. In these ways, the welfare state institutionalized labor market inequality by deeming some labor legitimate and worthy of federal support while placing other kinds of work outside the boundaries of protection.

People who did not qualify for employment-based benefits, mostly people of color and white women without male support, were instead relegated to the poorly funded public assistance programs. Public assistance was state run with only partial funding from the federal government and was stigmatized. The single mothers, disabled people, and elderly people living in poverty who qualified for these means-tested programs received smaller and less reliable stipends than people in the social insurance programs. These New Deal inequities created what Eileen Boris has called the racialized gendered state.[20]

But even within public assistance programs, there was inequality. AFDC, the program most closely associated with the term *welfare*, supported poor single mothers without a male breadwinner. When it was established in 1935, as part of the New Deal welfare state, AFDC was rooted in white, middle-class norms of womanhood and served "worthy" white women, most of whom were widows, albeit with meager monthly stipends. The mothers who received welfare were closely monitored. European immigrants, for example, were assimilated and taught "proper" housekeeping and child-raising practices. Still, in its early years, AFDC was small and noncontroversial, and few people objected to state support for white widows who were mothers and homemakers. In fact, it aligned nicely with the prevailing belief that white women's proper place was in the home.[21]

There was little attempt in these early years, however, to mold Black and Brown single mothers into better parents. For example, in the South in the 1940s, African American women were denied public assistance during cotton-picking season and only given support during the off season.[22] Indeed, societal ideas of worthiness and care have long been rooted in the belief that only some communities and families—white ones—needed to be cared for.[23] Opposition to women of color receiving welfare and its restrictive policies, then, were a racist attack on the labor of social reproduction that women of color performed for their own families. By and large, whether through administrative decisions, regulations, or the structure of programs, people of color were considered unworthy of public assistance and better suited to the labor market.

Compounding the problem of a lack of government protection, widespread racial violence, legal segregation, and systemic racism and sexism in the private sector ensured that people of color and white women received lower wages and therefore had fewer resources to sustain family life. They earned less because it was believed that their wages were supplementary or that they simply needed less to live on, or because employers knew they had few other options. They were excluded from unions that fought for and won higher wages. Nonnormative and nonwhite families relied on multiple wage-earners and struggled mightily to carry out the labor of social reproduction, often turning to friends, neighbors, and kin for support.

Some historians and political commentators nostalgically reference the period after passage of the New Deal as a "golden age" of US capitalism. Yet, large segments of the American working class were still mired in poverty and living precariously. Although the New Deal instituted a safety net and regulated the economy, it also built into federal policy inequalities of race, class, and gender. It shored up the white heterosexual two-parent family with job security, home mortgage guarantees, and health and educational benefits, while it further jeopardized non-normative families and families of color by limiting their access to public assistance and social benefits.

Even more troubling than the lack of government support for social reproduction of some groups, are state efforts to prevent the reproduction of Black and Brown people, evident in coercive sterilization programs. From the early twentieth century until the 1970s, state-run medical boards referred people, sometimes without their consent or knowledge, for medical procedures that would permanently prevent them from having children. This was part of a broader eugenics campaign that sought to encourage reproduction among white people and halt the reproduction of nonwhite, Indigenous, neurodivergent, and disabled people in the interest of improving the "stock" of the human race.[24]

Social reproduction vis-à-vis capital and the state cannot be analyzed without considering the bodies, especially racialized bodies, that were being reproduced—that is, how some people were deemed more valuable than other people. The differential status and treatment illustrate how social reproduction was always wedded to hierarchy and unequal valuation of both life and labor power. In short, social reproduction for most white families was protected and supported by the state and capital, unlike the social reproduction for people of color.[25] In addition, the labor of social reproduction that workers of color performed for white families was more highly valued than the same labor performed for their own families and communities.

After the passage of the New Deal, because of antiracist, labor, and antipoverty organizing, the welfare state slowly extended its reach. More women, like Tillmon, applied for welfare assistance, and previously excluded occupational sectors, such as agricultural and domestic work, were included in the Social Security Act and the Fair Labor Standards Act. The safety net was expanded with Lyndon Johnson's Great Society policies, which introduced food stamps, public housing, and health insurance for the elderly and poor.

Antipoverty activists also made a case that giving cash assistance to poor people outside the labor market was good for the capitalism because it fueled household consumption. Arguments about consumerism also drove Keynesian economists to push for lower taxes and lower interest rates so that Americans would have more cash in their hands. Although the welfare state still primarily rewarded and bolstered the white middle class with its generous housing and education assistance, it also uplifted many poor people (both white and nonwhite) with Social Security assistance for the elderly, monthly stipends for single mothers and disabled people, and a minimum wage for workers. By the end of the 1960s, more Americans were under the aegis of state protection. The number of families on AFDC, for example, increased from 800,000 in 1960 to 2.2 million in 1970. In addition, Congress created Supplemental Security Income (SSI) in 1972, making the patchwork of state programs for blind, disabled, and elderly poor people into a federal program that, by 1974, guaranteed a minimum level of income.[26]

Thus, during the post–World War II period, capital came to believe that support for social reproduction and household prosperity—whether from higher wages or government assistance—was an asset to the economy rather than a drain on profitability. One takeaway from the Great Depression was that capital wanted and needed stability—a stable and trained workforce, market predictability, and a robust consumer market—and they were willing to pay the costs associated with that for the next four decades.

Things changed with the rise of neoliberalism.

The shift from industrial capitalism to neoliberalism engendered a devastating crisis of social reproduction. Neoliberalism as a free-market ideology has its roots in the 1930s but took hold as policy in the 1970s. In the interests of maximizing profit and minimizing the costs of social reproduction, capital fled to places where production was cheaper; fought for lower taxes and smaller government in the US; and drove down wages to a point where a full-time salary did not support an individual, let alone a family. It led to a dismantling of the welfare state, the privatization of public services, and deregulation of the economy.[27]

Neoliberalism had a perceptible impact on the lives of many Americans. With fewer full-time industrial jobs, the erosion of union rights, and falling wages, the model of a male breadwinner and full-time homemaker—an ideal that some white middle-class families had achieved—was upended. White women's entry into the labor market, attributable in part to the women's movement but also because their families found it harder to make ends meet, made the dual-earner household the norm. In 1960, 25 percent of married couples with children under eighteen had dual incomes; in 2012, 60 percent did. Perhaps even more revealing is that, in 1960, 70 percent of two-parent families relied only on a father's income. This had dropped to 31 percent in 2012.[28]

With the state offering fewer services and supports for social reproduction and doing less to protect workers, families across race, class, and ethnic backgrounds find it increasingly difficult to care for children, the elderly, or others who need assistance. The crisis has become more acute as people live longer and require more years of care. Hospitals and insurance companies have cut back on coverage of institutionalized care for the elderly, ill, and disabled. Long-term care is increasingly diverted to private nursing or adult-care facilities, or to the home to be performed by family members or paid in-home workers. Disinvestment in public schools and limited public childcare options have strained families emotionally and financially. By the end of the twentieth century, neoliberal logics had more fully shifted the burden of social reproduction to the private sector.

Families are, out of necessity, devoting a larger portion of household income to the costs of social reproduction. They have turned to the private market for consumer products (prepared foods, robotic vacuums, and so on), thus expanding the trend toward commercialization of social reproduction. Parents pay for day care, after-school care, or private school tuition; hire supplementary tutors; or invest more of their own time to ensure their children are cared for and educated. They hire low-wage workers, patch together makeshift solutions, or are unable to achieve a level of household maintenance that meets their standards. An increasing number of families are going into debt and paying interest and fees to meet their basic needs.[29]

In the 1970s, countless policy makers predicted a decline in paid household labor due to technological advancements. Dishwashers, washing machines, and takeout food, they declared, would transform the modern household. They were only partially right. People did rely on the new technology, but they also depended on paid services outside the home and hired more private household workers to fill the care gap. Despite falling wages, people became care consumers because of the large pool of cheap labor, growing household indebtedness, or more employed adults in the household. Technology never did, nor could it, replace much of the hands-on work required in the household, whether nursing the sick, cleaning bathrooms, or putting children to sleep. As more and more of the work necessary to reproduce and sustain life is bought and sold, there has been a proliferation of health-care facilities, restaurants, assisted living and day care centers, education and enrichment programs, and hospice care, as well as in-home workers, who are disproportionately underpaid women of color.

Reliance on the private market to alleviate the crisis of social reproduction has led to a rise in service-sector jobs as the number of manufacturing jobs has declined. About 8 percent of American workers were employed in manufacturing in 2020, according to the Bureau of Labor Statistics.[30] In contrast, 28 percent were employed in social reproduction fields—community and social service, education, health care, food preparation, and personal care and service. The health-care and education sectors alone constituted 15 percent of the American workforce, nearly double the number of manufacturing workers.[31] The expansion of the paid labor of social reproduction is one indication of how the for-profit care economy is being tailored in response to the crisis of care and enabling capital to find new sources of economic profit.

The shift to neoliberalism also reconfigured who works, who doesn't, and what they earn—that is, the constitution of the working class. The working class was always diverse, but, since the 1970s, with the rise of the service sector, a greater portion of the working class in the US is people of color, white women, and immigrant workers. Sociologist Evelyn Nakano Glenn has tracked the movement of women of color out of paid household labor into the low-wage institutionalized service sector after World War II.[32] She argues that certain groups of women of color who left domestic work, especially African American women, ended up doing very similar labor in hospitals, schools, laundries, and restaurants.

Cities once dominated by manufacturing are now hubs of service work. The shift from an industrial economy to a service economy was not just a sequential process but a consequential one. For example, as historian Gabriel Winant has described, Pittsburgh morphed from an industrial heartland into a center of health care. The private insurance and health-care benefits of relatively privileged, mostly white, retired unionized industrial workers and their families laid the foundation for the expansion of a service economy. The growth of the health-care industry in Pittsburgh was fueled by multiple stakeholders—the financial sector, insured workers and retirees, and the state. In the absence of universal health benefits or robust redistributive state policies, it created a two-tiered system of those being served and those who serve them. Health-care workers were largely underpaid women, mostly women of color, who did not have the same benefits. Pittsburgh is just one example of how neoliberalism has helped usher in a private care market that has created inequalities, and how caring for some people comes at the expense of other people whose lives and labors are valued differently.[33]

As important as neoliberalism has been in shifting the political and economic landscape in detrimental ways, it cannot be considered "the singular paradigm," as American studies professor Tanja Aho argues.[34] Neoliberalism is only the latest iteration of a long history of inequality, exploitation, dispossession, and different valuations of life and labor that capitalism, and racial capitalism in particular, has constructed. What many middle-class Americans experience as a relatively recent crisis of social reproduction is a longer-standing problem for America's poorest populations. For generations, poor communities, especially poor communities of color, struggled to care for loved ones, put food on the table, buy basic necessities, and secure decent health care. They were subject to policies that sought to prevent them from reproducing, denied them welfare benefits to raise children and care for their families, or extracted profit directly from their labor of social reproduction. Poor and working-class families marshaled what they had. They established mutual aid societies and created alternative social arrangements and systems of social support. Still, the structural inequities sometimes resulted in family separation, untreated illnesses, and premature death.

What is new about the crisis of social reproduction in the neoliberal era is its scale. Neoliberalism has exacerbated the insecurity of poor communities and simultaneously pulled the rug out from under middle- and working-class families who had previously benefited from the social programs of the mid-twentieth century. Now, middle-class families are also struggling with how to care for themselves and their loved ones. We are reaching a critical threshold. People have fallen deeper into debt, are self-medicating, and have dropped out of school or the workforce. There are record numbers of children in foster care, families without access to affordable (or any) childcare, elderly people without caretakers, people who are unhoused and food insecure, and people with disabilities who are incarcerated. The crisis of social reproduction has reached a breaking point. [35]

What are we to make of the crisis of social reproduction? What does it mean for the future of families, the state, and capitalism?

Feminist social reproduction theorists, such as Nancy Fraser, Susan Ferguson, and Tithi Bhattacharya, argue that the crisis of social reproduction is not simply a crisis of individual families, as popular commentators sometimes frame it, but a systemic crisis of capitalism. The source of the crisis, they argue, is a fundamental contradiction between capital's reliance on social reproduction to produce labor power, which is a condition of the possibility for profit, on the one hand, and capital's drive to maximize profit, on the other. Producing labor power requires support for families and communities, which cuts into profit. Capital's drive for profit, by lowering wages and support for social programs, undermines the ability of families and communities to live securely. In short, there is a tension between care and profit. Ferguson argues that the "social labours involved in producing this and the next generation of workers sit in *a necessary but contradictory relation* to the capitalist drive to produce and accumulate surplus value." She continues: "It is *contradictory* because capitalists must—in order to remain competitive—create conditions whereby meeting human needs is subordinated to accumulation." The struggle between profit and care is what Nancy Fraser calls a "boundary struggle": capital moves to minimize support for workers, while workers demand more time and resources for care. Struggles around social reproduction, these theorists argue, are a space of political possibility and resistance. It is precisely in this arena of producing life, Ferguson and Bhattacharya argue, where workers have autonomy. [36]

Capital's relentless drive for profit, particularly under financialized capitalism, social reproduction theorists maintain, has accelerated the cutback of social services, falling wages, privatization of land and water, ecological degradation, and dispossession to such a degree that people are unable to maintain and reproduce life. In an important 2016 essay on the care crisis, "Contradictions of Capital and Care," philosopher Nancy Fraser argues that the capital accumulation is generating a deepening crisis "squeezing" our "social capacities" and has become acute.[37] This drive for profit, she predicts, could lead to the system's inability to reproduce itself and can only be resolved through "deep structural transformation of this social order."[38] In short, capital's failure to support social reproduction is jeopardizing capitalism itself. The crisis of care, social reproduction theorists argue, is an inflection point that contains a possibility for the destabilization of capitalism and the opportunity to create something new. It has led to renewed, widespread political protests around social reproduction, which I will discuss in chapter 4. Both the predictions of collapse and the promises of change are premised on the belief in the fundamental contradiction between social reproduction and accumulation of capital.

From the perspective of people of color and through the lens of racial capitalism, however, there is not, and never has been, a clear distinction or contradiction between production and social reproduction. Throughout US history, Black and Brown people have rarely been given the opportunity to produce life, except as profit. Their reproductive capacities have been used for the production of labor power and simultaneously have been a source of capitalist profit. Slaveholders saw no "inherent tension" between the production of commodities and social reproduction of enslaved people. The social reproduction of people held in bondage always created capitalist value. Financiers, insurance companies, and shipping companies benefitted enormously from the trade in enslaved people and the capital of human bodies—not just slave labor. Indeed, not only did the trade bring bonded workers to planters, but the process of enslaving and transporting people was profit-driven.[39] Enslaved people both produced commodities and were treated as a commodity that was sold separate and apart from those commodities produced by their labor power.

An analysis of racialized social reproduction calls into question whether the crisis of social reproduction will necessarily result in the destabilization of capitalism. Whether under institutionalized slavery, open immigration policies, or an expansive welfare state, capitalists have always accrued a certain amount of profit from social reproduction. Capital's historic extraction of profit from the social reproduction of certain racialized bodies has become a widespread feature of contemporary neoliberal capitalism. Under neoliberalism, capital has found even more ways to extract profit from social reproduction, primarily through the rise of the care economy.

Over the past few decades and especially the past few years, social reproduction has become a more significant part of the economy, measured by the kind of work that people engage in as well as in terms of profit. Because of the diffuse and decentralized nature of the care economy, there are many layers of profit to be made. A growing number of corporate firms are now dedicated to meeting people's social reproductive needs. Corporate capital, small businesses, and economically secure middle- and upper-class families all benefit from the crisis of social reproduction of the most vulnerable people, as I explain in more detail later in the book, or have found ways to make money from the care needs of people with resources. The current crisis of social reproduction is not an economic paradox that will undermine capitalism—as with so many other crises, capitalism finds ways to transform them into opportunities and, ultimately, to thrive. Capital is instead seeking out new forms of accumulation that depend on this very crisis.

Many scholars and political commentators assume that stable

economic and social relations are necessary for capitalism's health.[40] For decades, conventional wisdom was that capitalism requires predictable markets and a reliable workforce that reproduces itself to ensure a margin of profitability. Employers need to know that workers will show up to work the next day and still go shopping. The New Deal, the welfare state more broadly, and public infrastructure such as potable water systems, schools, and hospitals were premised on this logic. Stability is good for capital in certain moments and for certain communities. It is not, however, a universal truth. As the history of racial capitalism shows, capital has also made enormous profit from the destabilization of life, family, and community through slavery, settler colonialism, and imperialism. The enclosure movement in industrializing England and the massive dam construction projects in South Asia are additional examples of how capitalist profit and the disruption of social and economic relations go hand in hand. In the current moment, profit derived from the crisis of social reproduction also calls into question the presumed link between economic stability and corporate profitability.

Instability has become lucrative in other ways as well. In a financialized economy, as Marxist theorist David Harvey has written, capital accrues profit from insurance, speculation, debt, and buying and selling futures. Finance as a source of accumulation can reap enormous profit from instability and crisis. Although these financial transactions seem divorced from human bodies, they are, in fact, very much tied to people. Hedge fund managers bet on market volatility, and the banking sector earns loads of money from household hardship. When families default on loans, go into debt, or are slapped with fees and fines, someone is profiting. Market fluctuations, although bad for some, creates opportunities for generating wealth for others. I discuss further in chapter 6 how capital sees not devastation but dollar signs in other markers of instability such as foster care, welfare, the carceral state, and devolution of the safety net.

In addition, an unstable workforce—more pliable, manageable, and "deportable" (to use Nicholas de Genova's phrase)—has also been an asset to capital.[41] Precarious workers employed in the service sector, in both private homes and institutions, are locked into low-wage employment because of racism, sexism, legal status, and the dismantling of public assistance programs. These jobs do not offer upward mobility or economic advancement. Workers don't have benefits or job security. Employers, both household and corporate, benefit from the insecurity of workers with few legal or economic options and little choice but to work for whatever employers will pay and under any circumstances. Middle-class families, home care agencies, and cleaning companies, for example, are able to cope with and profit from the care crisis because of the availability of a large, cheap, and vulnerable workforce. In contrast to the stability that Henry Ford sought to create that became characteristic of the mid-twentieth century, employers today choose precarity over stability.

Capitalism has also found ways to profit from the "surplus" population, or what the South African apartheid government called "superfluous appendages": people who might be unable to work but still need services and care. This includes the elderly, disabled people, children, and people who are currently or formerly incarcerated. One might assume that the people capitalism finds unproductive are a drain on resources because they need to be contained, controlled, and managed. Indeed, Marxist analysis has traditionally seen people outside the labor market as a reserve army of labor that needs to be supported when not in the workforce. In a care economy, however, providing for people who may not be productive in capital's eyes has enormous value. As Ruth Wilson Gilmore has argued, the expansion of the prison-industrial complex—which simultaneously contained a surplus population, created jobs, and revived sluggish rural communities—served as a boon to an ailing California economy since the 1980s. Gilmore's brilliant analysis exposes how state policy works in tandem with capitalist economies to ensure new strategies of profit-making.[42]

More recently, as the move to find alternatives to incarceration has gained traction and sentencing laws have eased, the for-profit prison-industrial complex has expanded its reach beyond warehousing to treatment and care. Private corporations are benefiting financially from support programs inside prisons, such as health care, as well as from the halfway houses, counseling, and job training on which recently released people rely. The profit motive incentivizes keeping people entangled with the carceral state and under surveillance long after their sentences have been served.[43] Under the care economy, people outside the labor market have become a source of profit precisely because of their care needs and their precarious situation. Their value derives less from their labor power than from the sustenance of human bodies.

Most Marxist feminist social reproduction theory begins with the mode of production and then extrapolates what this tells us about social reproduction.[44] Thus, it analyzes how industrial capitalism relied upon and supported the labor of social reproduction and how deindustrialization and neoliberalism led to a disinvestment in social reproduction. I argue that not only has the mode of production (slavery, commercial capitalism, industrial capitalism, neoliberalism) shaped social reproduction, but the crisis of social reproduction has also shaped capitalism. The crisis of social reproduction has proven to be an opportunity for economic growth, particularly for the care economy. Under neoliberalism, social reproduction is not only a precondition for capital accumulation, as many feminist theorists argue, but also increasingly a source of capital accumulation for corporations, nonprofits, the state, and individual households.

Examining social reproduction from the vantage point of the most marginalized Black and Brown people suggests that there is no necessary tension between social reproduction and capital accumulation. In the care economy, the production and maintenance of human bodies, not only labor or labor power, has become a source of profit. Manufacturing still generates profit and there is still a need to produce labor power, particularly in the Global South, where a great deal of manufacturing has shifted. Indeed, the vibrant consumer economy of rich countries that runs parallel to and also feeds off of the care economy would not be possible without a manufacturing sector. But the way human survival has become a means for capitalist growth in deindustrializing countries is shocking and grotesque. Under neoliberal racial capitalism, the care for bodies with vulnerabilities and incapacities has become a source of wealth—whether those bodies are in jail cells, immigration detention centers, nursing homes, or day care centers. Those who cannot contribute their labor power contribute through their needs. Our love for them impels us to consume care services and buy products to ensure they are cared for. And, in the process, we deepen our relationship with the care industry and further exacerbate societal inequities.

Chapter 3

Social Reproduction, Coercion, and Care

Edith Mendoza arrived in New Jersey from the Philippines in January 2015 to work as a live-in domestic worker for the family of a German diplomat. Before coming to the US, she signed a contract specifying that she would be responsible for childcare and light housework. She was expected to work thirty-five hours a week at ten dollars an hour, with time-and-a-half for overtime, and was guaranteed Sundays off, transportation, and room and board.

The situation was different once Edith started the job. She worked eighty to one hundred hours a week and was never paid overtime. She was responsible for cooking three meals a day, cleaning the family's three-story, six-bedroom, six-bath house, doing the laundry, taking care of yard work—including shoveling snow—and caring for four small boys. On her day off, her employer bombarded her with questions about where she was going, making her hesitant about leaving the house at all. Although she wanted to flee, Edith was fearful of losing her visa and becoming undocumented. She developed a serious health issue, but her employer refused to let her go to the doctor. Edith went anyway and was threatened with deportation. She escaped in 2016 and contacted Damayan Migrant Workers Association. With their support, she filed a civil suit for stolen wages, but the case was dropped in 2018 because of her employer's diplomatic immunity. Damayan also helped Edith apply for her T visa—a visa for victims of human trafficking—which she received. This enabled her to reside legally in the US and bring her son and husband from the Philippines to join her.

Edith's story exemplifies how coercion underpins domestic labor. Although she was hired as a childcare worker, she was expected to do heavy house and yard work. As a live-in worker, her employer treated her as a round-the-clock servant. The threats and constant surveillance signaled that her employers were more interested in controlling her labor than ensuring her well-being. As an immigrant worker who was exploited and whose visa was tied to her employer, Edith's case is textbook labor trafficking.

Domestic work is a microcosm of structural inequality. It is one of the lowest-paid occupations, with workers earning, on average, fourteen dollars an hour and about sixteen thousand dollars a year, according to a survey conducted by the Economic Policy Institute. Domestic workers are three times more likely to live in poverty as other workers, only one in ten has an employer-provided retirement program, and one in five has employer-provided health insurance.[1] Domestic workers were originally excluded from New Deal labor protections—Social Security, minimum wage, and the right to organize. They got Social Security in 1950 because of lobbying by labor feminists and minimum wage in 1974 due to the domestic workers' rights movement, but they still don't have federal Occupational Health and Safety Act protections or the legal right to organize and bargain collectively. Even when domestic workers are protected by labor laws, there is little enforcement and oversight. Because of their vulnerability in the labor market, employers not only underpay domestic workers but get away with providing inadequate housing and food for live-in workers as well. Mistreatment is rampant. It is not uncommon to hear of workers who are physically or mentally abused.

Most people become household workers because they have few options. The working conditions are so miserable that as soon as they can, they flee domestic work and return to it only out of desperation. At the beginning of the twentieth century, for example, white women left the occupation in droves as opportunities opened in the sales and service sectors—opportunities reserved primarily for them. But, during the Great Depression, when there were few jobs, white women, who otherwise wouldn't have considered paid household labor, gladly took it up. Clearly, some measure of coercion—relying, for example, on state power, economic necessity or labor market discrimination—compels people to take these jobs.

Because domestic work has been an occupation of last resort, there have been frequent periods of labor shortage. In response, government agencies or employers' associations instituted labor contracting, immigration programs, training programs, and specific economic policies for the purpose of securing a steady supply of household workers, such as the 1930s New Deal program that trained and placed unemployed African American women in jobs as domestic workers. The state often worked hand in glove with employers and supported private initiatives or turned the other way when abuses occurred. Through regulation and enforcement, the state ensured the continued subservience of domestic workers, nearly all of whom were women of color.

Domestic work as a coercive occupation is intertwined with the history of gendered racial capitalism, so it is impossible to talk about paid household labor without also talking about race and gender. Domestic work, like every other paid occupation, is part of a structural power relationship, with a boss and a worker. From this vantage point, the labor of social reproduction is best understood not in terms of care but in the context of the history of slavery, racism, imperialism, and colonialism.

In this chapter, I examine how the devaluation of paid domestic workers' labor did not originate with familial ties and gender inequality in the home but rather with state power and racial inequality within the labor market.[2] Examining care work through the lens of labor and race makes visible the care economy's dependence on coerced racialized labor. Social reproductive labor, increasingly performed by migrant workers of color, also reflects shifts in the changing character of the American working class, which is more diverse, foreign, and precarious. Last, I delve into how social reproduction, and the gig economy more broadly, complicates our understanding of the increasingly blurry relationship between employers and employees—and even the definition of who is an employer and employee.

Racism and colonialism were the basis of many coercive state programs that placed servants in the homes of middle-class white families. For example, at the end of the nineteenth century, as part of the ongoing process of settler colonialism, the US Bureau of Indian Affairs (BIA) organized the removal of Indigenous children from their homes and sent them to boarding schools. The goal was assimilation and the destruction of Indigenous language, culture, and community. After their so-called training, Indigenous girls worked in the homes of white families as part of an "outing program" under the supervision of white BIA matrons. Although framed as social uplift and rescue to prepare Indigenous girls to manage their own households, they were discouraged from becoming mothers or housewives, and the BIA often forced them to give up their children. Both the government and em-

ployers wanted instead to groom them for possible future employment as household workers. The US program was not unique.
Similar programs were created in other settler-colonial countries,
including Canada and Australia.[3]

Colonial logics also shaped the US policy of recruiting domestic workers from Puerto Rico. In 1946, a Chicago-based private agency, Castle, Barton, and Associates, contracted with the
Puerto Rican Department of Labor to encourage Puerto Ricans
to come to the mainland US to work as domestics in the homes of
white families. This was possible, even during a period of restrictive immigration, because of Puerto Ricans' status as US citizens.
These household workers, some of whom were underage, worked
long hours and were underpaid and mistreated. Although the labor contracts were not binding, the head of the agency reportedly
told an employer that if a worker broke a contract, "we could
blackball them successfully from any other job," thus deterring
workers from quitting or complaining.[4]

In the wake of growing media coverage of workers' treatment, the Puerto Rican Senate launched an investigation and
halted the program.[5] In response to the controversy surrounding private contracting companies, the Migration Division of the
Puerto Rican Department of Labor initiated a separate, more
regulated training and migration program for household workers
in 1947. It offered information about employment opportunities
on the mainland, arranged contracts, and placed women in the
homes of white middle-class families in Chicago, Boston, and
New York. Government involvement didn't resolve problems of
overwork and isolation, however. Even in these government programs, workers who quit were cast as social deviants and sometimes arrested or institutionalized.[6]

Because of slavery and institutionalized racism, African
Americans were also bound to household labor. Enslaved men and

women in the Americas worked in the homes of slave owners, cooking, cleaning, serving, wet-nursing, and raising the children of the slave master's family.[7] During Reconstruction, the Freedmen's Bureau, the federal agency that aided the transition to freedom, trained freedwomen as domestic workers and financed their travel North to work in the homes of white families. Freedwomen sent North reduced government relief costs in the South and addressed the perpetual "servant problem"—the shortage of domestic workers—that Northern employers frequently complained about. Although the Freedmen's Bureau's purported aim was to "help" formerly enslaved people transition to freedom, this program was less about benevolence than enforcing wage labor and alleviating the labor shortage in the North.[8]

Domestic worker contracts for freedwomen created an especially oppressive work environment, where workers had limited mobility and were required, above all, to obey—essentially recreating the conditions of servitude. During Reconstruction, workers were convicted of vagrancy if they failed to enter into or fulfill the terms of a contract. In this way, labor contracts were a tool of labor discipline at a time when many freedpeople chose or would have chosen to withdraw from wage labor altogether. Freedwomen, in fact, often wanted to redirect their labor toward their own families. Forcing African American women to engage in social reproductive work as paid labor, rather than for their own families, underpinned Freedmen's Bureau policy, which was designed to turn formerly enslaved people into wage workers, often doing the same work they did when they were enslaved. It also shored up the gendered ideologies of the two-parent heterosexual white family. As women's and gender studies professor Priya Kandaswamy writes: "While bureau officials tended to see reproductive labor done by [African American] housewives as vagrancy, that same labor counted as legitimate and desirable work when done under white surveillance in the service of white families."[9]

State coercion didn't end with Reconstruction. In Georgia, from the early twentieth century until the 1930s, for instance, the carceral system served as an institutional and legal mechanism to force African Americans to labor in the homes of white families, which historian Sarah Haley has named "domestic carcerality."[10] After serving prison time, the vast majority of paroled Black women were sent to the homes of white families, where they were required to labor as domestics for at least one year. White employers did not have to pay these workers for their labor, although many paid a nominal amount. Parolees were always under the threat of being sent back to prison or having their parole extended. According to Haley, "They were subject to constant surveillance and the threat of return to the prison camp for any transgression; private individuals, many of whom were now white women, continued to serve as police and warders."[11] Caught up in a system designed to reinforce capitalist labor organization and white supremacist patriarchy, these parolees "imagined themselves as prisoners who had been transferred to a different carceral terrain."[12] This system addressed fears of labor shortage and provided labor for employers. The domestic sphere, in essence, became an extension of the prison regime; thus, release from prison did not mean freedom.

These patterns of racism and colonialism profoundly shaped how and why particular groups of people ended up as household workers. Connected to this was also the way they were racialized and how race shaped their experiences as workers.

Household labor in the US has always been a racially diverse occupation. At different points in US history, Irish, Japanese, Mexican American, Chinese, Indigenous, Caribbean, African, and African American people, as well as white women, all served as domestic workers. Domestic workers are often othered, even by well-meaning employers, who rely on notions of their workers' difference and inferiority to justify low wages and poor treatment.

At the end of the nineteenth century, Irish Catholic women were the predominant domestic workers in the Northeast, alongside African American women. In 1900, for example, 34 percent of domestic workers were Black and 39 percent were immigrant white women, the vast majority from Ireland.[13] As servants in white middle-class homes, Irish women faced harsh working conditions and were routinely referred to as "Biddy," a racially derogatory reference to someone who was unruly and unrefined.[14] At the time, the Irish occupied a racially ambiguous category: although European, they were not considered fully white. They experienced discrimination and exclusion, encountering want ads that specified "No Irish Need Apply" and commercial establishments that posted signs reading "Dogs and Irish Not Allowed."[15]

White women, both European and native-born, may have experienced discrimination and poor working conditions, as was the case with the Irish, but they also had privileges. They usually worked as domestics for only a short period of time before getting married. They got plum positions and earned the highest wages. On the other hand, women who were undocumented, non-English speaking, and/or of African descent were the most poorly treated, relegated to physically taxing labor, and earned the least. Women of color were more likely to work after marriage, and thus they experienced family separation because they juggled working in someone else's home while maintaining their own.

Various groups were racialized differently as employers ascribed to them specific characteristics. For example, in the nineteenth century, Chinese men were considered effeminate and nonthreatening to white female employers, as historian Andrew Urban notes.[16] Until the civil rights movement, African Americans were considered ideal domestic workers (although not for their own families). But, as formal segregation laws were dismantled and other job opportunities opened up, they left the occupation in droves. Those who stayed began to organize and came to be perceived by employers as too demanding and "unmanageable." Employers turned then to the growing number of immigrants. Caribbean domestic workers were stereotyped as "clean" and good at disciplining children, and Filipinos as "hardworking."

By shuttling people of color into domestic work and creating racialized hierarchies among them, racism served as a form of labor control.[17] Racial stereotypes made it seem as if some people were destined for that particular labor. Racialized ideology about domestic work also contributed to racialized ideas about the women doing the work and was extrapolated beyond the occupation—Black women, whatever their profession, came to be seen as cleaners or low-wage service workers; Filipinos were stereotyped as nurses and carers. Racism shaped the occupation and the occupation shaped ideas about race.

In the US, anti-Black racism was—and still is—especially salient in domestic work. Without discounting the large numbers of Chicanx women in the Southwest and Puerto Rican and Caribbean women in cities such as Chicago and New York who work as domestics, African American women, as well as women of African descent from Africa, Latin America, and the Caribbean were tethered to this labor in a way that other racial groups, particularly white ethnic women, were not. African American women were the largest number of domestic workers from the era of slavery until the 1970s. During Jim Crow segregation, many educated African Americans were locked out of other jobs and had no choice but to enter the occupation. As of 1960, for instance, African Americans represented 45 percent of all domestic workers, and more than a third of Black women worked as domestics.[18] When racial barriers were nominally removed after the civil rights movement and with the growing commodification of social reproduction, Black women continued to work in service, although in institutions rather than private homes, with little change in their social status.[19] This intensified with the dismantling of welfare in 1996. The most feasible option for poor Black women was to work as nurses' aides, hospital janitors, and school cafeteria workers.

For many African Americans, the parallels between domestic work and slavery were not lost on them. In the 1930s, two African American journalists, Ella Baker and Marvel Cooke, made a connection between slavery and domestic work in their exposé about the exploitative working conditions for domestic workers: "The Bronx Slave Market," where African American women were "pressed to the wall by poverty, starvation, and discrimination." The "slave markets" in this case were the New York City street corners where African American household workers waited to be hired for day work. The shortage of work during the Great Depression made competition fierce, with white women also vying for positions, and exploitation and mistreatment rampant. Baker and Cooke recounted what they witnessed on these street corner markets: "Fortunate, indeed, is she who gets the full hourly rate promised. Often, her day's slavery is rewarded with a single dollar bill or whatever her unscrupulous employer pleases to pay. More often, the clock is set back for an hour or more. Too often she is sent away without any pay at all."[20]

These parallels were further reinforced by household worker activists in the 1970s, who frequently pointed out similarities between slavery and domestic labor. Domestic Workers of America organizer Geraldine Roberts, introduced in chapter 1, explained her public posture of compliance and feigned emotion, and how this resonated with what she called "slavery time" in an interview in 1977:

> We were not satisfied; we were afraid we may not have the job—that we might get fired. So we was submissive to the boss lady to some degree; as we were to our mistresses in slavery time: the fear of the employer, the fear of not being able to get another job, no references being given if she got angry. We had to pretend and smile when we didn't want to smile and show our teeth and laugh loud and [act] stupid to make her feel that we were quite humble to her.[21]

In relying on the slavery trope, these activists assert that domestic work, like slavery, straddles the line between exploitation and expropriation. The slave metaphor is especially useful to dispel the assumptions of care and familial bonds that often framed the occupation. It also reinserted into the conversation the racialized power dynamics and coercion common to the work.[22] But the metaphor could only go so far. Slavery was a system of legalized and institutionalized ownership of human beings and their children, people who could be bought and sold on the open market. Domestic workers, on the other hand, possessed some rights—however limited those might be. Nevertheless, structural racism undergirded both slavery and domestic work. Race, and the intertwined histories of chattel slavery, imperialism, settler colonialism, and immigration, powerfully determined who was sought out and ended up in paid domestic labor, and how they were treated.

Today, domestic work is still a racially diverse occupation—perhaps more so now than ever—and a racial hierarchy persists. After changes in immigration law in 1965, more women from abroad came to the US as private household workers. Although statistics are notoriously unreliable, according to one survey, 90 percent of domestic workers in the US are women, and 58 percent are people of color.[23] Legal status, race, and language all shape workers' treatment and wages, becoming forms of discipline and control. African immigrant home health-care workers in New York and New Jersey shared horrific stories of racism, humiliation, and abuse with anthropologist Cati Coe. Employers frequently expressed preference for white workers, spewed racial insults at Black workers, and subjected them to harsher working conditions. Coe explains: "The home care market racializes care workers as African and migrant...It positions them as unskilled and in subordinate positions in relation to patients."[24] The workers Coe interviewed harbored anger about their low wages, lack of benefits, and poor treatment. Although they came to the US with high hopes, a racialized labor market and the abuse they experienced convinced many of them to return home rather than stay in the US.[25]

The visa system is one of the primary modern-day state technologies to recruit workers, compel them to work, and curtail their rights. Whereas the US Border Patrol polices borders with weapons, leaving a visible trail of trauma, death, and family destruction, the visa system quietly deputizes private employers to act as a kind of border patrol with the power to criminalize and sentence people to servitude. US Department of State officials determine who can enter, for how long, under what circumstances, and to whom the individual is accountable. The visa system endows both the state and individual employers with power over workers (much like the domestic carcerality Haley described in Jim Crow Georgia). Special visas enable foreign diplomats to bring with them "personal employees," attendants, domestic workers, or servants, who are legally bound to work only for the primary visa holder and are not allowed to switch jobs. Unsurprisingly, the system is rife with abuse.

Even before the formal visa and immigration systems were established, there were controls over who crossed the border, and certain accommodations were made for domestic workers. After the passage of the 1882 Chinese Exclusion Act, for example, the state created exceptions for employers who wanted to bring Chinese household workers with them. Employers put up a bond and were responsible for their employees—a system that foreshadowed the employer visa programs of today. The federal government, as Andrew Urban describes, facilitated and "brokered" domestic servitude.[26]

This is similar to Edith Mendoza's situation. Because her visa was tied to her employer, she found it difficult to challenge the mistreatment. But her case also illustrates the long-standing relationship between the US and the Philippines. Because of the history of US imperialism that impoverished this small island nation, Filipinos' independent sources of livelihood were destroyed. Facing high unemployment and a decimated agricultural sector, many Filipinos go abroad in search of work.

Since the 1970s, the Filipino government has actively facilitated the temporary deployment of Filipino workers abroad to address rising unemployment in the archipelago. Encouraging migration became a government policy and transformed the Philippines into what Robyn Margalit Rodriguez calls a labor "brokerage state."[27] The Filipino government trains potential workers, assists them with paperwork, and claims to ensure their well-being while abroad. An estimated 2 million Filipinos are formal temporary overseas workers. The total number of Filipinos living abroad is much higher, however, perhaps 10 percent of the population, about 10 million people, according to the Commission on Filipinos Overseas, a Filipino government agency.[28] This estimate includes officially registered permanent migrants as well as temporary and undocumented migrants and people who have been trafficked. Filipinos working abroad support families at home by sending back billions of dollars in remittances, which also serves as an important source of revenue for the Filipino government.[29]

Filipino migration has accelerated because of the growing need for care workers globally. They alleviate the care crisis in other countries by working in hospitals, in nursing homes, and for families as nannies and home health-care aides. Filipino migration, then, is a product of colonialism and the lack of economic development in the Philippines as well as neoliberal restructuring in more developed countries that has left people without the help they need.

The demand for care workers in places like the US has structured a labor market where Filipinos serve as low-paid care workers, often with limited rights and protections. They may have few other economic options or, as temporary workers, are sent home once they complete their terms of service.[30] They are on the front lines of health crises and have paid the price for it. During the pandemic, for example, Filipinos constituted more than 26 percent of US nursing deaths, even though they make up only 4 percent of registered nurses.[31] Particular groups of people end up doing the labor of social reproduction not simply by the individual choices of workers or employers—not, in other words, because one finds Filipinos "good" workers or because they supposedly enjoy doing this work. Rather, it has to do with a long history of immigration, imperialism, and state policies that have created hierarchical systems that deemed some people better domestic workers and gave them few other options.

Temporary workers who are not on diplomatic visas are able to come to the US with HB-2 visas designated for "low-skilled temporary foreign workers." This means that the US welcomes low-skill (and low-wage) workers from other countries if they are willing to work for a period of time and then return home once they no longer have a job. In 2021, 117,000 HB-2 visas were issued. The program is expected to grow because the Department of Homeland Security has the authority to increase that number if there is a shortage of workers.[32] Temporary workers are a product of historical global inequities—they come from places that have been disadvantaged because of imperial or colonial intervention. In the US, many ended up working in poorly paid and precarious jobs in the care economy, thus recreating the global inequities on a national scale.

The US contributes nothing to pay for the cost of raising this labor force—that burden is shifted to the laborers' home countries and family members, as I discussed in chapter 2. Nor does the US share any responsibility for their care while they reside in its borders. As temporary workers, they do not have access to benefits—Social Security, welfare, or unemployment—because their legal status is linked to their employment. They also do not qualify for Medicaid or the Supplemental Nutrition Assistance Program (SNAP), even if they are employed and meet income requirements. Despite their lack of eligibility, they are required to—and do—pay taxes into these programs through the use of a work identification number.

The HB-2 visa is an indication of how little value the US places on the lives of these workers. There is no concern for their social reproduction; that is, for their ability to care for themselves or their loved ones, only for their labor. Grace Chang refers to workers who are used and callously disregarded like this as "disposal domestics."[33] Open borders for capital and controlled borders for people—where certain people are allowed in under certain conditions—have benefited the employer sector immensely. But this dynamic is possible only because of a state-managed immigration system that places power in the hands of government officials and gives employers permission to bring in workers when needed and send them away when not.[34]

Labor contracting is still very much alive and expanding in the US. The health-care industry relies on mechanisms of outsourcing and recruitment of foreign workers. Workforce management companies contract workers from places like the Philippines with minimum three-year contracts with coercive terms, as Josh Eidelson has reported in *Business Week*. He tells the story of Novie Dale Carmen, a nurse from the Philippines who was hired by Health Carousel, a labor recruiting company for the health-care industry. Health Carousel claims to be building "the omni-channel health-care staffing business of the future," but it requires workers to sign binding contracts with numerous restrictions, exploitative work conditions, and little power to challenge the terms of their labor or leave the job. When workers breach their contract, the company sues them. Hundreds of workers have been sued by agencies like Health Carousel for trying to quit or refuse work.

Carmen worked a few hours outside Philadelphia at a branch of the University of Pittsburgh Medical Center—Pennsylvania's largest private employer, a nonprofit worth $23 billion. Paid less than her peer workers, she was instructed not to talk about work conditions, banned from going out of town without notifying the agency, and forced to work overtime—and she found that much of the time she worked was not counted toward her contract. When conditions became unbearable, she decided to leave but was on the hook for twenty thousand dollars to Health Carousel for breaking her contract. The twenty thousand dollars is supposedly for the up-front costs of the visa, transportation, housing, and other expenses. Carmen is suing the company for engaging in human trafficking.

Health Carousel is just one example. Medical staffing is a $30 billion industry, according to Eidelson. Other sectors with labor shortages are also turning to companies that specialize in the innocuous-sounding "workforce management solutions." They often rely on the EB-3 visa to recruit skilled and professional workers from abroad, who are also low-paid. Once workers complete their labor contract with the agency that arranges their visa, they are free to look for work with another employer. Prior to that, they are under the watchful eye and control of the recruiting agency. Hiring temporary workers, particularly workers from abroad, has become a means of profit, exploitation, and labor trafficking—not only for companies looking for cheap labor but also for agencies that match workers and employers.

Temporary and subcontracted workers, both US citizens and noncitizens, are part of a growing class of precarious workers that includes outsourced workers, independent contractors, consultants, and foreign and temporary workers. According to a survey by Staffing Industry Analysts, 51 million American workers—about 35 percent of the labor force—were contingent as of 2020.[35] This includes self-employed workers, people placed by staffing agencies, people hired directly by companies, and people hired on digital platforms. The state's role in creating an insecure workforce and the circumstances that allow labor precarity to thrive leads us to question whether we can turn to the state, in its current form, for solutions. If the state has been a primary agent in creating the care crisis, do we have confidence that it will take the lead in its resolution?

Although the paid labor of social reproduction is undoubtedly coerced, it is less clear whether the unpaid labor of social reproduction is carried out because of love or coercion. Power, however, undergirds unpaid household labor as well. Evelyn Nakano Glenn

argues that people are "forced to care" in two primary ways: racialized gendered labor, which includes slavery, immigration,
convict labor, and indentured servitude; and "status obligation,"
which is rooted in the construction of the nuclear family household, separation of work from home, and societal expectations
of women's unpaid caregiving.[36] So, although the structural inequities and character of unpaid labor are distinct from paid care
work, unpaid labor, too, must be viewed through a lens of power.

Many people choose to engage in unpaid household labor and
care work willingly and lovingly, whether they work outside the
home or not, or have the resources to outsource this work. They
care for their loved ones for a number of reasons—because they
want to; because they get joy from caring; because they love the
people they are caring for; because they want the best for them.
Anyone who makes that choice must be supported. As activists
have argued for years, unpaid household and care work must be
recognized and valued for its vital contributions.

But many women, in particular, feel overburdened, stressed,
and resentful, not because they don't care but because of the lack
of community and institutional support for the work. They want
better schooling and after-schooling for their children. They
want more reliable childcare. They want male partners to step up.
They are troubled by bosses who have no understanding of their
household responsibilities. Although care work is often viewed
as part of the struggle for a work/family balance, we should not
see it as an individual problem but instead should ask: Where is
the structural support? Where is the collective care? Why has this
kind of work become so taxing? Why are women the ones primarily burdened with this work?

Women's responsibility for the work of social reproduction
can be explained in part by the English common law doctrine of
coverture. Until the middle of the twentieth century, coverture

served as a legal foundation in the US for granting a husband legal power over his wife and her labor. Wives were obligated to provide uncompensated care and services for their husbands and children, and, in this way, coverture worked hand in hand with capital's need to support the labor of social reproduction. Coverture has been whittled away, and the stay-at-home mother is no longer the norm, but expectations and obligations that structure women's unpaid labor in the household still linger.[37]

The rise of wage labor and separation of "work" from "home"—economic and cultural shifts that gave rise to the breadwinner ideology that presumed that men would earn the wage and women would care for the home—laid the foundation for women to assume the role of primary caretakers, as discussed in chapter 2. Racialized constructions of mothers as caring and self-sacrificing erased both the hardship of this work and the outsourcing of difficult labor to women of color. Perhaps no labor is more clouded with sentimentality than that of wives and mothers. Ideas of motherhood, which applied primarily to middle-class white women, reached their peak in the 1950s, when motherhood was considered a bulwark against communism and foundational to US political security and economic prosperity.[38] In addition to being seen as a source of social cohesion and success, motherhood was identified as the cause of so-called depravity and dysfunction, as when social problems such as poverty and juvenile delinquency arose.

Decades later, these social, political, and economic pressures persist. Ideas about mothering (and care more broadly) shape women's relationship to unpaid care work and domestic responsibilities, which may generate joy but also stress and guilt as demands escalate and capacity diminishes. Women often feel forced to do this work because no one else will. Society expects them to. Family members expect them to. The law expects them to. They may suffer from stigma and isolation if they don't properly care for children and home. They might be arrested for abuse or neglect, and the state may take their children away. On top of all that, most workplaces do not accommodate parenting needs, and women's wages tend to be lower, so the "logical" conclusion is that women in heterosexual relationships will take on more of the responsibility for housework and childcare than their spouses.

At the same time, we cannot conflate paid and unpaid labor. There can be an element of choice or invested emotion in the unpaid household labor people do for their own families that simply does not exist in paid labor; however, neither choice nor emotion negate its economic necessity or degree of exploitation. Choice and emotion do not discount the elements of coercion that might include the threat of violence, state intervention, financial leverage, or social pressures. Despite this, in the context of unpaid labor, care and coercion can coexist. So, while I might make dinner for my family because I care and feel obligated to, if I stop by a local restaurant and pick up a meal, I do not assume that the restaurant workers are preparing it because they care or have an obligation. While the task is the same, the nature of the relationship, and thus the nature of the labor, is not—which is the most critical factor in analyzing the politics of care.

Examining social reproduction, both paid and unpaid, as racialized and gendered labor helps us understand how the care crisis is not primarily one of family politics. Although also located there, it is a particular manifestation of gendered racial capitalism rooted in coercive political, legal, and economic policies. Utilizing a racialized and gendered framework shifts our gaze from the burden on individual families toward the failures of the state, capital, and the market. Care work has not only impacted how people are able to care for their families but has also reshaped the labor market, widened the class divide, and redefined the very meaning of capitalist labor relations in the contemporary US.

The growing sector of contingent care work, which includes part-time, temporary, and subcontracted workers who are hired by individuals, third-party staffing agencies, or platform companies, requires us to rethink the employer-employee relationship. Traditional Marxists frame the labor struggle as between owners of capital and an industrial working class, where employers and employees occupy mutually exclusive categories. At the height of industrial capitalism, heroes and villains were easily identifiable: Andrew Carnegie, John D. Rockefeller, and Henry Ford all amassed fortunes through resource extraction, forced removal, and labor exploitation. The destruction they wrought was plainly visible in the lost limbs, tattered clothes, and poor health of workers and their families. Their tactics included calling on Pinkerton thugs to break strikes, pitting workers against one another, or organizing "company towns" to keep workers in a perpetual state of dependency. Their conspicuous consumption stood in stark contrast to the poverty wages they paid.

There are obscenely rich villains today. The health and hospital corporations, Big Pharma, and digital platform companies are fairly easy targets. They profit handsomely from the care economy and have demonstrated only marginal concern for their workers or their customers. But these dichotomies are less useful as the definition of who counts as an employer becomes more diffuse and extends far beyond the corporate elite. The corporate elite have shifted responsibility for directly hiring workers onto third parties or the individual employer-consumer. There is a growing number of people who don't fit easily in the traditional employer category, such as employers of nannies, gardeners, and housekeepers. Like incorporated businesses, they pay wages, establish working conditions, and benefit economically from hiring low-wage workers. But few see themselves as employers.

The once seemingly distinct categories of capitalists and laborers are becoming increasingly blurred in a neoliberal economy
because of greater diversity among employers and deepening inequality among workers. Two people could work for the same
company and have vastly different economic statuses. There are
well-paid tenured faculty and exploited contingent adjunct faculty at colleges and universities. There are Google workers directly employed by the company and other Google workers who
are outsourced. And millions of workers employed by US-owned
companies who do not live in the US make far below the wages
of their US-based peers.

The complex labyrinth that defines the paid labor of social
reproduction includes intermediaries, outsourced and subcontracted workers, solo household workers, and middle- and upper-class individuals who hire workers or utilize services through
a third party. The growing number of subcontracted workers
makes it hard to know who exactly is responsible for the wages
and working conditions of an employee. Subcontracting shields
the multiple entities that benefit from the exploitation of a single
worker. In the gig economy, including the individuals who turn
to platforms such as Care.com to find work or workers, there is
ambiguity about who is responsible for low wages and lack of
benefits. Are the platform companies or individual users the employers? Or are workers self-employed, as the platform companies
claim?

Although the digital platform companies that make money
off these workers cannot be let off the hook, we also have to
consider the "care receiver" or end user. Where do they fit into
the equation? Do they bear any responsibility for ensuring that
the people they employ are paid adequately and have health insurance or other benefits? The surrounding confusion should not
distract from the more important point. Trying to shift blame is

disempowering because it fuels the expectation that someone else ought to take responsibility. Ultimately, along with the platform companies, Uber riders, Care.com customers, and Instacart shoppers need to understand that they are part of a corporate, profit-making chain. They can simultaneously be consumers as well as employers hiring someone's labor.

Uniting the 99 percent was a rallying cry of the Occupy Movement in 2011. The slogan rightly pointed to the unconscionable gap between the wealth of the top 1 percent and the rest of us—a gap that has widened drastically with deregulated and unhinged capitalist profit-making strategies. We cannot lose sight of the fact that *that* is the real problem: people with unimaginable wealth control the media, shape our daily decision-making, and influence the political landscape. But the call for a politics of the 99 percent doesn't allow us to see who among us is hurting the most. Looking only at the villains discourages us from recognizing capital's new methods of extraction and examining our own complicity, and, in the end, is disempowering. Capitalism has evolved in a complicated way. Our response to it should take into account the multiple sites of power and structures of support that allow it to sustain itself. Campaigns for transformation ought to occur on multiple levels—a process that begins in our families and communities.

The paid care relationship is often framed as one between caregivers and care receivers, when we should be talking about employers and employees. The term *care receivers* obscures how the work is embedded in capitalist labor relations. The starting point for conversations about care work is not usually the worker but the person who needs care—even progressive advocates who seek to reframe political ethics begin with how to provide care for those who need it. As important as this is, there is a disproportionate focus on people who need care while people who do the work of caring fade into the background—yet, of course, these are not mutually exclusive categories. It is imperative to understand the paid care relationship as one of exploitation and power and to call the people who hire these workers what they are: employers.

The care economy today feeds inequality on multiple levels, including among households. Families of all economic backgrounds hire domestic workers and rely on the gig economy. Some employers make not much more than the people they hire. Many care workers are also in need of care and may hire other people to provide care, or their status may shift over time—from being a care worker at one stage of life to needing care and becoming an employer at another. People holding down multiple jobs and living on the edge of poverty also rely on childcare workers or call an Uber to get to work because they don't have a car. While they may not be part of the ruling class, employing other workers does make them employers as well.

Yet, it's different for families with resources who outsource work to low-wage, US-born or immigrant people of color. For those who can afford to pay more but don't, the difference between employers' wages and their employees' wages is a form of capital accumulation that further widens the class divide. Very often, market rationality and a cost/benefit analysis drive families with resources to outsource some of their labor. It may be cheaper for an employer to hire a domestic worker to clean or care rather than do it themselves: staying at work for an extra couple of hours is more lucrative, as the domestic worker is paid less. This is a calculus that fuels inequality. The family or individual can use that extra money from the wage difference to invest in educational enrichment programs, music lessons, private school education, and social networking.

In the context of the racial wealth gap—the fact that Black, Latinx, and Indigenous families, in particular, earn far less and have much less wealth than white families—private household workers bolster the racial and economic privilege of wealthy and primarily white families.[39] Acknowledging the relationship between wealth and poverty, understanding that racial inequality and white white privilege are intertwined, and treating employees with dignity, fairness, and respect are the first steps to social transformation. If we can't see it, we can't change it.

Chapter 4

"Tell 'Dem Slavery Done"

Social Reproduction
and the Politics of Resistance

The cavernous church was packed. All the chairs were occupied and people had begun to line up along the outer wall. Hundreds of domestic workers had trekked to Brooklyn, some of them after a long day at work, with children in tow, in the hope of building a movement to transform working conditions. This wasn't your ordinary labor meeting. An overwhelming number of attendees were women, although men were present as well. The women present crossed racial, ethnic, and cultural lines; they were old and young, outspoken and reticent. Some held infants only a few weeks old. Others brought their teenage children or were minding their grandchildren. Childcare was available in an adjacent room, and dinner was served. The commotion of children playing in the next room, combined with the low murmur of the interpreters and the architecture of the old building, made it difficult to hear the speaker with the microphone at the front of the room. Despite the imperfect acoustics, the message came across loud and clear: they needed to develop a strategy to ensure higher pay and better working conditions for domestic workers statewide.

This was a monthly membership meeting of Domestic Workers United (DWU), a coalition of domestic workers' rights groups from around New York City who had gathered in the fall of 2007. It included Andolan (Organizing South Asian Workers), the Committee Against Anti-Asian Violence, Damayan, and Haitian Women for Haitian Refugees, among others. Over the next few years, I joined with DWU on day-long journeys to Albany, the state capital, where we picketed, chanted, sang, and met with state legislators to pass a state bill of rights for domestic workers. Because of lobbying by DWU, in 2010, New York became the first state in the country to pass a domestic worker bill of rights.

Despite this powerful and visible movement that was drawing nationwide attention, the dominant narrative among labor experts and journalists at the time was about the precipitous decline of the labor movement. The disconnect between what I read and what I witnessed deepened my interest in how the labor movement was defined: claims about the death of the labor movement were only tenable if a good portion of the working class was excised from political analysis.

Mainstream histories of labor and capitalism are often written without reference to labor that does not fit the industrial model, especially that of women of color. Industrial unionism was birthed during the Great Depression when autoworkers waged their famous sit-down strikes. It took shape with the formation of the Congress of Industrial Organizations (CIO), a federation committed to industry-wide organizing across occupational and skill lines. The CIO and the American Federation of Labor (AFL), with which it later merged, were instrumental for solidifying the association of labor organizing with white male industrial workers.

In contrast to this traditional view of labor organizing, scholars of race, feminist labor history, and social reproduction have demonstrated a much broader landscape of class, labor, and organizing. It includes organizing by informal and service workers as well as unwaged workers: domestic workers, washerwomen, teachers, restaurant workers, nurses, housewives, enslaved people, and home health aides. Alongside this are demands for state care, regulations, or state resources so people can care for themselves: lower food prices, welfare assistance, unemployment compensation, pensions, disability assistance, and wages for housework. These are not only about employment but are economic struggles designed to ensure that people have the resources to sustain life, what theorist Cindi Katz calls "life's work." This body of scholarship widens the scope of labor organizing and the terrain on which capitalism can be challenged by taking into account the paid and unpaid labor of social reproduction that people engage in for their own well-being and to reproduce labor power for capital.[1]

This expanded frame of organizing that incorporates social reproduction blurs the boundaries between home and work. It reveals the potential for resistance and solidarity among paid and unpaid workers, as well as among people laboring inside and outside the home not just for work but for life. It situates community struggles such as access to clean water, decent schools, and affordable health care, which are critical for life, alongside the paid labor of social reproduction and unpaid caregiving. These workers and activists, who are disproportionately women, are forging a new, broader definition of feminism, as the authors of *Feminism for the 99%* argue.[2]

The scholarship around social reproduction as a site of resistance has shaken traditional Marxist theory out of its complacency and cynicism and awakened it to the political possibilities evident in the recent wave of organizing among teachers, nurses, and domestic workers. Marxist theorists who have historically put all their eggs in the basket of industrial workers are forced to reckon with this more complex definition of labor and organizing that sees race and gender not as divisive but as offering a more sophisticated analysis of how class operates in multiple locations and sectors of work. Such an analysis is longstanding among Black feminist Marxists, such as Communist Party member Claudia Jones; Esther Cooper Jackson, who worked with the Southern Negro Youth Congress; and Louise Thompson Patterson, a central figure in the Harlem Renaissance. These Black feminists produced a body of writing that theorized the place of Black women in working-class politics and social change. Patterson published a groundbreaking 1936 essay in the Communist Party magazine *Woman Today* examining the interconnections of race, class, and gender. "Toward a Brighter Dawn" analyzed the "triple exploitation" domestic workers experienced, "as workers, as Negroes, and as women." By homing in on the experiences of Black women, they articulated how class is inseparable from and is lived through race and gender.[3] Foregrounding the labor of white women and people of color, then, not only expands but also deepens the understanding of class.

Social reproductive struggle, like any class struggle, has the potential to challenge the racial capitalist system, but does not necessarily do so. There are many levels on which people can struggle—around wages, autonomy, services, and state support. Organizing around social reproduction can be reformist, meaning that it is in service to capital and can forestall change, or it can put forth "nonreformist reforms," meaning that it contributes to long-term change. For instance, a higher wage can be used solely for purchasing more consumer goods, thus boosting corporate profits; in another scenario, it can be donated to social movement organizing or used to reduce working hours. A higher wage, then, can be transformative if workers have control of it and use it for social change. Perhaps another metric is to determine if a campaign contributes to what in the 1960s was referred to as consciousness-raising: to gauge how participation in labor struggles enables people to develop a critique about the operation of political and economic power, or if it reveals for them the value of democratic participation and mass mobilization.

Organizing around social reproduction is sometimes explained as a product of neoliberalism, perhaps because of how the organizing has accelerated recently and become more visible. This perspective, however, erases the millions of workers who labored and organized in this sector under industrial capitalism. Grounding our analysis in the lives and labors of poor and working-class women—particularly women of color—who have operated on the margins of American economic society and the labor movement, offers a fuller picture of the multiple fronts of the labor movement, historically and in the present. Although considered unorganizable by traditional union organizers, poor, working-class people of color have been engaged in generations-long social reproductive struggles. Household workers demanded labor protections, sharecroppers challenged the terms of their contracts, consumers demanded lower food prices, renters opposed eviction, and single mothers fought for assistance to raise their children. These were not always called social reproduction struggles, but they are, nevertheless, part of a landscape of working-class struggle. This long view of social reproduction is important for setting the record straight and making visible the many workers who organized previously around social reproduction.

These lessons from the past offer insight into contemporary capitalism. If the prototypical worker in the mid-twentieth century was someone who worked for the same company their entire lives and retired with a pension and health care, today's prototype is someone who changes jobs frequently, often holds more than one job, has no job security, and doesn't have access to company benefits. There has been a proliferation of small-scale, precarious work arrangements in which workers are hired through a third-party agency or hired as contingent labor. More people, whether they are drivers, college teachers, factory workers, or accountants, tend to work part time, intermittently, or as independent contractors. And, because of the defunding of the regulatory apparatus, labor laws are inadequately enforced—compounded by the climate of fear and surveillance that discourages workers from addressing workplace violations regardless. The precarious conditions of employment in the US today have been a reality for workers of color for a long time.

We can, therefore, also take cues and glean lessons about organizing from the past. Domestic worker organizing, for example, offers a model of resistance applicable to a growing number of precarious workers in a neoliberal economy. The declining status and increasing precarity of other workers under neoliberalism is coming to resemble that of domestic workers, who have always been gig workers and independent contractors. The organizing strategies employed by domestic workers and other social reproductive workers point the way toward new forms of working-class protest. There is much to learn about organizing precarious workers from this group of people that has struggled historically to claim the benefits of social citizenship.

Social reproductive workers have created alternative labor formations and new sites and strategies of resistance. Resistance includes demands for wages or for higher wages, for better state care or the resources and structures to support radical or communal care. These workers have organized across occupation and industry lines, fought for state-based protections rather than employer-based rights, and organized in public spaces rather than workplaces. In the process, they have transformed how we think about labor organizing.[4]

Crafting a theoretical lens for organizing that fully incorporates the multiple iterations of social reproductive resistance suggests that we move away from a circumscribed notion of union struggle and perhaps even of labor organizing. Instead, we must consider a framework of working-class struggle, as Robin D. G. Kelley developed in his extensive writing about Black working-class resistance.[5] Some historians and political pundits mistakenly use union membership as a basis of analysis, thus missing a large portion of the working class. We cannot be laser-focused on union membership as a barometer of working-class struggle. Redirecting attention to workers outside formal labor unions and people who were excluded from unions gives us a more nuanced understanding of working-class politics. Labor organizing suggests that someone is working, whether paid or unpaid, and it can include people engaged in social movement unionism who are part of labor struggles and campaigns without formal membership. Many people involved in domestic worker organizing or those who participated in the "Fight for $15" minimum wage strikes, for example, did not formally join organizations.

Working-class struggle is a broader term that includes people who are waged and unwaged and can also include other forms of community-based struggles around housing, food, and water. It includes all people—workers and nonworkers, housewives who organized for wages, consumers who protested for lower food prices, people who cannot work, the unemployed, welfare recipients, pensioners, disability activists, antieviction campaigners, and people who are fighting for economic security. If we consider this rich array of working-class struggle, we derive a very different understanding of protest today: one that rests in the enormous potential for political resistance to neoliberal racial capitalism. From this vantage point, labor organizing is not on the decline but is experiencing an upsurge.

Domestic workers have always organized, whether through day-to-day resistance or mass mobilization. There are countless examples of individual actions, such as pan-toting, work slow-downs, and quitting, as well as collective struggles.[6] As early as 1881, African American washerwomen in Atlanta formed an association called the Washing Society. They gained the support of nearly three thousand washerwomen, went on strike for higher pay rates, and nearly shut the city down, as Tera Hunter has written in her path-breaking book *To 'Joy Our Freedom*.[7] After World War I, when African Americans migrated north, domestic workers, in a quasi-collective assertion of their labor power, refused live-in work so that they could come home to their families every night.[8]

In the 1930s, at the height of the Great Depression, household workers across the country organized. In New York City, Dora Jones mobilized one thousand mostly Finnish and African American household workers—a group that became a local chapter of the Building Services Employees International Union. They established a hiring hall that offered employment services to its members and sought to replace informal arrangements with contractual relationships.[9] Likewise, in the later postwar period, as sociologist Mary Romero has documented, Chicana workers in the Southwest shifted from full-time work with a single employer to the "business" model of cleaning for multiple families.[10]

In 1971, African American women household workers established the first national movement of domestic workers. The Household Technicians of America (HTA), an organization with a membership of twenty-five thousand was dedicated to pay, professionalism, and respect. It included Dorothy Bolden, in Atlanta, discussed in chapter 1, who helped form the locally based National Domestic Workers Union of America; Mary McClendon, who took the lead in establishing the Household Workers Organization in Detroit in 1969; and Geraldine Miller, who was active in the National Organization for Women and founded the Household Technicians Union in the Bronx.[11]

These workers challenged the servitude and low pay that characterized household labor and, in the process, pushed the boundaries of traditional labor organizing. The movement advocated for standardization of the occupation, employment contracts delineating rights and responsibilities, increased political power vis-à-vis employers, training and professionalization programs, and minimum wage coverage under state and federal laws. They dispelled the notion that they were "part of the family," disputed that they did this work because they cared, and critiqued the emotional demands on them. They made claims to labor rights, political inclusion, and equal recognition for their labor.[12]

They received minimal support from labor unions and turned instead to civil rights, Black power, and women's organizations. They also developed their own strategies: Dorothy Bolden rode bus routes in Atlanta to recruit women into her organization. Geraldine Miller relied on the commuter train as a site of organizing. Carolyn Reed, also discussed in chapter 1, recruited domestic workers in laundry rooms in New York City. They organized women regardless of their immigrant status or their racial, ethnic, and linguistic backgrounds.

One campaign that best illustrates the goals of equality and recognition was for inclusion of domestic workers in the minimum wage provision of the Fair Labor Standards Act (FLSA). Domestic and agricultural workers were excluded from New Deal labor protections, including minimum wage, Social Security, unemployment insurance, and the right to organize and bargain collectively. Over time, some states offered labor protections and, by 1950, because of lobbying by labor feminists, domestic workers received social security. But when the HTA emerged, they still did not have a federal minimum wage.[13]

Household workers' primary goal was to secure the same legal recognition and social standing for domestic work that was afforded to other forms of work. Edith Barksdale-Sloan, one of the early middle-class leaders of the movement, argued: "Pay must be increased to provide a livable wage. Second, workers must receive the so-called 'fringe benefits,' which long ago stopped being 'fringes' in every other major American industry."[14] They staked their claims both on the value of the work and on the rights of the worker. For them, domestic work was not distinct from other kinds of work—it was work, period, and deserved the same treatment. They did not call themselves caretakers, family members, maids, or domestics, and preferred to be known as household technicians. In this way, the domestic workers' rights movement at its core was a labor struggle centered on a fight for expanded rights and protections. As organizer Carolyn Reed put it: "Household workers are the last frontier of labor organizing."[15]

Domestic workers lobbied on behalf of the proposed amendments to the FLSA, testified before Congress, and mobilized employers to support them. In 1974, with the passage of congressional amendments, they won inclusion in the FLSA, moving one step closer to full equality. In the wake of this victory, their press release stated:

> Minimum wage coverage for household workers gives to these one and a half million employees a legal mandate, a recognition of the value of their services and basic equality with other workers.... For the domestic worker, whether she is Black, White, Red or Brown, or lives in the North, East, South or West, it means a new respect—for her service and her person—and the ability to support herself and family.[16]

In a context of expanding state protections and the federal government's presumed commitment to mitigate formal inequality, domestic worker activists made important strides toward winning a measure of recognition and legal protection and shedding the paternalism that underpinned their exploitation.

This was a significant historical moment. It was the final gesture of the New Deal welfare state before the shift to a ruthless neoliberal order, the last gasp of an economic program that was never designed to be inclusive and thus created momentum for a turn away from a safety net. But it also signified the historic outcomes made possible by an alliance among policy makers, middle-class allies, and grassroots activists when that comradery was built on the work and vision of the most marginalized.

The relationship that HTA developed with middle-class housewives in making claims for a federal minimum wage was particularly significant. It was a partnership premised on a common understanding that both paid and unpaid household workers were negatively impacted by the devaluation of domestic work. Josephine Hulett, field organizer for the HTA, explained in an interview: "After all, there's a sense in which all women are household workers. And unless we stop being turned against each other, unless we organize together, we're never going to make this country see household work for what it really is—human work, not just 'woman's work': a job that deserves dignity, fair pay, and respect."[17] This campaign for rights was a far cry from demands to support workers on the basis that they care for middle-class people, which has marked the contemporary care discourse.

More recently, a new generation of domestic workers has organized. Beginning around 2000, dozens of groups, including DWU, took shape around the country. They addressed the ongoing exploitation of household workers, egregious instances of abuse, and the practice of what they, like earlier organizers, called "modern-day slavery."

In the summer of 1989, Christine Lewis came to New York City with her five-year-old daughter from Trinidad, where she had worked as an early childhood educator, and moved in with her older sister in the Bronx. Shortly after arriving, Christine went in search of work so she could pay rent, put food on the table, and buy clothes as the weather turned cold. She traversed the city, she explained, and "discovered Central Park, the 'creme de la creme' of all the parks I had seen. And women who looked like me— brown—pushing alabaster babies in stylish Maclaren [strollers]."[18]

She became a nanny. It was gratifying work, but she found that, in addition to providing childcare, she was expected to run errands and clean the house: "Nanny work morphs into taking your shoes to the shoemaker, taking your coat to the dry cleaner, cooking food for the house." Clear-eyed and confident, Christine never hesitated to assert her rights. She told her employer: "My focus is on your child...I will cook for the kid. I will do the kid's laundry. I will help the kid with home lessons...I'm not doing anything extra that's not centered around the child."[19] Still, she worked from 8:30 in the morning until 10:30 at night and was paid $350 a week with no overtime compensation, which translated to five dollars an hour. For Christine, the exploitative pay and unrealistic expectations stemmed from the fact that she was a woman of color engaged in women's work: "It's immigrant women of color who feel the brunt of this pain. A white girl will come to the job and get more money and less time because she's white."[20]

Christine connected with other domestic workers in the park. "This park was truly the crossroad of the United Nations. There were women from Nepal, the Philippines, Trinidad and Tobago, Barbados, the Congo, Mexico, Peru, El Salvador, Bangladesh, England, Ireland, Russia, and Poland."[21] Through conversations with other domestic workers, Christine learned the value of organizing. As she explained, "New York was my new home, and it was at my new job, during these tattle-tales with the other babysitters that I realized we have to empower each other around what is acceptable and not acceptable in an industry that is rife with exploit[ation] and disrespect."[22] She was aware of the risks of speaking out. "Speaking truth to power could have gotten you fired," she observed. But she had a fighting spirit and never let fear deter her.[23]

Christine became one of the stalwart leaders of DWU. The organization provided support and offered legal advice to domestic workers. Their slogan, "Tell 'Dem Slavery Done," spoke to the fact that, in Christine's words, "We were working for poverty wages. We were working for long hours. Women were being talked down to. Women were treated like slaves."[24] She was a key organizer for the New York State Bill of Rights campaign in the early- to mid-2000s, which granted domestic workers the right to overtime pay, one day off every seven days, three days of paid vacation after a year of work for the same employer, and protection from racial and sexual harassment. It was an important victory but, according to Christine, fell short of what domestic workers needed in terms of wages, paid time off, health insurance, and social security.

On top of the lobbying and legal support, DWU also fostered a sense of community by practicing a kind of collective care in which people helped one another out. They offered food, childcare, housing, and stipends for people in economic need. "We have a community. We have what you call the village. Everybody looked out for everybody," Christine explained. She also relied on "the village"—family and friends, especially her sister and nephew—to help care for her daughter when she worked fourteen-hour days at her first job.[25] She was there during DWU's early years and is one of the leaders of the organization today.

Like DWU, Damayan—the Filipino migrant workers association that helped Edith Mendoza, as we saw in chapter 3—also mobilized workers. It was cofounded by Linda Oalican, who was born and raised in the Philippines. One of ten children in a poor family, she excelled at school and studied at the University of the Philippines, where she joined a radical youth group. During the autocratic presidency of Ferdinand Marcos Sr., when the Philippines was in the throes of social unrest and political disaffection, Linda dedicated herself to confronting poverty, inequality, and fascism. In 1971, she dropped out of college and joined her comrades to organize farmers and factory workers. On the cusp of the declaration of martial law in 1972, she was arrested and detained for six months—and spent three of those in isolation. After her release, she married, had children, and continued to organize while working for the National Housing Authority in the Philippines.

In the 1990s, when her children were a little older, Linda immigrated to the United States. She became a domestic worker because it was one of the few occupations open to her. In her first job, as a live-in worker in New Jersey for a young couple with three children, she worked from six in the morning until ten at night. When things became unbearable in one job, she found another. During her eighteen years as a domestic worker, she was never paid overtime. The marginalization and second-class citizenship Linda experienced while working infuriated her. When she injured her back, her employers' indifference became clear to her. Employers cared little for the health and well-being of their employees, she realized, and often saw them as disposable. She heard of employees who went to work in the morning only to find their personal items in a garbage bag, left with the doorman, who told them that they were no longer needed: "Many times domestic workers like myself had to work through their illnesses, and if they got that misfortune of being inflicted with a deadly, fatal, terminal illness, then that's the end of the road for them."[26]

Linda knew she needed to organize. She looked for a job in Manhattan in order to be in close proximity to other domestic workers. She eventually pulled together a small group of workers to strategize about how to address the abuses in the occupation. At first, they were a little unsure of how to move forward, but they soon began to work with the Committee Against Anti-Asian Violence (CAAAV) and then formed the Damayan Migrant Workers Association.

Damayan worked with DWU to lobby for the New York State Bill of Rights. Like Christine, Linda believed the bill could have been stronger. She recounted, "I was quite disappointed with the outcome of the New York Bill of Rights because we were able to win very minimal of the demands that we put out there...But we did not stop organizing, because personally I know, having been an organizer in the Philippines, that the only chance of workers to have genuine rights and a fighting chance in the city is through … genuine worker's organization."[27]

One of the most striking characteristics of this wave of organizing is its racial and ethnic diversity. A large number of these workers come from abroad and many are undocumented. DWU, for example, brought together Southeast Asian, South Asian, Caribbean, Central American, African, and East Asian workers in an unprecedented example of interracial labor solidarity.

The mainstream labor movement often saw race as an obstacle to class solidarity, where nonunionized, nonwhite workers were used as strikebreakers. Cross-race alliances were viewed as rare but significant instances of transcending race and forging class solidarity. For domestic workers organizing under neoliberalism, it was necessary to build cross-race coalitions, given the diversity of the workforce. Solidarity was not premised on "color-blindness" or an erasure of difference. Rather, workers' understanding of class and their common experience of exploitation was bound up with their ethnic, racial, and cultural identities, and, as a result, they embraced their differences. This was evident in their organizing strategies and at meetings, where they sang calypso songs, ate Jamaican curries, and recited Spanish-language poetry without missing a beat.[28]

Priscilla Gonzalez, a steering-committee member and Latina coordinator of DWU, helped shape the interracial politics of DWU. Priscilla sought out DWU to assist her mother, a domestic worker who was having difficulties with her employer. She was so impressed with the organization that she decided to stay on as a volunteer. As Ai-Jen Poo, one of the key leaders of DWU, shared in an interview:

> [Priscilla] always tries to frame difference, ethnicity, and culture as opportunities... for us to strengthen our organizing. I think that that shift in orientation has actually helped us a lot because we have worked hard to create a multilingual organizing space that is truly multilingual where non-English speaking folks can actually participate and exercise their leadership equally with English-speaking members.[29]

Erline Browne, a nanny and steering committee member of DWU in its early years, attended an international gathering of domestic workers in Amsterdam in 2006. She was profoundly influenced by the similarity of experience, regardless of race and nationality: "Wherever you go the story is the same. Once you are doing this work, you just do not get respected. You get very little pay. You get abused."[30] The interracial alliance was premised on an understanding of how minoritized and marginalized workers across the globe are similarly exploited and the realization that they could counter vulnerability through collective pressure.

Thirteen domestic workers' rights organizations from around the country, including DWU, came together at the US Social Forum in Atlanta in 2007. They founded the National Domestic Workers Alliance—the organization that launched the Caring Across Generations campaign discussed in chapter 1. They continued and expanded the fight for federal, state, and international protections as well as the enforcement of laws, including the FLSA, which the HTA had worked so hard to pass.

Globally, domestic workers won passage of the International Labour Organization's convention "Decent Work for Domestic Workers." The 2011 convention recommended global standards for the occupation: the right to organize, freedom from abuse, guaranteed rest one day per week, minimum wage, and a clear definition of terms of employment in accordance with national laws.[31] Convention 189, as it is known, was a watershed moment. Although it did not drastically transform working conditions for household workers, it indicated that domestic workers were able to influence policy at the international level.[32] Two years after the passage of Convention 189, the network that lobbied for it, including NDWA, became the International Domestic Workers Federation and elected as its president Myrtle Witbooi, general secretary of the South African Domestic Service and Allied Workers Union. The international federation formally brought together domestic worker organizations from around the world and pushed for the convention's ratification and implementation by individual countries. As of 2022, it represented 670,000 workers from 67 countries.

As we can see, domestic workers' exclusion from mainstream labor unions led them to form alternative labor associations with distinctive tactics. Domestic workers turned to lobbying, legislation, and shaming abusive employees because strikes were not always effective.[33] They campaigned for legislation to protect all workers in the occupation, not just the organized. They also developed alliances with middle-class constituencies—students, lawyers, and employers—whom they hoped to educate and encourage to abide by a model contract. They couldn't organize in their workplaces, so they turned to ethnic associations, public spaces such as playgrounds and bus stops, or workers' centers—neighborhood spaces where workers could gather—and brought together documented and undocumented workers. Neighborhood centers and public venues enabled them to organize independent of a particular employer or even of a particular occupation because these efforts were rooted in the community rather than the workplace. Instead of formal union membership structures, they have pulled workers into "social movement unions," and are committed to broader social justice goals bridging workplace interests and other political and economic issues. Unlike traditional unions, which are primarily interested in representing current workers and negotiating better contracts for them, social movement unions aim to build a working-class movement.[34]

Organizing among other service sector workers, many of them engaged in the labor of social reproduction, has also escalated. In the 1960s, public sector workers, teachers, transport workers, airline attendants and nurses, unionized and won bargaining rights.[35] Since then, a broad swath of social reproductive workers have launched powerful and promising labor campaigns. Home health-care attendants organized in the 1970s under the leadership of the Service Employees International Union (SEIU), the American Federation of State County and Municipal Employees Union (AFSCME), and District 1199, which represents health-care workers. Although home health care had long been used by the health-care industry as a cost-saving strategy, the expansion of home health care since the 1980s is a result of neoliberal shifts, such as cutbacks of publicly funded hospital care and rule changes that allow Medicaid funds to go to the for-profit sector. From the point of view of the health-care industry, it is more profitable to fill hospital beds with acute patients and shift nonacute patient care to the home. Home health-care workers move between private households, nursing homes, and hospitals. Through their organizing, they have established a new form of representation for workers paid through public funds, the public authority, which acts as an employer for the purpose of collective bargaining for workers from scattered worksites.[36] Home health care is one of the fastest growing sectors of the labor movement.

More recently, there has been a renewed wave of resistance by teachers, nurses, and restaurant and other low-wage workers. One of the most pathbreaking actions was the strike led by Chicago public school teachers in 2012, the first in that city in twenty-five years. Under the leadership of a group of women of color, including Karen Lewis and the Caucus of Rank-and-File Educators, the Chicago Teachers Union (CTU) addressed not only pay and benefits but also educational reform, learning outcomes, and community issues. Parents and teachers were regarded as allies in the struggle to improve schools—in fact, many teachers were also parents in the community, illustrating that these two groups were not mutually exclusive. The union built support among parents and community members by demanding more music, art, and gym programming for students, increased school funding, and smaller class sizes, and by challenging the reliance on high-stakes testing. Theirs was not only a struggle for higher pay for teachers but also a fight for public education, which they saw as tied to broader social inequities of poverty and crime, thus creating the possibility for a more inclusive movement.[37]

In 2018 and 2019, a wave of teachers' strikes, concentrated in "red states" in the South and West, took place across the country. Thousands of teachers walked off the job in West Virginia, Arizona, California, North Carolina, and Georgia in response to low pay and staffing shortages. The platforms very often included better working conditions and higher pay for support staff to improve educational outcomes for children. Much like the CTU, these workers were moving closer to the expansive possibilities of a social reproductive campaign that combined workers' rights with community issues.

Another example is the Fight for $15 movement, which first emerged in November 2012 and demanded a minimum wage of fifteen dollars an hour. Fight for $15 included a large number of low-wage workers, from home-care attendants to fast food workers to childcare and airport workers. It began as a one-day strike in New York City by mostly Black and Brown fast food workers who earned so little they often qualified for public assistance or had to work multiple jobs to make ends meet. The movement, backed by SEIU, grew rapidly. Fight for $15 is a working-class movement rather than an organization with a membership structure, and workers can participate without formally joining. They may benefit from higher wages without signing a contract or even attending a demonstration. Equally important, the movement organizes workers across occupational lines. The Fight for $15 is part of broader living-wage campaigns that seek to increase the wages of the most poorly paid.[38]

For these workers, the question of class cannot be extricated from the politics of race, gender, household, and resources necessary for survival. These campaigns illustrate the possibility of social reproduction as a site of class struggle that is diverse and wide-ranging in its political outlook and connects economic security, family, community, and social issues. Because social reproduction is essential for the functioning of capitalism, systemic struggles that challenge it contain the power to shut things down and have the potential to disrupt capitalist profit.

Shifting our gaze to the labor of social reproduction expands the terrain of struggle beyond work sites, reinforcing that the distinctions between home and work, public and private, have always been hazy. Both the work that one engages in and the daily labor of survival have historically been vibrant sites of class-based struggle. With the rise of the care economy, the possibilities for resistance among paid social reproductive workers are even clearer. During the COVID-19 pandemic, a wave of protests and demonstrations by teachers, renters, warehouse workers, and nurses—some of the largest in generations—further fueled working-class struggles.

Recently, feminist activists have called for an International Women's Strike that unites women in a one-day strike and foregrounds women's paid and unpaid labor. The possibility of such a strike—of a "feminism for the 99 percent"—is admirable for its attempt to center class and labor as foundational to feminist politics and counter the corporate feminist vision of individual advancement. A one-day strike can raise awareness and energize people. It can draw attention to the essential work that women do. But, to have a long-term impact, such a strike requires the follow-up of local organizing. Strikes by nurses and teachers over the past few years, for instance, won concessions for members and raised awareness while also helping to nurture a generation of labor leaders—people like Nicole McCormick of the West Virginia Education Association—who continue to be advocates, speaking out and contributing to social change. Transformational change happens with the tedious day-to-day work of engaging people beyond a one-off commitment.[39]

In addition to the challenge of sustained engagement, bridging the divisions among women to build a feminism for the 99 percent seems difficult at this moment. Within the broad category of women—even excluding the most privileged women—there are political differences, racial antagonisms, competing class interests, and contested definitions of feminism. As we have seen, the economic success of some women is dependent upon the exploitation of other women. In addition, the potential costs of a one-day strike are much higher for a low-wage precarious worker, particularly someone who financially supports other people, than for a more economically secure worker. Carolyn Reed, the formidable leader of the HTA, hoped to organize domestic workers to strike, although she was never able to pull it off—in part because domestic workers had a lot to lose by going on strike. Community and organizational support are critical for such a strike to reach the most marginalized workers. A lack of such infrastructure may explain why so many of the recent women's strikes have been largely white.

However, cross-race, cross-class solidarity is possible, as the domestic workers' rights movement of the 1970s has shown by building alliances with white middle-class employers around a platform of uplifting paid household labor. But, in the current climate, particularly with a care discourse that privileges the needs of employers and speaks primarily to the predicament of women with economic security, more work needs to be done for a widespread women's strike to be logistically possible. On top of this, the political viability of such a strike needs reexamining: the shifting demographics of the labor of social reproduction raise the question of whether this should be a "women's strike" or a low-wage worker campaign. Low-wage workers, mostly women but men as well, are organizing on a global scale, across gender lines in multiple sectors, both production and social reproduction—agriculture, garment work, retail, tourism, and health care—as historian Annelise Orleck has powerfully documented.[40]

In addition to organizing as workers, activists have also demanded care and support from the state to better care for themselves— higher wages, yes, but also lower food prices, a guaranteed annual income, unemployment insurance, housing, veteran and old-age pensions, and compensation for unpaid care work. Collectively, these illustrate that the state was often seen as a potential source of support for social reproduction. People of all backgrounds have sought to leverage state resources for a more comfortable and secure home life.

The Wages for Housework movement, for example, demanded that the state pay women for unpaid household labor, which, they argued, was essential to the functioning of the economy and society, more broadly. The movement believed that the state and capital worked hand in hand to ensure the continued exploitation of women in the home and to erase their contributions. When activist and theorist Selma James attended a national women's liberation movement conference held in Manchester, England, in 1972, she called on housewives to organize as workers. James wrote and circulated a pamphlet, *Women, the Unions, and Work, or What Is Not to Be Done*, arguing that women did not need to join the wage labor force and unionize in order to participate in class struggle because they were already workers— unwaged workers in the home. James, who was a member of London's Notting Hill Women's Liberation Workshop Group, had long been involved in antiracist struggles in the United States and Trinidad. Her goal was to expand class analysis to consider the many unwaged workers, including housewives, colonial subjects, and enslaved people, who contributed to capitalist wealth. The pamphlet, apparently, was "selling like hotcakes."[41]

Shortly after the Manchester conference, activists formed the International Wages for Housework Campaign. Led by James and socialist feminists Mariarosa Dalla Costa, Silvia Federici, and Margaret Prescod, who founded and led the Black Women for Wages for Housework, the movement had bases in the United States, the United Kingdom, and Italy. In contrast to other feminists of the period, Wages for Housework activists saw paid employment outside the home as simply another form of exploitation rather than a source of liberation for women.[42] As James and Dalla Costa wrote in *The Power of Women and the Subversion of the Community* in 1972, women must "refuse the myth of liberation through work."[43]

The movement had as a central goal not only compensating housewives and expanding the analysis of unwaged work, as James argued, but also transforming household and gender relations and the supposed "natural" role of women in the domestic sphere. Federici, in her classic 1975 treatise *Wages Against Housework*, wrote that unpaid household labor was packaged and sold to women in terms of love, care, and family to mask oppressive and exploitative laboring conditions. Housewives were compelled to do housework, she suggested, because it was transformed into "an act of love."[44] The demand to care, then, was emotional labor. Paralleling Hochschild's analysis of emotional labor in the context of paid employer–employee relationships, the Wages for Housework movement explored how familial love served as a form of coercion to justify no pay and was not only imposed but also internalized—women themselves came to believe that they did this work because of love.

Recognizing household labor as work worthy of wages was a way to build power, to organize women as part of the working class, and to refuse "precisely the female role that capital has invented for us."[45] That is, giving women a wage would acknowledge their status as workers and invest them with economic power, or, as Federici insisted: "From now on we want money for each moment of it, so that we can refuse some of it and eventually all of it."[46] They refused the work as well as the ethical imperative to do it and the premise that it must be done out of love. As Dalla Costa and James wrote: "We must discover forms of struggle which immediately break the whole structure of domestic work, rejecting it absolutely, rejecting our role as housewives and the home as the ghetto of our existence."[47]

The Wages for Housework movement did not believe that the nuclear family should be the primary site for the labor of social reproduction.[48] The long-term goal was to recognize and collectivize this labor, so it would eventually be done in nurseries and communal kitchens. This movement was particularly compelling for its political analysis, which dispelled the mythology of middle-class motherhood and placed it in a larger structural and economic context. They offered a framework that expanded the scope of class struggle and had the potential to disrupt the privatized, family-based model of household labor, which fuels inequality and has given rise to the care economy.

Another powerful example comes from the welfare rights movement, which demanded state assistance for mothering work. Led by Johnnie Tillmon, chairperson of the National Welfare Rights Organization (NWRO), introduced in chapter 2, the welfare rights movement sought to overturn the discriminatory rules and regulations that were used to deny assistance to African American women. Caseworkers wielded discretionary power and monitored recipients' behavior, by, for instance, showing up at odd hours in search of evidence of a man who might be present. These infamous "midnight raids" were grounds to cut off a recipient's benefits if anything, even a man's razor, was found. Welfare rights activists developed handbooks informing recipients of their rights in clear, accessible language. They let recipients know, for example, that they could appeal a caseworker's decision or take an advocate with them to a hearing. They held sit-ins and protests, demanding that the local welfare department give them all the items, such as a telephone, that the department deemed essential for a basic standard of living. They refused the work requirements instituted in the 1960s, and insisted on their right to stay home and care for their children. With help from lawyers, they successfully overturned state laws that required residency for a period of time prior to submitting an application and that denied recipients the right to due process before the termination of benefits.[49]

In a context of the denigration of the social reproductive labor of Black women, the demands for a right to mother were significant. In 1971, Tillmon wrote, in the inaugural issue of *Ms.*, the premier feminist magazine of the time: "Nobody realizes more than poor women that all women should have the right to control their own reproduction."[50] The welfare rights movement campaigns dispelled the racist and sexist stereotypes that deemed Black women unfit mothers and succeeded in affording them a degree of control and autonomy over their lives. For Tillmon and her allies, the goal of economic security that would enable them to mother their children was inextricably bound up with the struggles for racial justice and feminist liberation.

Lobbying, advocacy, and organizing by the welfare rights movement were crucial for expanding the conversation about comprehensive economic support. By the late 1960s, momentum built among grassroots activists, policy makers, and government officials to address the racial and gender inequities in public assistance, most clearly with proposals for the implementation of a government program that provided an income floor. The welfare rights movement aimed to replace AFDC with a guaranteed annual income to bring every poor person up to a minimum standard of living, which they established at $5,500 a year for a family of four, an amount well above the poverty line in 1968. NWRO's guaranteed income was introduced into Congress, along with numerous other proposals, including one by Republican president Richard Nixon. None of these plans ever passed Congress, however, in part because of the deepening racial hostility directed at women of color on public assistance. Nevertheless, NWRO's proposal was a historic milestone. The standard bearer for the guaranteed income campaign was a group of poor Black women who were demanding both the right to live and the right to mother. It is also significant that, for a moment, the nation considered providing direct cash assistance to every needy American to ensure that no one lived in poverty.[51]

Guaranteed annual income is distinct from the universal basic income. Most universal basic income proposals would provide an unconditional, federal government payment to all citizens regardless of income, family status, or work history. The guaranteed income, in contrast, would be paid to the poorest Americans, with the amount decreasing as recipients' earnings increased. Functioning much like a negative income tax, a guaranteed income would effectively bring all Americans up to a minimum standard of living and ameliorate inequality, rather than giving everyone—rich and poor—the same amount.[52]

Guaranteed income pilot programs and research initiatives have flourished in recent years. In 2018, Springboard to Opportunities in Jackson, Mississippi, launched Magnolia Mother's Trust, a program to give poor Black mothers a no-strings-attached cash stipend of a thousand dollars a month for one year. Mother's Outreach Network in Washington, DC, has endorsed a guaranteed income and is starting its own pilot program for mothers who are entangled with or at risk of becoming entangled with the DC Child and Family Services Agency. For them, a guaranteed income is an alternative to state intervention and family separation; it also represents part of an effort to dismantle the agency.[53]

The demand for a guaranteed income reflects activists' beliefs that a minimum standard of living is a fundamental right, and the onus is on the federal government to provide it. The guaranteed income would help realize self-determination and a person's ability to maintain day-to-day life. Providing economic security promises to alleviate the most extreme cases of poverty, ameliorate racial inequality, liberate poor women from economic dependence

on men, and give people the opportunity to care for themselves
and their dependents. Any feminist theory of justice requires a
guaranteed income, as political scientist Almaz Zelleke argues.[54]

Although the welfare rights movement was not explicitly anticapitalist, its demands were a form of radical reclamation. Black
women in the welfare rights movement demanded a right to do
domestic and household labor for their own families rather than
enter the labor market; in other words, to engage in the labor of
social reproduction on their own terms. They represented a sector
of the Black community that was denied the basic right to care
for themselves and their loved ones—people who were deemed
"valueless" by capital and whose labor power may not have been
needed. And if their labor was needed, public assistance would
give workers a viable alternative to degrading and exploitative labor conditions. In that regard, the movement subverted dominant
capitalist norms and attributions of worth.

The Wages for Housework movement and the welfare rights
movement helped shift the political terrain of class struggle to
the domestic sphere. They believed that the labor performed by
mothers was economically and socially valuable and should be
compensated by the state. Although the Wages for Housework
movement rejected the language of love and care for their own
families, welfare rights activists rooted their claim to assistance
in that language. Wages for Housework activists were speaking
to women for whom the language of love was deployed to co-
erce them to provide unpaid care. Welfare recipients, however,
embraced a politics of love for their own families because they
had historically been denied the opportunity to be with and care
for them. Foregrounding love, then, challenged the social expectations and normative ideologies that forced them into the low-
wage labor market at the expense of family responsibilities and
community connection.

Other activists, as well, organized around the premise that state resources could be utilized for the benefit of the community and to ensure individual autonomy. In the 1960s and 1970s, public housing residents in Baltimore, as historian Rhonda Williams has documented, took control of their housing complexes to use public housing as a platform for grassroots activism and to demand accountability from the government.[55] Similarly, welfare recipients in Nevada, led by the formidable Ruby Duncan, used federal resources from the War on Poverty to "wage their own war on poverty" in the 1970s and 1980s, as Annelise Orleck has written.[56]

Domestic workers, welfare recipients, the Wages for Housework movement, and other radicals in the 1960s and 1970s were all organizing at a time when it seemed that the state could be leveraged. This was not born from naivete but from a thoughtfulness about the political possibilities before them. The state had, after all, taken bold public action to protect individual rights and expand the welfare state. Civil rights activists pushed for federal assistance to dismantle legalized segregation and protect voting rights, leading to a pitched confrontation with racist Southern officials. In the context of a "federal war on poverty," resources were allocated for new programs to eradicate poverty and address racism. Activists were rightfully skeptical about the motivations of the federal government—they understood the limits for meaningful change in that context and were aware of how federal agencies' covert operations undermined movement organizing. Nevertheless, they hoped to ameliorate foundational inequalities by advocating on behalf of people who had been "left out" of the rights and privileges associated with citizenship. There was widespread agreement among progressives about the positive role of the welfare state and the need to extend its reach. Although the federal government fell short in many ways, there was commitment to holding its feet to the fire.

Because the state has been a key player in the exploitation and expropriation of paid and unpaid social reproductive labor, leveraging the state means ensuring that control of resources and decision-making can rest with families and communities. Considering how best to engage the state, George Caffentzis and Silvia Federici distinguish between the "the public," an institution that is managed by the state, and "the commons," which is controlled by the people.[57] Organizers in the 1960s and 70s, in their demand for control, were tending toward a model of the commons, in part because of long-standing distrust of the state. Welfare rights activists were adamant that they should decide how to spend their monthly stipends, without caseworker involvement. In her 1974 pamphlet *Wages Against Housework*, Federici argued similarly that state resources must be controlled by community members:

> It is one thing to set up a day care centre the way we want it, and demand that the State pay for it. It is quite another thing to deliver our children to the State and ask the State to control them, discipline them, teach them to honour the American flag not for five hours, but for fifteen or twenty-four hours. It is one thing to organize communally the way we want to eat (by ourselves, in groups, etc.) and then ask the State to pay for it, and it is the opposite thing to ask the State to organize our meals. In one case we regain some control over our lives, in the other we extend the State's control over us.[58]

Federici's call for cooperatives, communal kitchens, and land occupations was in essence anticapitalist resistance because these institutions and resources would be democratically controlled.

Neoliberalism, however, constructed a different political landscape. The possibility of securing state resources and being granted the kind of autonomy demanded by radicals in the 1960s and 1970s is rapidly diminishing. The state has retreated from its purported commitment to achieving equality and, in fact, is moving ahead full force to exacerbate inequality. With the transformation of the welfare state, which I discuss in the next chapter, and the rise of the for-profit care economy, discussed in chapter 6, it is not clear that public dollars end up in the hands of the people who need it most or that recipients are able to maneuver in a way that gives them real control over that money. More often, state programs serve to discipline people by drug testing or mandating work. Programs for the poor, because they are often subcontracted to the private sector, are being used to enrich the wealthy (covered in more detail in chapter 6). Given that, the demand for state resources must be made prudently, and people making those demands must ensure that resources are going to the right people. Campaigns for direct cash assistance have been the most promising in this regard.

The broad terrain of social reproductive organizing suggests that working-class movements should link home- and work-based labor; organize the unemployed, underemployed, unpaid, overworked, documented, undocumented, and guest workers; and push for an expansion of social benefits and public services, alongside demanding better work, less work, and decent wages. Such struggles are the key to building people's power, which is a cornerstone of social transformation. Grassroots organizing can foster solidarity and lay the foundation for a movement that could, in the long run, undermine capitalism. A broad-based intersectional movement led by women of color can move us in a direction of transforming what both care and capitalism look like.

Chapter 5

Who Cares?

Caring (or Not Caring) for the Poor

Sandra Killett has been a community organizer for close to thirty years, a role she came into because of her hardships as a single parent. After separating from her husband in the mid-1990s, she moved with her two small boys from one relative's home to another in New York City as she searched for a permanent place to live. Although employed for a period, she found it difficult to simultaneously care for her children, work, and secure reliable housing. Because Sandra wanted to care for her children, going on public assistance was the only option.

Applying for public assistance was a degrading experience, with a probing questionnaire and multiple forms of verification that signaled distrust rather than compassion. Once she was on welfare, things were not much better. Temporary Assistance to Needy Families (TANF), the program that replaced AFDC, required periodic, seemingly random, requests for further documentation, frequent meetings with caseworkers, and thirty hours of employment per week. The demands and mandates of TANF defeated Sandra's purpose for going on welfare: to raise her children. As she explained, all the jobs she got while on welfare were about "trying to figure out how it would allow me to be with my children because it wasn't enough just to say [to welfare officials] you wanted to be home with your children. Raise your children. Nurture your children." Frustrated with the protocol, she decided to join Community Voices Heard, which organized around welfare.

Although Community Voices Heard provided her with support and information and connected her to other parents, it couldn't protect her from a child welfare system that ultimately separated her from her children. Sandra was a loving mother, but, as a single parent, she struggled with her sons when they were teenagers. Her older son harbored a lot of anger, especially about his parents' separation. At thirteen he became disobedient, and they had volatile arguments. Sandra had never dealt with a situation like this—it was quite unlike her own relatively tranquil childhood—and she was at a loss. Her son crossed boundaries and pushed her to the limit. During one incident, she grabbed him by the neck and told him that she would not put up with his disrespect. She went to child protective services, hoping to get counseling for him. The social worker saw the scratch on her son's neck and concluded that she beat her children—despite their protestations—and opened a case.

Child welfare workers searched her apartment weekly and questioned her and the children. One day Sandra and her son had another physical altercation: her son pinned her on the ground, and she hit him on the hip with a bat. She was so fearful of his violent behavior that she called the police for help. The cops spoke to her son privately and then arrested Sandra. She spent three days in jail and the boys went to her brother's home. It was one of the most difficult periods of her life. Although her younger son eventually returned home, her older son ended up in foster care for two years—against both of their wishes. She visited him regularly but worried that he was not cared for. For her, the separation was "like death." She described "laying in my son's bed [at night] and crying because he wasn't there. Not knowing where he was... I couldn't know or they didn't allow me to know where he was, not even a phone call. And how is that even possible that you could do that to parents?"

Years later, her son was diagnosed with bipolar disorder, which explained a lot of his behavior. Counseling and an earlier diagnosis would have dramatically altered the trajectory of the family. As Sandra says: "You could take [the children away] and forever traumatize the family, change the family dynamics." Things were never quite the same after the intervention. Her younger son was deeply troubled by his brief separation from his mother, as well as how his relationship with his brother was transformed by his extended absence. Fifteen years later, now living in Harlem, Sandra explained that she and her older son have reunited, made peace, and have a healthy, loving relationship.[1]

Sandra's situation illustrates the hypocrisy of the care discourse, which has failed to address the care needs of the poor. It has offered few solutions for how single parents like Sandra can care for their children or how to put an end to parent-child separation—now a hallmark of the child welfare system. What should be the cornerstone of the country's care agenda—a system of care for the poor and needy—is sadly missing. Although nearly everyone, regardless of race and class background, is facing a crisis of social reproduction, people's ability to cope depends on their resources, benefits, and systems of support. Advocates of expanded care policies have fought for flexible work options, tax credits, and higher pay for care workers, but these policies mean very little to the poor. Middle-class and wealthier people benefit from unpaid family leave and childcare tax credits. Higher pay for care workers is designed to meet the needs of well-off working parents.

Most care policies are premised on assumptions of whiteness, full employment, and ample economic resources. Too many people are left out of solutions that rely on the market economy or are geared toward people who can outsource childcare and take advantage of tax credits. Such policies do little for people outside the formal economy who are unable to work or work intermittently. For the single mother with a disability and no wealth. For a formerly incarcerated single father who cannot find work. Or for a family living out of their car. The shredding of the safety net, rhetoric of self-sufficiency, and the trend toward privatization have left people to fend for themselves. One of the cruelly ironic things about our care policies is how badly the people who need the most care are faring.

People on the economic margins have been devastated by the cutback of public services and declining government support. The poor are increasingly entangled in a punitive welfare state bureaucracy, the carceral state, or the low-wage or no-wage labor market, with few tools at their disposal to pull themselves out of it. The closing of schools has been accompanied by the opening of prisons. Deindustrialization has been coupled with the implementation of work requirements for social benefits. Over the past few decades, as welfare was transformed from a program supporting single parents to one that punishes them, the number of children in foster care skyrocketed. And many poor and working-class families turned to debt as a survival mechanism. Mainstream campaigns to uplift and revalue care sit alongside educational, zoning, welfare, labor, and funding policies that have frayed poor communities.

Despite claims about the universal nature of care and proposals to address the care crisis that will supposedly benefit us all, core safety net programs are rarely part of this discussion. The Care for All Agenda, a comprehensive care infrastructure plan introduced by two progressive Democrats, Elizabeth Warren and Jamaal Bowman, resolves "far-reaching public investments" in hospitals, schools, housing, transportation, public parks, and libraries. It aims to increase pay and benefits for care workers, protect the right to organize, ensure paid time off, and implement a federal jobs guarantee and universal public programs for health care and childcare. It is by far the most promising of legislative proposals and is premised on the idea that "we are interdependent…and everyone will give or receive care." Yet, it makes no mention of guaranteed income support or people caring for their own children. It promises to support unpaid caregiving, but it's not clear what that means.[2] There is much that is worthwhile in the Care for All Agenda, and supporting it is a strategic decision. But, either way, we have to push for economic support for people outside the formal economy and to care for their own loved ones.

Because much of the care discourse is wedded to a care economy, rather than alleviating inequality, it benefits from—and perhaps inadvertently contributes to—widening race and class divisions. Ruth Wilson Gilmore refers to this failure to address the needs of the poorest as "organized abandonment." There is a glaring contradiction between an agenda that presumably cares for all and the growing challenges of the poorest Americans.

Nothing exemplifies the disconnect between the universal promises of the care discourse and the declining fortunes of the poor better than the fate of public assistance programs. Since the 1970s, there has been a systematic dismantling of programs serving poor people and a shift away from direct government economic assistance. The welfare state has been replaced by the carceral state, which has both exacerbated the care crisis and created new opportunities for growth in the care economy. Meanwhile, poor people are left in a dire situation with very little care support.

The growing numbers of women of color on public assistance in the postwar period generated a fierce racist backlash beginning in the early 1960s, which transformed public perceptions of welfare. Because of the rising numbers of single-parent families, the migration of African Americans to northern urban areas in search of work, deindustrialization, and racism in the labor movement, the proportion of African American people on welfare increased from 31 percent in 1950 to 48 percent in 1961.[3] An outcry charged "welfare fraud" and accused "migrants from the South" living off other people's tax dollars. In 1965, *U.S. News and World Report*, for example, attributed the growing number of welfare recipients to the "mass migration of unskilled Negroes from the South to Northern cities" and expressed concern about "the high rate of illegitimacy in the self-perpetuating breeding grounds of city slums."[4] The attack on the welfare state emanated from public hostility toward women of color receiving any kind of aid, what political scientist Ange-Marie Hancock calls "the politics of disgust."[5] The racist and sexist stereotypes that Black and Brown welfare recipients were lazy, sexually promiscuous, and undeserving of assistance were rooted in long-standing assumptions that women of color were primarily workers, not mothers, and should be self-supporting.[6]

By the 1970s, the racialized discourse became the basis for the "welfare queen" stereotype. Popularized by presidential candidate Ronald Reagan in 1976, the trope signified an inner-city Black woman with multiple children from several different fathers who fleeced the system. Poor single mothers of color, especially African American and Puerto Rican women, were scapegoated and blamed for rising taxes and the growing economic insecurity of American families, even though welfare accounted for less than 1 percent of the federal budget. Roger Freeman, an economist with the Hoover Institution, wrote in 1971, for example: "By imposing an excessive and lopsided tax burden [the welfare state] has sapped the natural growth potential of our economy."[7]

The demonization of women of color led to the transformation of AFDC from a program that provided some financial support for eligible people into a temporary program that offered services more than cash and regulated rather than assisted.[8] In 1996, president Bill Clinton signed into law a bipartisan bill to dismantle the welfare system, ending the entitlement to assistance for poor families. Republicans and Democrats banded together in a show of unity to abdicate any responsibility to ensure economic support for the needy. AFDC was replaced with TANF, which remains in effect today. TANF imposes a five-year lifetime limit on assistance—regardless of need. In addition, large swaths of poor people are excluded from federal assistance. For the first five years of their residency in the US, legal immigrants are barred from applying for TANF, Supplemental Nutrition Assistance Program (SNAP), Medicaid, and the Child Health Insurance Program (CHIP). Undocumented people did not qualify for any public assistance before 1996 and still don't today. States may use their own money to cover people, but they cannot use federal funds.

States have enormous leeway about how to spend federal TANF funds. They can provide services or outsource their bureaucracy to private companies rather than provide direct assistance. Few TANF dollars support recipients with monthly cash stipends. In 1997, close to 75 percent of the money spent on welfare went to basic cash assistance, whereas in 2020 only about 20 percent did.[9] The rest was spent on job training, marriage classes, childcare assistance, tax credits, after-school programs, and subsidizing wages for companies that hire recipients. The rationale behind TANF is to move recipients from "welfare to work," although few people get meaningful job training or end up in decent-paying jobs. TANF requires nearly all recipients to work at least thirty hours a week. For that thirty-hour workweek, they receive a welfare check rather than a paycheck, which translates into working for far less than minimum wage.

In 2017, Congress mandated that able-bodied SNAP recipients without dependents work at least eighty hours per month. And some states are eager to extend work requirements to Medicaid recipients as well: Georgia is on the verge of instituting the first such requirement.[10] At the very moment of deindustrialization, when work became harder to find, less rewarding, and more precarious, the welfare program's work requirements became more coercive, pushing the poor deeper into an inhospitable labor market or mandating work at below-market wages.

With the implementation of TANF, public welfare programs decidedly moved away from providing economic support and toward criminalizing the poor.[11] The cumbersome and nearly insurmountable bureaucratic hurdles kept assistance out of reach for qualified people. The application process assumes that recipients are criminals or engage in illicit behavior. Fingerprinting was instituted in some places as part of the application process for SNAP and TANF in the first two decades after welfare reform, although nearly all states have since dropped those requirements. Many states still require a substance abuse screening questionnaire for TANF, which can serve as a justification for drug testing the poor. The restrictions on the use of federal money have made it more burdensome for states that want to provide a stronger safety net. TANF has been of limited benefit to the poor. Because of the 1996 reform, the number of families on welfare declined precipitously from 4.8 million in 1995 to 800,000 in 2021.[12]

The simultaneous rise of the carceral state alongside the dismantling of the welfare state further illustrates the shift in social policy from support and assistance to containment, coercion, and surveillance. Criminalization of welfare recipients and policing went hand in hand, as poor people of color found themselves entangled in the legal system for petty offenses, including low-level drug possession, loitering, and panhandling. It is no coincidence that prison became the most likely alternative to public assistance. As Elizabeth Hinton has argued, the War on Poverty was closely linked to the War on Crime, and federal law enforcement programs were implemented as part of an antipoverty strategy. During the three decades following the passage of TANF, more and more poor people of color were locked up. The history of the carceral state is rooted in deindustrialization, the shredding of the safety net, and management of the poor.[13]

The 1996 reform marked a turning point: welfare incontrovertibly became a punitive program, and the federal government turned its back on the poor. Today, a cash assistance system for the poor is pretty much nonexistent in the US. Of course, the welfare system had always disregarded the labor of social reproduction that Black and Brown women performed for their own families. But AFDC was a federal entitlement—if states accepted federal money and the applicant met the established criteria, assistance was federally guaranteed. As discussed in chapter 4, the welfare rights movement used that to their advantage in the 1960s to make demands for state support for their own families' care work,

The dismantling of welfare at best disregards and at worst demonizes the care work that welfare recipients engage in for their own families. Moving recipients "from welfare to work" implies that the care work that they engage in is not work—contradicting what is at the center of today's care discourse: broadening the notion of work to include social reproductive labor and taking into account everyone's care needs. If the aim is to be universal, then the care discourse must reorient its political agenda and prioritize

the economic security that would enable everyone—especially
poor people—to care for their loved ones without mandatory
work and with the resources to live decently. With the dismantling of welfare, the poor have few places to turn.

An especially tragic consequence of the gutting of the welfare
state and declining financial support for poor parents is the rise
in the number of children in foster care. Children in poor families, especially poor Black families, are more likely to end up in
foster care either because parents are unable to care for them or
because their families have been targeted by the child welfare
system. The percentage of Black children in foster care is double
that of their percentage in the general population.[14] A study in
the *American Journal of Public Health* found that half of all Black
children and half of all Native children have experienced, before
the age of eighteen, an intervention by child protective services.[15]
A disproportionate number of children of color end up in foster
care for a longer than average period, even when other factors
are considered and when their parents would prefer to keep the
family together.

The child welfare system, like the welfare system, is less about
providing support and more about punishing the poor. Parents
are surveilled and sanctioned, and children could be taken away
at a moment's notice, as was the case with Sandra, introduced at
the beginning of this chapter. Dorothy Roberts, the country's
foremost expert on child welfare, has argued that surveillance has
turned child welfare into a family policing system: "The prison
and child welfare systems impose excessive policing on African
American mothers under the guise of protecting children and the
public from harm."[16] Undoubtedly, abused children should be removed from the home, but many children are taken away when
parents just need help.

Roberts illustrates that the treatment of the same behavior by wealthy white versus poor Black parents differs drastically. Black families are more likely to be reported for child abuse than are white families. Child welfare workers provide less in-home support for families of color, disregard Black familial bonds, and stereotype Black parents. The vast majority of families experience state intervention not because of abuse but because of "neglect"—a vague and subjective category that is often conflated with poverty. Once families are in the system, they are closely monitored, and caseworkers have nearly unfettered access to the home and possess enormous power to remove children. The overrepresentation of children of color in foster care, then, is a result of systemic racial bias.

The child welfare system's individualized analysis of poverty and violence fails to account for the source of parent-child conflict or "parental neglect," which might include racial discrimination, unemployment, alcohol or drug use, health or disability issues, or lack of social support systems. Consider a mother who leaves a child home alone because she does not have access to childcare: a social worker might deem her neglectful rather than try to assist her by providing childcare. Things may have turned out differently if Sandra had access to the counseling she desired and the medical help her son needed. Instead, officials quickly labeled her a neglectful and abusive mother. The removal of "at-risk children" disciplines and punishes Black families, causing long-term damage and creating greater instability for families in an already precarious position.

Child protective services' narrow definition of violence also erases institutional forms of violence that children encounter in schools, with police, or in the foster care system that tears families apart. Sandra was labeled violent, but the emotional and destructive violence of the police and family separation went unaccounted

for. Thus, parents are blamed for their own hardship, and institutionalized social inequities fade from view. The end result, according to Roberts, is to "maintain unjust social hierarchies."[17] Beyond
that, child protective services and foster care have become profit
making schemes, as I will outline in the next chapter.

The very poor have been erased from or play a marginal role
in the care discourse. The care discourse asks how we can make
it easier for people to care for children, the elderly, and disabled
people. The most obvious answer is to ensure that they have the
economic resources to do care work. What Sandra wanted more
than anything was the economic support to raise her children and
psychosocial support in difficult moments—two things every parent needs. Instead, because the child welfare system is narrowly
focused on surveillance and discipline, the questions of care and
actual child welfare have fallen by the wayside.

The growth of child removal policies is just one example of
the widespread disregard for the people who need care the most:
other examples include the dismal status of Black women's maternal health, failure to provide services for transgender people,
inadequate health care for Indigenous communities, inadequate
nutrition for children living in poverty, and schools that warehouse rather than educate. To push for a truly caring society
means enabling people, by providing resources and social supports, to do social reproductive work for themselves, not just as
workers caring for others.

Although support for the poor has dwindled, federal and local
governments have instituted some programs with the intention of
offering support for care. The Affordable Care Act has given more
Americans access to health insurance. The Earned Income Tax
Credit has lifted millions of working Americans out of poverty.
The Child Tax Credit has reduced childhood poverty. Universal

pre-K, now offered in a handful of states and cities, offers free public education for three- and four-year-olds and is welcomed by families that cannot send their young children to private day care or hire nannies. These are presumably universal programs championed by advocates of expanded state care. As important as they are, there are too many people in need of assistance who don't benefit from these programs.

Most antipoverty and care legislation is rather modest and fails to address the deep structural inequities that are the source of the care crisis. One of the most celebrated is the Family Medical Leave Act (FMLA) passed in 1993. It requires employers to offer unpaid leave with job security for employees who have a qualifying family or medical emergency, which might include serious illness or the birth or adoption of a child. This means that no one can lose their job because of a family or medical emergency. Its scope is limited, however. It only applies to companies with fifty or more employees; only 56 percent of American workers are covered by FMLA.[18] In addition, the narrow definition of family includes spouse, child, or parent but not extended family, such as aunts, uncles, or grandparents, who are often an integral part of family support networks. Moreover, if employers do not cover the wages of workers, the benefit is more or less worthless for families without the resources to take unpaid leave.

The Child Tax Credit (CTC), first instituted in 1997 in the wake of welfare reform, is another important initiative. The CTC, which gives families a $2,000 credit in 2023, is vital for working- and middle-class families. During the pandemic, the federal government expanded the CTC. Unlike the regular CTC, the temporary expanded CTC had no earnings requirement, gave parents direct monthly payments rather than tax credits, and allocated a generous $3,000 per child ($3,600 for children under six). In 2021, the CTC lifted nearly 3 million children out of poverty, about 2 million of them because of the temporary expansion, according to a paper produced by the US Census Bureau.[19] But the expansion has been phased out and officially lapsed at the end of 2021.

Although the CTC has helped some families, the claim that it is universally beneficial is false. Workers must make a minimum of $2,500 a year to receive any of the $2,000, and they must make at least $13,200 in order to receive the full amount for one child, according to the Tax Policy Center. Because of these earnings rules, 19 million children don't receive the full credit. So, the CTC does not benefit the lowest-earning families.[20] In addition, the CTC excludes undocumented children. Further, because of "child-claiming rules," children who do not live with the same caregiver for six months of the year, whose primary caregiver is a distant relative or friend, or who are not claimed on the household's taxes don't qualify for the CTC. This means that children who move frequently between households, are unhoused, are involved in the child welfare or the juvenile justice systems, or who are not claimed on a tax return—many of whom are immigrants and/or children of color—do not benefit.

The CTC is presumably intended to offset the cost of childcare for working families. Yet, the problem of lack of reliable and affordable childcare assistance persists. Although the wealthy can hire nannies and afford top-tier day care centers, most poor, working, and middle-class families cannot. There has never been universal childcare in the US, even though some feminists fought tirelessly for it in the 1960s.[21] One bill came very close to passage in 1971 but was vetoed by President Nixon. More often, people have to construct makeshift solutions, relying on friends, family, and neighbors.[22] Universal day care, not just tax credits for people who rely on a private childcare market, should be a part of any comprehensive care package, available to any parent who needs it.

The Earned Income Tax Credit (EITC), first enacted in 1975 with bipartisan support, was conceived as a way to get people off welfare and into low-paying jobs, as well as to push back on racist arguments that stereotyped poor women of color as lazy. It's both carrot and stick. It reduced direct economic support and created financial incentives for low-wage work by boosting the income of low-wage workers. Like most tax benefits, however, it does not help the unemployed—people who seek work but cannot find it because of racism, lack of training or education, discrimination, illness, a history of incarceration, or household care responsibilities. In addition, people who receive public assistance—Supplemental Security Income, disability, or military pensions, for example—do not qualify for EITC, even if their monthly benefits are below the threshold. And undocumented immigrants who pay taxes with an individual taxpayer identification number rather than a social security number cannot receive the EITC benefit. Thus, the determining factor for EITC is not how much people need to live but whether and how they have worked, as well as their legal status. Tax credits and other assistance programs have lifted some working poor out of poverty but have done little to address the precarity of the labor market.

In addition, tax credits like the CTC and the EITC deflect from the real problem: low wages. Why should the government supplement the wages of working Americans? Why aren't workers paid enough to live securely? The paradox of a booming stock market and wages that fail to keep up with inflation is not a contradiction at all—low wages simply mean more profit for shareholders. The EITC, then, serves as a taxpayer-funded subsidy for greedy employers. Subsidizing low-wage work does not solve the problem of low wages; it encourages the expansion of low-wage work. It takes the burden off employers who pay less than workers need, passing that cost onto the taxpayer.

In this discussion about jobs and tax credits, the underpaid or unpaid household labor required to care for the young, the elderly, and people with disabilities is also obscured. Many of these proposals that address the care crisis—childcare assistance, unpaid leave, tax breaks, refunds, and increased pay for care workers—are tied to employment and designed for a market economy. They primarily benefit businesses, well-off employed people, and people who take care of people who work. People without formal employment are excluded. And the definition of work is circumscribed—unpaid care work does not count. Tax credits do not benefit people who choose to engage in unpaid care work or undocumented people doing this work for pay.

A comprehensive care agenda, on the other hand, would include people who are formally employed as well as people who are not. It would create support for care work for one's own family, not just to ensure that corporations function efficiently but because people need care. And it would include the myriad definitions of *family*: single parent, extended family, temporary care situations, LGBTQ, intergenerational, chosen family, and whatever arrangements people make to ensure care for their loved ones. Such an agenda would align with the spirit of both welfare rights activists in the 1960s and Wages for Housework movement activists, who insisted that household labor and childcare should be economically supported.

Alongside government policies, some corporations have instituted programs to create "caring workplaces." Google, for instance, has sought to distinguish itself from its competitors by instituting care policies for employees and to enable employees to care for loved ones. Google's web page explains, "How we care for Googlers." The company offers a range of benefits from prepared meals to yoga classes and has been lauded for flexible, family-friendly, and progressive policies. It provides health care, vacation time, and eighteen weeks of paid family leave for new mothers and six weeks for new fathers. New parents get "child-bonding bucks" to help with the cost of diapers, food, and formula. Google office buildings have a "Mother's Room," backup babysitting, a parent support group, and a parent guru. They also have free infant childcare and onsite childcare for tech workers at their main campus.

Google's benefits cater to the needs of its most privileged employees rather than the least privileged. For example, the company runs four childcare centers at its California campus for employees. But, the childcare workers employed in these centers cannot realistically take advantage of the childcare benefit because of their long commutes, since the cost of housing near Google headquarters is prohibitive. Most of these workers are paid twenty dollars an hour, higher than many childcare workers but far below a living wage in Silicon Valley. In May 2021, during the pandemic, Google reopened its childcare centers but, because of safety concerns, did not restart its transportation services, which were especially useful for workers who lived far away.[23] When childcare center workers requested a transportation stipend, the company stated that transportation was a "perk" and not a benefit.

Chelsea Price-Gallinat, a Google child educator, explained in an interview: "Transportation is a perk, just like childcare is a perk. And who's using that perk? . . . It's the wealthy White families who live close to campus that need the childcare. And it's the BIPOC [Black, Indigenous, People of Color] folks who live all spread out who need the transportation.[24] In response, Price-Gallinat and other workers organized the Alphabet Workers Union. The Alphabet Workers Union is a minority union, which means it does not have National Labor Relations Board (NLRB) protection. At the same time, it is not restricted by NLRB regulations, so it can organize a larger swath of workers. Alphabet brings together full-time workers, temporary workers, vendors, and contractors into a single entity.

Google's policies are indicative of the way corporate care is circumscribed and driven by the concerns of middle-class women and families. The caring responsibilities of relatively privileged women and care as an obstacle to their professional success and economic advancement have dominated certain strains of the care discourse. In 2013, Sheryl Sandberg, chief operating officer of Facebook, published her bestselling book *Lean In*. She suggests that in their efforts to combine workplace and household responsibilities, women are holding themselves back professionally. That is, because of seemingly minor everyday decisions, working women "step back" in anticipation of the work/family balance. Addressing the problem of gender inequality in the workplace, she proposes, requires that women be more assertive, take risks, and "lean in." Like other corporate feminists, Sandberg individualizes the challenges of professional and working women. The idea of a "work/family balance" implies that women need to make different choices, embrace more of one thing, and let go of something else to maintain a "balance."[25]

Unlike Sandberg, lawyer and political scientist Anne-Marie Slaughter aims to transform thinking about work in general and care work in particular. Revaluing care, she suggests, requires more family-friendly work policies, higher pay for care workers, and government support for care work. She asserts that we should hold space for moments when we need to prioritize family and put work on the back burner. Slaughter herself did just this: she left a top-level position at the State Department and returned to her job as a professor at Princeton in order to make time for her family. As compelling as Slaughter's propositions are, it is simply not feasible for working-class women to take time off for long stretches or demand that their employers take into account their care work. Slaughter and Sandberg have differing solutions to the problem of work/family balance, but they converge in their preoccupation with the lives of better-off women.[26]

Family-friendly corporate policies are designed to recruit and retain women in the interest of diversifying their workforce. Gender equity in the workplace has become equated with women occupying the highest ranks of the corporate and professional world—where they have no doubt been underrepresented. This particular battle, however, does not address the needs of the vast majority of employees and the larger issue of occupational segregation—that is, how most women who work in corporate America are relegated to low-paying, low-valued work. Tackling that would require rethinking the occupational structure and rectifying disparities in pay and benefits between those at the top and the bottom, not just equity between men and women in the top ranks. Family-friendly policies are admirable, and every workplace should support care work. But, so far, corporate care initiatives have given us a kind of tunnel vision about who needs care and the scope of the care agenda.

Their narrow focus on gender equity and care for a particular kind of worker indicates the indifference these companies have for lower-level as well as outsourced workers. Under Sandberg's leadership, Facebook instituted several progressive workplace benefits. Full-time employees get four months of paid leave so parents can bond with their new child, and ten weeks of paid family leave if an employee has to unexpectedly care for a child or relative. As the company says on its website, "We're here to support our people as they grow their families." Additionally, the Menlo Park campus has a Wellness Center that offers medical, dental, vision, and mental health care on campus.[27] But Facebook outsources a large portion of its work. It contracts out the labor of more than fifteen thousand content moderators, mostly overseas. Content moderators in Nairobi, Kenya, for example, are paid as little as $1.50 an hour. In addition to low wages and the psycho-logical trauma they experience from hours of viewing violent, racist, and misogynist posts, these workers have also been denied the right to form a union.[28]

Similarly, Google's very generous benefits package does not apply to all employees. The benefits are reserved for full-time em-ployees directly hired by Google. More people are part of what has been called Google's "shadow workforce," made up of about 150,000 temporary and contract employees, compared to 140,000 permanent employees. According to an investigation by *The Guardian*, Google knowingly and illegally underpaid its tempo-rary workers.[29] The stratification and inequity at companies such as Google and Facebook illustrate not only how some employees ben-efit and others do not; they also show how the care privileges that some people receive are dependent on the exploitation of others.

These companies are able to pay some workers well and offer generous benefits because much of the company's work is carried out by an exploited workforce—their underpayment subsidizes this system of care for a select group of employees. The benefits packages for privileged workers widen the class divide. The result is a growing pool of low-wage workers that service the well-off and contribute to their ability to survive and thrive. Underpaid workers at large companies may have to get second jobs as Uber or Instacart drivers, serving and subsidizing the wealthy in an-other way. In that regard, these generous benefit packages are part and parcel of the care economy.

The family-friendly policies are troubling in another way as well. Rather than creating space for valuing home life, these com-panies ask workers to contort their home life to fit the needs of capital, bringing children to day care at work, breastfeeding while on break, and receiving parenting advice from their employer. While the children of the poor are left uncared for, the children of white-collar workers are folded into the structures of the work-place, perhaps even to cultivate the next generation of Googlers.

Most care policies are piecemeal and premised on the expectation of full-time professional employment and a two-parent hetero-sexual household. The experiences of middle-class and upper-class women have come to dominate the terms of the care discourse: their struggle to achieve a work/family balance, their difficulty in finding good care, and their obstacles to career advancement. Meanwhile, the class divide widens and poverty deepens.

Poverty is a systemic problem in the US. By some measures, the working class is doing better now than it was twenty years ago. Wages have increased, the unemployment rate is at a record low, and the poverty rate has declined. But official statistics are notoriously flawed. Unemployment rates, for example, only count people actively looking for work. People who have given up looking for work are called "discouraged workers." They are not even counted as part of the unemployed. The unemployment rate also doesn't consider underemployment—people who are employed part-time but would like full-time work.

Measuring poverty is way more complicated than it seems. Poverty is usually assessed by calculating the cost of living. But how exactly do we do that? And is that the right approach? The official poverty threshold, established in 1963, relies on an "emergency" food budget that is multiplied by three. It is widely considered an outdated metric of what people have—because it relies on pretax income—and also of what they need, since the food budget used was meant to be temporary, and the costs of other items have increased relative to food in the past sixty years.[30] A lot of people who land above the poverty threshold are objectively poor. A living-wage calculator, developed by economists at MIT, takes into account the real cost of housing, childcare, medical

care, and education and establishes a much higher poverty threshold.[31] An alternative approach is to consider not just household
income but also community conditions such as access to good
schools, job opportunities, health care, transportation, and protection from violence and discrimination. This approach, which
recognizes material needs as well as an individual's capacity to
pursue life plans and exercise freedom, as economist Amartya Sen
puts it, is undoubtedly a better measure of well-being.[32]

Even if we rely on official measures, the picture is bleak.
Close to forty million Americans live in poverty.[33] That's a
shocking number. More troubling is that most marginalized
Americans are worse off than a generation ago. A growing number of people in the United States live either in deep poverty
(which the United Nations defines as people earning less than
half the poverty threshold) or in extreme poverty (people who
live on less than two dollars a day). Although extreme poverty is
not part of everyday vocabulary in the US and is usually associated with "elsewhere," one and a half million American households live in extreme poverty today—nearly twice as many as
twenty years ago.[34]

In 2017, Philip Alston, the United Nations (UN) special rapporteur on extreme poverty and human rights, conducted an investigation and a fifteen-day tour of poverty in the US.[35] His team
visited Alabama, California, Puerto Rico, West Virginia, and
Washington, DC. They documented housing insecurity, unsafe
sanitation, police surveillance, criminalization, and harassment of
the poor. Their subjects are people who reached their five-year
lifetime limit on TANF, do not qualify for any other programs,
cannot find work, live in remote areas, or are disconnected from
both the safety net and the job market. To quote the UN report:
"The American Dream is rapidly becoming the American Illusion, as the U.S. ... now has the lowest rate of social mobility of

any of the rich countries."[36] At the same time, income inequality has grown steadily. The share of wealth of the top 1 percent equals that of the bottom 90 percent of Americans.[37] The report concluded that the pervasiveness of poverty and inequality "are shockingly at odds with [the United States'] immense wealth and its founding commitment to human rights."

Particular categories of people are hurting the most. Single mothers of color are more likely to be poor than most other demographic groups. In 2021, poverty rates for families headed by women were 43 percent for Native, 37 percent for Black, 36 percent for Latinx, 25 percent for white, and 20 percent for Asian families, according to Census Bureau data analyzed by the National Women's Law Center.[38] By comparison, for married-couple families, the poverty rate was 5.4 percent.[39] The deepening poverty of some groups can be explained partly by the absence of a safety net. When people are in trouble, they rely on their private safety net—that is, if they have one. According to a study by the Federal Reserve, in 2019 the median wealth of white families was $188,000, $36,000 for Latinx families, and $24,000 for Black families.[40] This includes everything from home ownership to retirement accounts to cash in the bank. Black and Latinx people have significantly less personal wealth to fall back on when times get tough.[41]

The racial wealth gap is compounded by other social inequities as well. Formerly incarcerated people have a particularly difficult time working their way out of poverty. Forty-five percent of formerly incarcerated people were unemployed one year after their release from prison, according to a 2018 Brookings Institution study. For those who did find work, median annual earnings were only ten thousand dollars. This group was much less likely to take advantage of programs such as the EITC and the Work Opportunity Tax Credit (WOTC), even though they were eligible, possibly because they did not know about them or did not have the where-withal to claim them because of the complexity of the tax code.

One of the most visible indicators of the rise in poverty is the increasing number of encampments of unhoused people. Although the unhoused are a permanent feature of US society, the scale of encampments is unlike anything we have seen since the Great Depression, when "Hoovervilles" popped up all over the country. Encampments emerged on a mass scale after the 2008 financial crisis. The National Law Center on Homelessness and Poverty has reported a fourteen-fold increase in camps between 2007 and 2017. In 2021, an estimated 3.7 million people experienced housing insecurity, and an additional 7.7 million were behind in paying their rent.[42] Encampments are a product of the lack of affordable housing, economic instability, and unsafe conditions in public shelters. But instead of countering housing insecurity with secure housing, mayors around the country have responded with sweeps led by riot police.

People who are unable to cope economically are also going into debt. Household debt increased from $8 trillion in 2004 to a record-high $16.5 trillion in September 2022. Seventy percent of household debt comes from mortgages; the remainder comes from student loans and automobile debt, both of which have increased dramatically over the past twenty years. Student loan debt has increased six-fold since 2004.[43] The explosion of household debt is a mark of "the growing privatisation of social reproduction," as described by Adrienne Roberts, professor of international politics at the University of Manchester.[44] Housing, medical care, and education are part of the care economy—which people need to live. If they can't pay for basic needs and government services are unavailable, they go into debt.

Growing household debt is one outcome of dwindling public support for care work and the dismantling of the safety net. To address the care crisis, families have turned to the private sector, often borrowing money for childcare, education, and other basic needs. The care economy has fed off the privatization of care and flourished in the process. When corporations and businesses go into debt, they can declare bankruptcy, close down shop, and reopen under a different name while principals are protected. There is no such endgame for ordinary Americans. Unpaid debt and bankruptcy can destroy one's ability to borrow money, obtain a credit card, or open a bank account. Daily transactions like cashing a check become more expensive, and the purchase of large items, such as a car or house that requires financing, are next to impossible.

There is a growing movement to address how debt is a barrier to economic security. The Debt Collective, "a membership-based union for debtors and our allies," believes that no one should have to go into debt to meet basic human needs. It has called for the abolition of bail and other carceral debt, assisted debtors in legal cases, and organized a student debt strike that led to changes in federal law, including around for-profit colleges.[45] As of early 2023, the organization claims to have facilitated the abolition of an estimated $100 billion in debt.

Although discussions about poverty and public assistance often center on Black and Brown people, who are disproportionately affected, the largest single majority of poor people in the United States are white. In 2022, there were 24 million white Americans living in poverty and 9 million people of African descent.[46] Racism turned welfare into political fodder and targeted and delegitimized antipoverty programs that served poor white people as well. Now, food stamps, Supplemental Security Income for the disabled, and Medicaid are all increasingly under attack. The toxic debate about welfare has had a detrimental impact on all poor people, regardless of racial or ethnic background, and is a reminder that race and class politics have always been intertwined in the US.

Although people of all class backgrounds have been negatively impacted by the care crisis, we have witnessed bifurcated policies to address the needs of poor families of color as compared with wealthy white families. Over the past thirty years, neoliberal policies have shredded any semblance of a public support system for the poor. There has been a steady decline in how people at the very bottom are faring. The reliance of middle-class families on privatized forms of care became more feasible precisely because of the widening inequalities of class and race and the availability of cheap labor. And the growing number of low-paying jobs has exacerbated the class divide, as poor women of color are funneled into these occupations.

Despite an assumption that everyone benefits equally from policies that support parents and caregivers, the mainstream care agenda has been almost exclusively focused on those with economic means or at least a job. The 2021 American Rescue Plan includes funding provisions to help families with care: assistance for childcare providers, Head Start, and the Child Care and Development Block Grant to assist low-income parents with childcare. It increases the CTC and EITC, invests resources in home and community-based assistance for elderly and disabled people who qualify for Medicaid, and offers assistance to states that want to increase wages for care workers. The plan is a welcome shift in the political discourse for its intention to support ordinary Americans. Still, most of this assistance is tied to the care economy or to enabling people to participate fully in the workforce. And it is temporary. There are few provisions to ensure basic income support or support for people who want to care for their own families, and it offers no guaranteed improvements for workers. Even president Joe Biden's more ambitious American Families

Plan, which was defeated by the opposition, did not offer direct income support.[47]

Employer-based care policies, tax credits, and programs like FMLA will not solve the problems of deindustrialization, carcerality, and housing insecurity. Proposals to expand and support care work are intended to ameliorate the care crisis for employers. They may, in fact, result in an even deeper care crisis for childcare workers, who are often separated from their own children for extended periods of time. Ironically, the people caring for others are least able to care for themselves and their loved ones. Perhaps they would prefer resources to care for their own children rather than higher wages to care for someone else's children.

If some of the neediest people are excluded from government care policies, can we call these policies "universal"? Our yardstick for a robust care agenda should be how well *they* are doing. A care discourse that fails to address inadequate housing, access to education, economic opportunities, racial and gender inequality in income and wealth, and punitive government programs will fail to ameliorate the crisis of care that is a hallmark of the contemporary US. We need to expand our notions of who needs to be cared for to ensure that the most vulnerable are not left behind. We need an antipoverty plan without conditions: one attuned to the challenges of our uncertain times that recognizes paid and unpaid care work, regardless of age, personal status, employment, or "worthiness." We have to fight for adequate public support and expanded welfare assistance, workplaces that accommodate household and family responsibilities, and support for the unpaid caregiving of the poor and the working class.

As it stands now, for most Americans, the care economy is broken. But it is not broken for capitalism. As I detail in the next chapter, care and the care crisis have been a site of economic extraction. Demanding more state resources is not enough. We must also ask who makes the decisions about the allocation of resources. A truly just and caring society cannot be achieved by relying on a care economy embedded in the marketplace and profit-making world, which, unfortunately is the direction we are currently moving in.

Chapter 6

In Bed with Capitalism

The State, Capital, and Profiting off Those in Need

Welfare fraud is a massive problem in Mississippi. But not the kind that most people think of when they hear that term—recipients earning unreported cash under the table or spending their money in ways that some people deem irresponsible. Anna Wolfe, a reporter for *Mississippi Today*, has pieced together a shameful story about John Davis, the now former director of the Mississippi Department of Human Services, and his alleged use of welfare money to enrich himself and his friends, take fancy vacations, and purchase luxury vehicles. As head of the department, Davis gave the nonprofit Mississippi Community Education Center, founded by Nancy New, up-front payments of more than $60 million in welfare grants over four years. New, who worked with her son, Zachary New, donated thousands of dollars to Mississippi Republican politicians from 2017 to 2019.

The welfare grant to the News was for a program called Families First of Mississippi, which purported to help poor families get off assistance. Because Families First was a nonprofit, there was little transparency about how the money was spent. The News allegedly embezzled $4 million for personal use—buying expensive cars, paying back personal loans, and paying rent. In addition,

Nancy New transferred $6 million to private schools owned by her family, $1.4 million went to a fitness program designed by former Mississippi State University football star Paul Lacoste, and $9,500 toward the mortgage on the ranch of former NFL player Marcus Dupree. Five million was spent to build a new volleyball stadium at the University of Southern Mississippi at the request of retired NFL quarterback Brett Favre, whose daughter played volleyball at the university, which was also, incidentally, Favre's alma mater.

According to Wolfe, Davis also funneled millions of dollars in welfare funds through the News to his good friends, the DiBiase family. He paid former wrestler Brett DiBiase $48,000 to teach opioid addiction courses, knowing full well that DiBiase was in a drug treatment program in Malibu at the time. Davis also allegedly directed the nonprofit to use state money to pay for DiBiase's four-month stay at the luxury rehab. Ted DiBiase Jr., Brett's brother, was paid $3 million to conduct professional development workshops. And their father, Ted DiBiase, a minister and former wrestler known as the "Million Dollar Man," got $2.1 million in welfare funds for his nonprofit, Heart of David Ministries, in part to develop an app to send bible verses to troubled teens. The amount of misused welfare funds in Mississippi almost equals the total annual welfare budget in the state, nearly all of which comes from the federal government.[1]

The saga in Mississippi is framed as an anomaly, and the purchase of personal items clearly crossed a legal boundary and raised a red flag. Yet, the doling out of public funds to friends and associates is indicative of a larger and perfectly legal trend: how politicians and for-profit companies have turned welfare, the core program to assist the needy, into a source of profit. But it is not only programs for the poor: social reproduction more broadly, including health care and education, is an increasingly important source of profit and a massive part of the US economy. Many public responsibilities—health care, education, welfare, garbage pickup, road maintenance, security, and policing—have shifted to the private realm of family, community, nonprofits, and the market. Politicians, investors, nonprofit leaders, and CEOs have made a fortune by turning to lucrative public service contracts. In the US, care has exceeded manufacturing in terms of its importance to the economy. Of the top ten Fortune 500 companies (defined by revenue), four are part of the care economy: CVS Health, United Health Group, McKesson (a pharmaceutical and medical supply company), and AmerisourceBergen (a wholesale drug company). CVS alone raked in $292 billion in revenue in 2022.[2] In 2021, national health expenditures were almost $13,000 per person—$4.3 trillion.[3]

The care economy is fueled by a crisis of social reproduction that has been exacerbated by the rise of neoliberalism. Privatization and limited public services have made providing human services the go-to strategy for generating revenue for the private sector. Individuals spend money—in fact, must spend money—to ensure that they, their loved ones, their homes, and their communities are cared for. A wide range of for-profit companies fills the care deficit and finances people's care needs. These companies provide products and services like childcare, cleaning, elder care, food delivery, dog-walking, short- and long-term loans, tutoring, and health and education supplies and apps. The sick, elderly, disabled and poor people, parents and guardians, children without guardians, housing- and food-insecure people—all have become potential sources of profit for capital.

Both private and public dollars have fueled the growth of the care sector, indicating how the state is embedded in and partially responsible for the rise of the for-profit care economy. The state is shaping capitalism through the massive infusion of funds into health care and social services. At the same time, the state has relied more heavily on the private sector to carry out its functions while it has retreated from oversight. This has created a system in which public officials and private stewards are driven by a desire for personal profit rather than concern for the needy. As we will see, these ideas have influenced welfare, health care, child welfare, the food rescue program, housing, the financial sector, and the adult guardianship system.

The rise of the contemporary care industry parallels that of the military-industrial complex during World War II and the postwar period, when billions of federal dollars went into the private sector in the form of defense contracts and funding for education and science research for the purposes of war, military preparedness, and national safety. Defense spending not only fortified the military arsenal but also magnified the power and wealth of the private defense industry. Massive defense spending transformed the labor geography of the nation, shifted political and educational priorities, and impelled the construction of new infrastructure.

Similarly, the infusion of public and private dollars into the care industry has created a new occupational landscape, new corporate entities that depend on care, and new forms of profit-making. The defense industry remains powerful, and manufacturing is still an important component of the US economy, although its center of gravity has moved abroad in search of cheaper labor and fewer regulations. There are also no hard distinctions between these economic sectors; manufacturing can also include supplies and hardware for health care and education; and health care, education, and pension benefits go to military veterans. But, today, defense is dwarfed by the care industry, which has ballooned in terms of sheer size and dollars, even if we use pre-pandemic measurements. In 2019, federal defense spending was $732 billion.

In the same year, the federal government spent $1.2 trillion on health care.[4] Total health care spending, including state and federal governments, businesses, and households, was $3.8 trillion.[5] If the defense industry profits from death and destruction, the care industry profits from disability, dependence, and disease.

Neoliberal public discourse, the attacks on the welfare state, and buzzwords like *austerity* and *government inefficiency* create the impression that the state is no longer investing in social programs. Indeed, state priorities have shifted away from entitlement support. We are told that there are simply not enough resources to properly fund schools, offer universal day care, or provide generous social benefits—or that doing so would require higher taxes or fuel inflation. But the language of austerity masks how many public dollars are going into the private sector and the billions in profit made off the state-managed care economy. Although comprehensive statistics are not available, there is plenty of evidence of government money going to the private sector, some of which I detail in this chapter. The state outsources many of its functions by giving grants to private entities to provide public services.[6] The largesse of the state has been vital to the growth of the care economy, creating jobs and sustaining a faltering economy, although little of this money has benefited the poor directly. Public officials, the nonprofit sector, businesses large and small, and well-connected individuals all benefit from and have stakes in the care economy.

Advocates who call for greater investment in care have not effectively addressed how care dollars are allocated. Given the current role of the state, deepening public/private partnerships, and lack of accountability, we have to ensure that demands for more state assistance and an expanded care system do not simply funnel more money into the hands of the private sector and corrupt politicians at the expense of the poor.

Health care, one of the biggest areas of economic growth in the US, is deeply implicated in pain profiteering. Hospital systems, insurance companies, pharmaceutical companies, medical practices, legal firms, collection agencies, and finance companies all profit when someone is sick or injured and needs care. Staffing cuts and work speedup—imposing longer shifts, requiring staff to attend to more patients, and instituting time-managed care— have transformed the experience for both the people doing the care and the people being cared for.[7] Medicaid, for example, has become "a business opportunity for care industries," often leading to ableist abuse of low-income disabled people, argues gender and women's studies professor Akemi Nishida. And for this assembly-line care, patients, even those with health insurance, are left with hefty bills. The astronomical cost of health care has eaten up more and more of Americans' disposable income. The typical non-elderly family in good health spends about 10 percent of their income on health care. For a family earning $50,000 a year with employer-provided insurance, that's about $5,000. This includes insurance premiums, out-of-pocket costs, and taxes earmarked for health care. It does not include their employer's contribution.[8]

The health-care industry has little compassion when it comes to billing. Hospitals, including nonprofit hospitals, are some of the most aggressive debt collectors, often disregarding the economic hardship of low-income patients. Methodist University Hospital in Memphis, for example, has earned a reputation as one of the most notorious and ruthless debt collectors. A tax-exempt hospital affiliated with the Methodist Church, it provides "charity care," yet offers little charity to its low-income patients. According to reporting by MLK50 and ProPublica, it not only sends unpaid bills to collections but also routinely sues patients. In fact, Methodist sued more than eight thousand patients between 2014 and 2018, many of whom were low-income. The hospital almost never gave patients, even very poor patients, a discount as part of a settlement and would instead get a court order to garnish their paychecks if the full amount could not be collected immediately. In some cases, the defendants were low-income Methodist employees.[9] After the ProPublica story broke, perhaps because of the negative publicity, the hospital erased $12 million of patients' medical debt.

Medical debt is not isolated to a few predatory hospitals; millions of Americans are mired in medical debt. Forty percent of Americans—100 million people, a disproportionate number of whom are Black and Latinx—have some medical debt, according to a survey by the Kaiser Family Foundation in 2022.[10] Medical debt is the number one source of debt collections.[11] In 2021, Americans owed $195 billion in unpaid medical bills, according to the Census Bureau's Survey of Income and Program Participation, as analyzed by Kaiser.[12]

Americans' massive medical debt is only one example of the financialization of social reproduction. Accessing medical care, along with rearing and educating children, caring for the elderly, and purchasing and maintaining a home, all have implications for the financial sector, especially if families do not have the cash to pay for goods and services up front. Financial stakes in social reproduction can include pension investments, interest on debt, collection fees, health and disability insurance, late payment fees, mortgages, and student loans.[13] The finance industry has become central to the new care economy, growing at a record pace to assist people with paying off medical and household debt. One example is CareCredit, a credit card company that finances health care costs. Its annual interest rate in early 2022 was 15 percent—quadruple the prime lending rate of 3.5 percent annually. And that's available only to people who qualify for a line of credit.

If people don't have a sufficient credit score or enough reliable income to borrow money to pay off debt, they may end up defaulting. Credit card companies and health-care providers sell debts to these private firms for a fraction of their total value. A number of publicly traded companies have emerged around defaulted loans and unpaid bills. Companies with innocuous sounding names such as Encore Capital, the largest debt buyer in the country, and Portfolio Recovery Associates have made millions of dollars. For Portfolio, 2021 was one of its most successful years, with a net income of $183 million, a 23 percent increase over the previous year.[14] This success contrasts with what the company describes as a "challenging environment," or one in which consumers are actually able to pay off debt and delinquency rates decline. Good times for consumers are bad times for Portfolio. Similarly, Encore Capital's stock price nearly doubled over the course of the pandemic and the company's net income grew by 66 percent in 2021 to $351 million.[15]

The growing market of financial equity firms relies on existing race and class inequities to prey on the poor. Low-income Black and Brown people, who don't have the resources to wage a protracted legal battle, are most frequently targeted by debt collection companies that file lawsuits and subsequently have wages garnished. Two professors of politics, Genevieve LeBaron and Adrienne Roberts, have chronicled how debt-buying firms are turning to the legal system to force payment, leading to the rise of "debtors' prisons." The result is that in some states, courts are issuing arrest warrants for people with, in most cases, small amounts of debt.[16] The combination of predatory lending and punitive collection practices is deadly when people are unable to get the care they need or end up on the street when their assets are repossessed. This is another example of how carcerality is supplanting economic security in the state's dealings with the poor.

Although health care might be the best example, the paramount drive for profit has infected other areas of social reproduction as well, including education, housing, and dependent care. Over the past several years, private equity firms such as Blackstone, BlackRock, and Kushner Companies have made forays into the low-income housing market. Corporate interest in low-income housing was driven in part by the shift beginning in the 1970s from publicly owned and managed housing projects to the housing voucher program (Section 8) in which low-income people rely on the private market and the federal government covers a portion of their rent. Companies were able to take advantage of the shortage of housing for the poor and tap into the federal dollars flowing into the housing market.

Jared Kushner and his partners own and manage thousands of dilapidated low-income units, many of which are rented by people receiving housing assistance from the federal government. Reporter Alec MacGillis uncovered that Kushner Companies ruthlessly issued fees and penalties for unpaid rent and broken leases, often in violation of tenants' rights or in cases when tenants had received written permission to end a lease. A private law firm hired by the company pursued cases relentlessly. Residents, who often did not have the time or resources to go to court, had their wages garnished. On top of those predatory practices, properties were poorly maintained, leaving tenants to live in unsafe conditions and deal with rodent infestations, broken appliances, leaks, and mold.[17]

Housing provides one more example of how the financialization of social reproduction was well underway before 2020. Capitalist social reproduction has always been tied to profit and finance, as discussed in chapter 2. But neoliberalism and then the COVID-19 pandemic increased the scale of extraction by allocating large sums of public money that created unforeseen possibilities for profit-making. The pandemic exposed how companies, both in the US and abroad, make money off of illness, death, and debt. While some of the trillions of pandemic dollars went to direct cash assistance for individuals in need, the federal government gave massive amounts of money to public agencies, institutions, nonprofits, and corporations.

Apart from Amazon, whose profits far outpaced that of other companies, some of the biggest winners during COVID were the pharmaceutical companies, particularly those that developed and produced vaccines and treatments, creating what Tithi Bhattacharya refers to as "vaccine capitalism."[18] When the pandemic hit, the federal government launched Operation Warp Speed, a public-private partnership to develop, manufacture, and distribute vaccines and treatments for COVID. Biotech company Regeneron received $450 million from the federal government to develop an antibody treatment for COVID-19, REGN-COV2, which was granted an emergency use authorization by the US Food and Drug Administration to treat COVID patients. The company claims on its website that the drug was "made free" by the US government. But nothing is free—someone always pays the price. In this case, the government covered the cost of the drug. Although the public footed the bill for its development, Regeneron holds the patent and has artificially raised its price. According to Doctors Without Borders, a full treatment of REGN-COV2 costs about $240 to manufacture, yet the market price was $2,100, giving Regeneron a profit of $1,860 per dose.[19] This price gouging makes the treatment much less accessible to people in poor countries and led to further fleecing of US taxpayers. A year after the development of the drug and with the expiration of the initial contract, the federal government purchased an additional 1.4 million doses at the market rate—to a tune of $2.94 billion.

Although Regeneron's stock price has fluctuated somewhat, it has more or less doubled since the start of the pandemic. Regeneron CEO Leonard Schleifer earned a whopping $135 million in compensation and stock options in 2020. After an outcry from investors, Schleifer's stock awards were eliminated, but with salary and incentive compensation he still earned about $6.5 million in 2021.[20] For owners of capital in the care industry, the pandemic was not a tragedy but a historic windfall. Regeneron is just one example. Johnson & Johnson CEO Alex Gorsky made $26 million in 2021. UnitedHealth Group, a health insurance and managed care program, posted a record profit of $17 billion in 2021, $2 billion more than the previous year. Cigna earned $5.4 billion.[21]

The crisis of social reproduction generally, and during the pandemic specifically, led to greater financial profits for investors, banks, stock traders, pharmaceutical companies, the health-care industry, and venture capitalists. Who lost out? Ordinary Americans, particularly Black and Brown people. Poor people pay overdraft fees. People with money do not. Poor people pay interest on credit card debt. People with money do not. Poor people pay check-cashing fees. People with money do not. The multiple and overlapping crises of social reproduction that many poor people face have become a source of profit in the health/hospital, credit, insurance, and housing sectors. These are the same people who are disproportionately represented in the ranks of low-wage health-care and essential workers and who, during the pandemic, experienced high rates of illness and death. Temporary measures to increase unemployment compensation, expand the child tax credit, put a moratorium on evictions, expand Medicaid, and suspend student loan repayments have expired or will soon. The poor and middle class will be left with even more bills to pay. And more bills for the poor mean more lucrative opportunities for the financial industry.

The emergence of the care economy could not have happened
without the collusion and strategic interventions of the state. The
state has always created the conditions for the accumulation of
wealth: from imperial wars waged over raw materials to legalized slavery and institutionalized racism and sexism; from the
systemic displacement and/or genocide of Indigenous people to
the jailing of anarchists and communists who threatened capitalist
profit-making. More recently we have seen the devolution of the
welfare state, outsourcing of state responsibilities, and a failure to
regulate businesses, nonprofits, and government agencies that get
state resources. This has become a form of redistribution from the
public to the private sector.

Public assistance, which once offered aid to poor people even
as it regulated the labor market and served to discipline recipients,
has become the newest profit-making scheme. Rather than a cur-
tailment of public spending, under neoliberalism there has been
a shift in the allocation of resources. The role of public money in
the expansion of the private care economy indicates that more
money for government programs does not translate into more
money for the needy. In some cases, it was never intended to. In
other cases, there is a lack of public transparency and accountability about how resources are spent. Today, a lion's share of money
that is presumably for the poor ends up benefiting for-profit companies or service providers. Public social welfare dollars purportedly to help the poor, ill, and needy have been critical for the
growth of the care economy. If the care economy is essential for
the health of capitalism, then neither the state nor capital has any
real incentive to ensure that people are able to disentangle themselves from it.

Although there is no longer an entitlement to welfare assistance, federal, state, and local governments still spend trillions of dollars on antipoverty programs and social and human services. In 2020, total state and federal spending on Temporary Assistance for Needy Families (TANF) was $31 billion. Federal health-care spending—Medicare, Medicaid, the Children's Health Insurance Program (CHIP), and the Affordable Care Act—was $1.4 trillion. At the federal level, the Department of Health and Human Services, which includes Medicare, Medicaid, and TANF, among other programs, had a budget of $2.8 trillion in fiscal year 2021, which was 18 percent of federal budgetary resources and more than double the $1.3 trillion that was spent in 2020.[22]

The huge budget, however, doesn't mean that these resources are mitigating poverty and helping the poor. The TANF budget has not increased since 1997 because it is a fixed block grant without adjustments. But because states have flexibility about how to spend the funds, the share that goes directly to the poor has declined dramatically. People in need are given job training rather than jobs and offered services rather than money. Public dollars designated for support programs, services, job training, education, administration, or surveillance, are routed through private non profit or for-profit companies. Or they end up in the hands of public officials such as Mississippi's John Davis, or their friends and business associates. Either way, the poor end up with very little.

The scandal in Mississippi is the largest public embezzlement in the state's history. The funneling of state welfare dollars into a nonprofit served as cover for public officials to use the money for their own personal benefit. Money that was supposed to go to poor families in Mississippi went to welfare officials and their allies. According to a state audit in early 2020, $90 million in welfare funds was misused by the state.[23] The annual state budget for welfare is $100 million, with about $86 million coming from the federal government. Because of the audit, the state now requires more comprehensive financial records. As shocking as the scandal is, it is only one small piece of the much larger problem—which predates the tenure of Davis—of who has access to assistance in Mississippi.

As state officials sort out how welfare funds were stolen and misused, poor mothers in Mississippi continue to struggle. Mississippi led the attack on reproductive justice that resulted in a Supreme Court decision triggering a ban on abortion in the state (as well as many other states). Yet, Mississippi has the highest infant mortality and child poverty rates in the country, calling into question whether the state actually values the lives of babies. The state consistently fails to deliver necessary assistance to poor families. It has one of the lowest monthly TANF payments, which was raised, in April 2021, for the first time in two decades, to $260 a month for a family of three with no other income.[24] That is not a typo: less than nine dollars a day, for a family of three.

Even that meager monthly payment is hard to get. Mississippi has found creative ways to ensure that families have a very difficult time applying for and staying on assistance. Only about 5 percent of eligible families in the state—1,800 households, just over 3,000 people—received TANF in 2021, according to the Mississippi Department of Human Services.[25] This is a reduction of almost 98 percent from the 130,000 people who received cash assistance in the state in 1996, when welfare was dismantled.[26] The state requires that families who have already qualified for and are receiving TANF and Child Care Payments (the Mississippi program to help poor mothers on welfare pay for childcare) undergo, every year, an "application redetermination process." Recipients must reapply annually rather than simply reporting a change in their status. They have to produce multiple forms of documentation, use an online system with no support from navigators or case managers, and be approved within a strict sixty-day timeline. In some cases, families submit documentation on time, but case managers claim it was not received, according to a 2021 survey by the Mississippi Low-Income Child Care Initiative (MLICCI), which advocates on behalf of childcare providers and parents in the state. In other instances, the department fails to render a decision within the required sixty days and the family is deemed ineligible even if the application was submitted on time.[27] This is nothing but bureaucratic red tape that intentionally deters people from applying.

Since the passage of TANF in 1996, poor mothers in Mississippi have struggled to find childcare in order to fulfill the federal mandate that TANF recipients work at least thirty hours a week. For single parents who want state childcare assistance, Mississippi, until recently, required that they cooperate with the state's Child Support Enforcement division in filing suit against the parents who are not present. Although child support enforcement is federally mandated in order to receive TANF, this is not the case with childcare assistance. By requiring child support enforcement, Mississippi's childcare program has financial claims on and can pursue legal judgment against the parents of children who are not with the child and not seeking aid. This has proven to be a major obstacle for parents who avoid contact because of a history of domestic violence, who know that the other parent has limited resources, or who are distrustful of getting entangled in the criminal justice system. Thousands of poor Mississippians have been denied or deterred from applying for assistance because of such regulations. For those who do jump through all the hoops and successfully apply, the approval rate for state childcare assistance is 35 percent; for TANF, the approval rate was 8 percent in 2022.[28]

Despite dire need, Mississippi has a history of simply not spending welfare funds or diverting TANF and childcare assistance money to other state agencies, such as the child welfare program. In 2021, the state received half a billion dollars of federal money from the American Rescue Plan for the Child Care and

Development Block Grant. Part of the money was for childcare providers and part of it for the Child Care Payment Program, which gives vouchers to low-income families who need help paying for day care so that they can work. These vouchers are then redeemed by the childcare centers. Although poor parents and childcare centers alike struggled during the pandemic, the state set unrealistic guidelines for how this money should be spent. It gave childcare centers only six months to spend the awarded funds and required prior approval for any expenditures from an understaffed and slow-to-respond state agency.[29]

MLICCI, a grassroots Biloxi-based organization, advocates for the expansion of affordable childcare and the safety net as a way to ensure racial and gender equity and women's economic security. It works closely with low-income women and childcare providers, most of whom are low-income as well. Founded and directed by Carol Burnett, MLICCI has built statewide relationships with low-income childcare providers and convened meetings and summits. Burnett has been on the front lines, lobbying the state for over two decades to expand childcare assistance for the poor. A recent report released by the organization argues: "The most critical work support that single moms need to be economically secure is stable and affordable childcare."[30] Mississippi's failure to allocate childcare funds highlights clearly that the goal of welfare reform is not to encourage job training and work or to foster "independence," but to punish the poor.

Grassroots organizations like MLICCI provide much-needed support to poor parents, helping them navigate the state bureaucracy and become knowledgeable about the rules and regulations. MLICCI connects childcare providers across the state, many of whom live and work in isolated communities and have little time or individual capacity to effect policy changes, giving them a platform and the power to speak with a united voice. In 2023, after years of lobbying by MLICCI, Mississippi dropped the child support requirement for childcare, a huge victory that will be implemented after this book goes to press. Although skeptical of state officials, members of MLICCI feel they must—because of the dire need among Mississippi mothers—continue to hold public officials accountable, even as they strive toward a more just and equitable system. They are the most visible advocate for childcare for poor women in the state. By forging statewide unity, they have emboldened local activists, built a base for a political movement, and won concessions for the people who need it most.

Mississippi could be an outlier. Or it could be a harbinger. In policy after policy, we see the proliferation of "public-private partnerships," in which the government awards social service contracts to private companies. Over the past few decades, programs ostensibly for the "public good" have been repurposed for the private good. With the easing of restrictions on how public dollars can be spent, both nonprofit agencies and for-profit companies are doing work that the state ought to be doing, with little oversight, and amassing cash in the process. Private-sector profiting from welfare dollars at the expense of the poor has become standard operating practice, and is, in fact, a hallmark of neoliberal governance.

State-based care programs that people on the left valiantly fought for are now a source of private wealth accumulation. Businesses have cashed in on a range of state-funded services, from managing foster care to disbursement of welfare funds. Young-Williams, a private child support service firm, has made enormous inroads running government health and human services. As a private company, its revenue and salaries are not publicly available, even though most of its revenue comes from government contracts. Companies like Lockheed Martin, Northrup Grumman,

Maximus, and the Public Consulting Group (PCG) that have public welfare contracts benefit from tough times. That's when business ramps up and they can capture more tax dollars.

Maximus is one of the largest health and human services contractors with local, state, and federal governments, and its backstory and growth are tied to the welfare state. Founded in 1975, Maximus manages the administrative complexity of social services. The more convoluted the program is, the greater the need for a company like Maximus, whose motto is "helping government serve the people." Maximus received the country's first privatized welfare contract in 1987. Its size, scope, and profit margin grew exponentially with federal welfare reform in 1996 and even more with the passage of the Affordable Care Act in 2010. Maximus went public in 1997 and is beholden to investors. Promising to reduce overhead costs and root out fraud, Maximus has brought business management to the care industry, which means reorienting from people to profit, from needs to efficiency. It operates state health insurance exchanges, welfare-to-work programs, child support enforcement, and job training, and administers Medicaid, Medicare, and the Child Health Insurance Program (CHIP).

In the winter of 2020, Maximus had $3.7 billion worth of state contracts in New York alone, contracts that had been renewed without competitive bidding.[31] Maximus manages the New York State health insurance enrollment centers for the Medicaid and Affordable Care Act programs. And since 2014, it has run the state's Medicaid Managed Long-Term Care program, determining which patients are sick or disabled enough to get coverage. This means a private, for-profit company is making decisions about who gets covered by a state program. Through managing the government's bureaucracy, Maximus is able to, according to reporter Tracie McMillan, "police the poor."[32]

Maximus's approach to child welfare is particularly egregious.

Since the 1990s, child welfare agencies have accelerated the rate at which children are removed from their families. These policies have echoes of Indigenous child removal in the nineteenth century, although the context is different. Indigenous child removal was a complicated process tied to the aims of settler colonialism and genocide under the guise of assimilation. In the twenty-first century, the removal of Black and Brown children has similar destructive consequences on family and community life but is driven primarily by the stipend attached to their care.

Maximus helps state child welfare agencies reduce costs and maximize revenue. Foster care is a matching-grant program, which means it is run by the states but paid for by both state and federal funds. One way the company brings economic efficiency to foster care is to garnish the benefits of children who are entitled to disability or Social Security payments because their parents have died. Maximus describes foster children, as law professor Daniel Hatcher writes in *The Poverty Industry*, as a "revenue generating mechanism."[33] It examines personal health and school records and caseworker notes to determine if a child could be deemed emotionally or physically disabled and qualify for assistance. Decisions about whether children should be taken into state care or remain with their families are determined in part by Maximus's revenue goals. Hatcher writes:

> Once a child becomes a ward of the state, numerous additional and overlapping revenue strategies come to life. The child is engulfed by revenue maximization efforts that all too often are not aimed at determining how to best meet the child's needs, but rather at how to best use the child to meet the fiscal needs of the agency and the state.[34]

Children are evaluated and ranked using data analytics to determine who among them might be most economically valuable to the state, and those children are pursued by Maximus.[35] This means that, in states like Mississippi, where welfare dollars are distributed among other state agencies, the money that should be used to support families can be sent to agencies that take those children away.

Even as it profits off the poor, Maximus is creating its own class of poor people. It has 38,000 direct employees and 14,000 contingent workers.[36] This company that is supposed to ensure people get access to health care offers a health-care plan that most of its employees cannot afford because of a $2,500 deductible—a hefty chunk of money if you earn just above the fifteen-dollar-an-hour federal-contractor minimum wage.[37] And Maximus does what it knows best: it sanctions its own workers. If workers miss more than forty hours of work a year, they are given a verbal warning. If they miss sixty-four hours, they can be fired. The company does not accept doctor's notes for this unpaid time off.[38]

Private companies are not the only ones in the business of making money off vulnerable children. The very state agencies charged with looking out for the children's interests view them as possible sources of revenue. When a state agency becomes the child's representative, in many cases, it also acts as the child's guardian. As such, it manages and can apply for federal benefits to which the child is entitled, such as Social Security or disability. In practice, some state agencies do not even inform the child of an application for disability benefits, and instead they keep those funds. The confiscation of funds is justified as going toward the care of the children; in other words, poor children are expected to reimburse the state for their foster care. In fact, those funds do not support those individual children but go into state coffers or to the private firms that make a profit from managing the state's child welfare programs. Seizing the state benefits of children in state custody violates the mission of child welfare programs, which are mandated to support children in need with state funds, not the child's personal funds.[39]

When Maximus and other similar companies make money off programs targeted to the poor, those public dollars end up in the hands of stockholders and CEOs. The growth strategy for Maximus, as outlined in its 10K filing to the SEC, is the increasing demographic of people "experiencing financial hardships and other barriers that require a combination of social safety-net programs and support into work."[40] Maximus profited handsomely during the pandemic, moving into areas of unemployment insurance and COVID-19 response, and formed a new arm: Maximus Public Health. Stock prices rose from $70 a share in April 2019 to $96 in April 2021. In 2020, its revenue was nearly $3.4 billion and its profit margin more than $700 million.[41] This is clearly another form of allegedly legal welfare fraud or fleecing of the government. Hatcher puts it bluntly: the poverty industry "is strip-mining billions in federal aid and other funds from impoverished families, abused and neglected children, and the disabled and elderly poor."[42] Companies benefiting from this hardship have a powerful incentive to exacerbate the problem of poverty rather than alleviate it.

Government positions have become enticing not to serve and represent the people, but because officials have nearly unfettered control over state and federal coffers and are able to channel these funds toward personal and financial interests. A strong indication of the private sector's interest in the public care economy is that in 2011, campaign contributions from the health-care industry were four times that of the defense industry.[43] In 2022, the for-profit childcare industry ramped up donations to West Virginia senator Joe Manchin because of his opposition to universal childcare, essentially rewarding him for his position, as reported by Common Dreams.[44] The industry's lobbying is another indication of how profit and personal benefit shape policymaking.

There is a revolving door between government officials and business leaders. As Hatcher argues: "Vast contractual interconnections between government and private contractors—focused on revenue maximization strategies—are undermining the legal and economic structure of America's government assistance programs and siphoning billions in aid from those in need."[45] What we are witnessing comes dangerously close to state capture, where the largess of the state is used for private benefit. In light of the stunning lack of integrity that informs public programs, it should be incumbent upon us to think strategically about how the welfare state or government assistance might fit into any progressive agenda.

The adult guardianship system is another example of how care for those purportedly unable to care for themselves has become a source of profit. As a legal concept, guardianship dates back centuries. It establishes a power differential and hierarchy by stripping rights from so-called dependent populations. Lately, this has been used as a basis for profit extraction. When certain individuals— usually disabled and elderly people—are alleged to be incapable of managing their personal and financial affairs, decision-making authority is transferred to another person.

The guardianship system came under public scrutiny recently with the high-profile case of the performer Britney Spears. Spears's father served as her court-appointed guardian for fourteen years—apparently because of her mental health challenges—and legally controlled her assets as well as her professional, medical, and personal decisions, even though she was thirty-nine years old when the guardianship was finally dissolved. Although Britney is now free, millions of disabled people, elderly people, people with an addiction problem, people with mental illness, or others whom the state has deemed unable to care for themselves or make informed decisions are assigned state-appointed guardians. The guardian assumes control of and manages their financial assets and health care.

The guardian system has been fertile ground for fraud. Strangers, acquaintances, or family members who do not have the best interests of the individual at heart can present a letter from a physician, petition the court, claim that the individual is mentally incapacitated, and, if the court agrees, be appointed a guardian. The individual under guardianship may not have knowledge of the process or an opportunity to contest the court order because the court believes they are unable to advocate on their own behalf. Their home and other assets may be sold to cover the cost of care and legal fees, a process with little oversight.

Recent investigative reporting has uncovered how the guardianship system has become predatory and corrupt, targeting the elderly in particular. In a 2017 exposé in *The New Yorker*, reporter Rachel Aviv revealed how "professional" guardians, hoping to get rich quickly, seek out potential victims. People who may be perfectly healthy and capable of living independently have been deceptively placed under guardianship and involuntarily removed from their homes. According to Aviv, in 2017, a million and a half adults in the US had guardians, who, in turn, controlled $273 billion in assets. As Aviv writes: "Under the guise of benevolent paternalism, guardians seemed to be creating a kind of capitalist dystopia: people's quality of life was being destroyed in order to maximize their capital."[46]

The scheme is permeating other sectors as well. A quarter of guardianship petitions in New York were brought by nursing homes and hospitals, sometimes as a strategy to collect overdue bills, as a recent study conducted by Hunter College of the City University of New York found.[47] Because guardianship involves both property management and health-care management, the health-care industry has a vested interest in controlling the assets of patients under their care or of former patients who owe them money.

Much like foster care, the guardianship system, under the guise of caring for someone, has been utilized as a profit-making scheme. Guardians are private individuals, some of whom have become adept at defrauding people. But they are able to do so only with the complicity and sanction of the court. How widespread such fraud and abuse are or how far back they date is unclear. The US Government Accountability Office found hundreds of allegations of financial exploitation, neglect, and abuse of seniors in forty-five states and the District of Columbia between 1990 and 2010.[48] This is a relatively small percentage of the estimated 1.5 million adults under guardianship, but it is indicative of care programs that have become sites of financial extraction.[49]

The guardianship system may be well-intended, and there are undoubtedly many responsible and conscientious guardians—people who are investing their own time and resources to ensure that others are well cared for. But the combination of investing the state with the power to deem some people "dependent" and unable to advocate or care for themselves, along with predatory individuals motivated by profit, has created a tragic situation. The state has created and sanctioned a system with the potential for abuse, and has been silent in the face of theft.

Like the for-profit sector, the nonprofit sector has benefited from an infusion of public money, including grants and contracts, and it expanded enormously in the second half of the twentieth century. By slashing direct cash assistance in favor of services and in-kind support, the state created an opening for the nonprofit sector. Fueled by perceived public fiscal constraints and assumptions of the state's inefficiency and bureaucracy, in combination with flexibility about state spending, nonprofits have, in some cases, been contracted to run entire government programs or agencies.

Lyndon Johnson's Great Society, in the 1960s, was a turning point for the issuing of government contracts to the private sector to implement social programs. Nonprofits became beneficiaries of the state's largesse as part of a larger governmental strategy to stem urban decline and mitigate poverty through the creation of service sector jobs in the fields of "eds and meds," or education and health care. The Great Society encouraged nonprofit and for-profit interest in publicly funded social service programs. As professor of public policy Claire Dunning writes, "Social scientists, policy makers, bureaucrats, and local administrators recognized the economic transformation occurring in American cities, and deliberately, though not always explicitly, buttressed the human service sector in a strategy to create jobs for the unemployed and underemployed." Although these jobs had federal funding and were promised to be a route out of poverty, they made little impact on the urban crisis and may, in fact, have deepened it by reinscribing the racialized and gendered labor market. Most workers, particularly African American and Latinx women, performed menial tasks for poverty-level wages with little hope of advancement.[50]

The business of distributing food to the hungry is a powerful example. Feeding America, formerly known as Second Harvest, is the seventh-largest nonprofit in the United States. Founded as a food bank over four decades ago by John van Hengel, Second Harvest accepted a government grant in 1975 to open eighteen food banks. It soon learned the benefit of this public-private partnership and grew into what is now Feeding America.[51] The idea behind Feeding America was simple: take food donations from farmers, manufacturers, and retailers that would otherwise go to waste, and give it to the hungry. A tax code change in the 1970s led to an increase in donations of unused food from corporations, which took advantage of the tax benefits. As a result, Feeding America grew into a massive operation. It claimed in 2020 to have rescued 4 billion pounds of groceries, including more than 1.8 billion pounds of fresh produce that fed the poor.

But the discarded food industry is not really about the needs of the hungry, as Theresa Funiciello, a former welfare recipient, organizer, and policy advocate, argues in her book, *Tyranny of Kindness*. Rather, it is a system designed to feed and sustain itself. Funiciello traces how antipoverty dollars have been diverted from the poor to the nonprofit social service sector, which has been transformed into a business serving primarily middle-class professionals: "The real beneficiary is the system itself, and the tens of thousands of people who have become employed through this secondary market—each with a stake in its preservation."[52] She considers the overhead costs of transportation, refrigeration, storage, staff salaries, office space, computers, and other equipment, which raise the price of "table scraps" far beyond what they were initially worth. A "formerly free 'product,'" she explains, "now has value added at every level as it takes a journey...You can give a mother 50 cents to go and buy a head of lettuce (on sale). Or you can send a head of lettuce through this crazy system and keep increasing the original price as it moves both literally and figuratively through layer after layer of do-gooders." Leaving aside the environmental damage, by the end of the process, Funiciello estimates, the head of lettuce costs "triple the original store price, but since it was deemed unsalable in the first place, just how much is it worth?"[53]

Another problem with the food distribution model is that neither Feeding America nor the pantries they serve can select what they need. They take what national food distributors as well as local businesses no longer want or cannot sell. Corporations donate items that they would otherwise discard because they are past the sell-by date, overproduced, improperly packaged, or for some other reason cannot be sold. Normally, the corporations would have to pay for disposal. Now, not only is someone taking the worthless items off their hands, but they also get a tax break and good PR to boot. Some of this food is unusable and discarded by Feeding America, the food pantries, or feeding centers because it may be contaminated, infested, or too far past the sell-by date. What remains is an eclectic assortment of products that may not be needed by the poor families for whom they are intended: meat marinade without meat and an overabundance of sweets and snacks. According to Funiciello, the costs associated with the Feeding America strategy of "rescuing" food could be better spent by giving money to the poor to purchase groceries. Rescuing food suggests there is a shortage of food. In the US, the problem is not the availability of food—there is plenty of food available on store shelves—but people's lack of financial resources.

Nonprofits like Feeding America are funded by corporate donations (often from the very same companies that are getting tax breaks for discarded food), individual donations, and government contracts. Some of this money goes to transporting food, but it is also spent on glossy brochures, comfortable offices, fancy fundraisers, and generous salaries. The irony of how this public money was spent was not lost on Funiciello, who observed:

> One common reaction to the notion of giving mothers money directly has always been 'If you give them the money, how will you know they will spend it on food?' In light of the monstrous developments in this discard market, I'd have to ask that question of them. For that matter, if you give the *hunger activists* the money, how do you know *they* won't spend it on their Christmas parties

replete with booze?[54]

Feeding America's expenses were about $3.8 billion in 2020, according to the latest numbers they posted. CEO Claire Babineaux-Fontenot earned close to a million dollars in 2020—a lot less than Big Pharma CEO salaries, but quite a lot for a hunger organization. In 2020, a year when the demand for food was at its highest in decades, Feeding America made an enormous surplus of $162 million, twenty-three times more than the previous year, which leaves us to wonder, were they profiting from the pandemic?[55]

As the public welfare state and government social services were systematically dissected at the end of the twentieth century, with some parts tossed in the bin and other parts sold to the highest bidder, the nonprofit sector benefited enormously. It has grown in leaps and bounds, becoming ever more reliant on government funding. Even as the state steadily retreats from ensuring public health and well-being, it continues to allocate money to those ends, with little accountability. Over the past fifty years, we have seen what political scientist Steven Smith and public policy analyst Michael Lipsky describe as an "interpenetration of government and the voluntary sector."[56]

Not only have government grants and public monies been vital to the growth of the private sector, but nonprofits and for-profit companies in human services have also become crucial for governing and the health of the economy. State and local human services agencies have become so dependent on the private sector, both for-profit and nonprofit, that severing this relationship or holding the organizations accountable would jeopardize the government's ability to function. In an article in *The City* in February 2020, New York assemblymember Richard Gottfried noted, of Maximus and its contracting for New York State's health services: "There's just no way to hold any private company account-able when the state says it would stop functioning without it... A $3 billion contractor might as well be a state agency, except that a state agency is ultimately responsible to the democratically elected governor who appoints its leader, while a private contrac-tor is ultimately responsible to its shareholders."[57] The govern-ment's hands are tied because of its reliance on the private sector.

The nonprofit sector is vast and diverse. It includes religious institutions, universities, schools, and hospitals, as well as commu-nity-based and social-service organizations.[58] What distinguishes them from for-profit companies is not whether they make profit but how that profit is distributed. Historian Jonathan Levy ar-gues that nonprofits are corporations that earn profit from invest-ments, contracts, or commerce, although they call it *surplus* rather than *income*.[59] Instead of profit going to owners or shareholders, nonprofits reallocate money to program expansion, salaries, or company infrastructure. Nonprofits are supposed to operate in-dependent of the existing structures of power, uninfluenced by government or business. Much like nongovernmental organiza-tions (NGOs), nonprofits are presumably engaged in a mission of selfless work for the betterment of humanity or the common good—hence their special exemption from paying taxes.

The on-the-ground reality is more complicated. Nonprofit or-ganizations, funded by corporations, the wealthy, and the state, have become a massive part of the economy. In 2016, over 12 million people were employed in the nonprofit sector, representing more than 10 percent of private-sector employment, according to the US Bureau of Labor Statistics.[60] In 2021, with 12.5 million workers, the nonprofit sector was the third largest employment sector, behind retail and only slightly below manufacturing.[61] Nonprofits contrib-uted $1.4 trillion to the economy in the last quarter of 2021, accord-ing to *The Nonprofit Sector Quarterly*.[62] Their role is so outsized that one could argue, in addition to the financialization of the economy, there has been a "nonprofitization" of the US economy.[63]

Of course, not all nonprofits are the same. We should distinguish between grassroots, collectively run nonprofits that are committed to social transformation and those that bring in millions and are run by a paid middle-class staff that speaks on behalf of its constituency. For example, Damayan Migrant Workers Association is a nonprofit—a worker-run organization that has maintained its commitment to democracy. Its leaders do not draw hefty speaking fees or take home fat paychecks. Executive director Linda Oalican says, "I'm still a low-wage earner in the US. Why? Because we're a nonprofit, but people can look at our wage scales: it's small and that's deliberate. Because we wanted to focus on more important things for our community like genuine organizing, genuine empowerment."[64] Nonprofits can sometimes be advocacy organizations or platforms for the poor, giving the disenfranchised a voice in policymaking. Nonprofits have the potential to become what Levy calls "a vehicle of expression" for the marginalized.[65]

Even though there are nonprofits doing very good work, the larger context of capital infusion into the nonprofit world has hamstrung real activist work. Oalican expressed ambivalence about the relationship between nonprofits and grant funding:

> In nonprofit work there are pitfalls, and I would say it's meant to be. You'll get grants, you'll have deliverables; that is a scheme to tie you down, to take you away from meaningful organizing for your community.... I really believe in movement building and many times the work in nonprofit organization will prevent you from doing that. Most of the grants that we receive are for services, honestly, to take you away from movement work.[66]

Similarly, author and activist Arundhati Roy has argued that the rise of NGOs in India has had a detrimental effect on activism—what she calls "the NGO-ization of resistance":

> NGOs give the impression that they are filling the vacuum created by a retreating state. And they are, but in a materially inconsequential way. Their real contribution is that they defuse political anger and dole out as aid or benevolence what people ought to have by right. They alter the public psyche. They turn people into dependent victims and blunt the edges of political resistance.... They have become the arbitrators, the interpreters, the facilitators.... They're what botanists would call an indicator species. It's almost as though the greater the devastation caused by neoliberalism, the greater the outbreak of NGOs.... The NGO-ization of politics threatens to turn resistance into a well-mannered, reasonable, salaried, 9-to-5 job.

Nonprofits, like the state and for-profit sector, are deeply implicated in a care economy that fuels inequality by transferring public dollars intended for the poor to the better-off.

For many people on the left, a national care infrastructure program, like the Care for All Agenda discussed in chapter 5, is the most promising strategy to rein in the excesses of neoliberalism, revive a sluggish economy, resuscitate a robust liberalism, and unify the country. An expansion of the care economy, we are told, will create jobs, help us confront climate change, enable women to enter or reenter the labor market, address gender inequality, provide for the neediest among us, and revalue care as an ethic. Care has become the new silver bullet for progressive politics and a possible solution for an array of social, political, and economic problems. Yet, in most cases, either there is little clarity about the role of the market or the for-profit care economy, or proposals are tethered to a private-sector or profit-oriented model and depend on a labor market stratified by race and gender.

Meanwhile, the corporate sector, acutely aware of the potential for growth and profit on a large scale, is strategizing ways to capitalize even further on the care economy. Pivotal Ventures, a company founded by Melinda French Gates and committed to social progress, has produced both an Investor's Guide and an Entrepreneur's Guide to the care economy.[67] The Boston Consulting Group report that I cite in the introduction to this book valued the paid and unpaid labor of care at $6 trillion. It concluded that investing in care is critical to the health of the overall economy and "pays dividends" because it encourages more women to enter the workforce: "Without a healthy care economy, the workforce falls apart."[68] Although the report acknowledges and quantifies the unpaid labor of care, that, ironically, does not translate to proposals for economic support for this work. The implication is that unpaid care labor is an opening for new capital investment. Families must turn care work over to the market and enter the formal labor force in order to keep the economy healthy. An indication of the scope of these conversations is that the Boston Consulting Group report was featured at the 2023 World Economic Forum in Davos. The nation and the world are poised to define a care agenda that will have implications for generations to come. We need to have a say in shaping that agenda. We need to say that we and our loved ones are not for sale.

Chapter 7

"But Some of Us Are Brave"

Radical Care and the Making of a New World

In 1969, the Black Panther Party for Self-Defense organized a Free Breakfast for School Children Program in Oakland, California. Operating out of St. Augustine Episcopal Church, the program served eggs, bacon, grits, toast, and orange juice to children in the neighborhood. In addition to this hearty breakfast, they were given mini-lessons in history and Black Power. The Free Breakfast Program was one of more than fifty community survival programs launched by the Panthers. The survival programs filled a void that had resulted from the failure of the state to provide basic social reproductive services to the Black community. Managed largely by Panther women, the free breakfasts as well as free medical and dental clinics served impoverished Black communities. In addition to exposing the inadequacies of the state, the survival programs, according to historian Robyn C. Spencer, made people question the commodified relationship that mediated their basic human needs.[1] By offering these services, the Panthers asked, "Shouldn't food, shelter, and medical care be freely available to all people?"

The Black Panther Party's survival programs embodied a commitment to *radical care*—care that is collective and antihierarchical, sits outside capitalist profit-making structures, and contributes to long-term social transformation.[2] The Panthers were a Black Marxist organization seeking revolutionary nationalism and the creation of a democratic, socialist state—embodied in their slogan "Power to the People." The survival programs were one part of their agenda. The radical essence of the Free Breakfast Program was not lost on the Federal Bureau of Investigation (FBI), which monitored, surveilled, and worked to undermine the Panthers. In an internal memo, FBI Director J. Edgar Hoover wrote that the Free Breakfast Program "represents the best and most influential activity going for the BPP and, as such, is potentially the greatest threat to efforts by authorities to neutralize the BPP and destroy what it stands for."[3]

The Young Lords Party, a Puerto Rican Marxist organization based in East Harlem, also organized collective care projects when it witnessed the failure of the state to provide services. Members organized street cleanups and garbage pickups, a health clinic, and an ambulance service. These programs enabled them to cultivate relationships with community residents and raise awareness about the failure of city services in places like predominantly Puerto Rican East Harlem, subjecting its residents to rotting garbage and filthy streets. In 1969, the Young Lords organized a direct-action campaign, a Garbage Offensive—what historian Johanna Fernández calls "creative urban disruption"—by blocking traffic at major intersections with uncollected garbage and setting it on fire.[4] Their sustained five-week protest was intended to politicize community members and force local officials to implement systemic reforms. Pablo "Yoruba" Guzmán, one of the leaders of the Lords, reflected on the Garbage Offensive a year later: "Our objective...[was] to move on the government for allowing the garbage to pile up in the first place. By questioning this system's basic level of sanitation, our people would then begin to question drug traffic, urban renewal, sterilization etc [*sic*] until the whole corrupt machine could be exposed for the greedy monster it is."[5] For both the Black Panthers and the Young Lords, these programs were intertwined with their long-term goal of radicalizing people: getting people to recognize that inadequate social reproductive services were a product of broader inequities. The Panthers and the Young Lords sought to simultaneously improve the lives of community members, raise consciousness, and contribute to long-term social change.

These are not the only historical examples of radical care emerging out of organizing with the aim of social transformation. In the 1960s, feminists opened domestic violence shelters and rape crisis centers to assist women experiencing abuse, sexual assault, and unsafe conditions at home. They offered pregnancy counseling and organized underground abortion clinics at a time when abortion was illegal, and the consequences of self-managed abortion attempts were often deadly. Trans people, who experienced isolation, vulnerability, and violence, also organized radical care collectives in the absence of other forms of support. In 1970, trans activists of color Marsha P. Johnson and Sylvia Rivera founded Street Transvestite Action Revolutionaries (STAR) as a safe space for trans youth of color in New York City. Trans and feminist radical care work grew directly out of movement organizing and combined service, political activism, and social change.[6] Indeed, there is a long history of grassroots practices that model the transformative potential of radical care.

What makes *radical care* radical? Radical care is nonhierarchical, anticapitalist, and collective. Mainstream care intends to ensure that people's care needs are met so that they can become "productive" members of society—that is, wage earners or consumers—and it is wrapped up with self-management, neoliberal productivity, and capitalist models of individualism. It creates boundaries between the people who need care and the people who provide care. Radical care rejects the paternalistic notion that some people are dependent while other people provide care for them, and acknowledges how we rely on one another. It rejects the idea that care givers and care receivers are mutually distinct categories and that policies are needed to encourage people to become caregivers. Radical care moves us from self-care to what Cara Page and Erica Woodland call healing justice.[7] It imagines care as a horizontal practice, while being attuned to how care needs vary from individual to individual.

Below, I uplift several examples of radical care: mutual aid programs, disability justice, antilabor trafficking, Indigenous organizing, Black food justice, the Movement for Black Lives, and the prison abolition movement. These examples help us make sense of radical care practices and chart a new path forward. Most radical care grows out of dire community need that emerges from the calculated failure of social welfare programs, profit extracted from social reproduction, and the justifiable distrust of a predatory and surveillant state. Many of these activists are embedded in social movements, and radical care is one strand of their political organizing. Radical care initiatives are models of democratic practice and community engagement, practices that are often a first step to movement building and cultivating a commitment to long-term social transformation.

Radical care is not only a survival strategy—it goes beyond care as social service or a "good deed"—and is outside the dominant individualist and profit-making structures. It is an example of prefigurative politics, which Harsha Walia defines as "envisioning and actualizing egalitarian social relations."[8] Although these models may seem small-scale in the context of an invasive care economy, they are in fact an indication, using a phrase that animated the World Social Forum, that "another world is possible." Examples of prefigurative radical care are not only an alternative to capitalism—they sit in opposition to capitalism because they work to dismantle and rebuild. They aim to provide care and transform. They offer ways of thinking about communal care as a form of radical relationality that is unambiguously anticapitalist and part of a larger political struggle.

Few people would disagree with an aspirational goal of a truly caring society—but what is a truly caring society? And what is the role of the state in a radical future? What kinds of reforms move us closer to a goal of a caring world, rather than setting us back? Care is often invoked as an alternative to the carceral state. But, as we have seen, these alternatives, which sometimes take the form of social services, can be extractive or destructive. Where does that leave us? If the prison abolition movement calls for the dismantling of all prisons, should a transformative care politics call for a dismantling of all profit-oriented or state-controlled care systems? Care is messy and complicated. We cannot reject all care institutions wholesale, but need to carefully weigh which caring policies do harm and which provide necessary support for survival.

I hope to illustrate what radical care looks like in practice and how it can be part of a transformative politics that can move us toward a more liberatory future. On-the-ground activists are reimagining care and generating alternative models for more effective challenges to capitalism. We have so much to learn from campaigns for radical care and from what people are already doing, even as we grapple with how these struggles connect with one another and build toward long-term social transformation.

Grassroots activists have established systems of communal support in response to state neglect, violence, and the unequal allocation of resources. Their examples of radical care were born out of state abandonment, or what communications professor China

Medel calls "strategic abandonment"—when people are simply
left to die. These practices are not always intentionally organized
as alternative—they evolve out of community need, sometimes
without a specific political orientation—but they have the potential to become alternative. They are often cooperative, antihierarchical practices outside the state and profit-making systems. If
we understand radical care as not just taking care of people in the
present but also as part of constructing models for a new collective
future, these would serve as inspiring models.

The Nollie Jenkins Family Center in Holmes County, Mississippi, models a communal approach to the problems of gendered violence, state and family abuse, and economic insecurity.
It provides a physical space and a social safety net for girls and
young women in a region where little government social support
exists. Started by local resident Ellen Reddy in 1994 as a childcare center, the center serves and empowers the local community.
Its foundational premise is that every family needs to be cared
for, and everyone has a responsibility to look out and care for
one another. The community—not child protective services, the
police, or school officials—becomes the means to address behavioral problems, mental health challenges, and domestic violence at
home or school. Beyond Holmes County, the center is developing an agenda of expanding economic opportunities in the Delta,
ending corporal punishment in schools, ending the school-to-
prison pipeline, addressing domestic violence, supporting sexual
autonomy for young people, and empowering African American
girls. One of my students described Ellen Reddy's work as "the
abolitionist future."[9]

The kind of everyday care practiced at the Nollie Jenkins
Center is also recounted by Sandra Killett, whom we met in
chapter 5. Sandra's childhood in Brooklyn was shaped by collective care. Born in 1962, Sandra was raised by a single mother

with a substance use disorder who couldn't provide the care her seven children needed. The family was on public assistance and money was always tight. Despite the hardship, Sandra's aunts, neighbors, older siblings, and family friends stepped in, looked out for one another's children, and helped out whenever necessary—what Sandra calls a "community wraparound," something she undoubtedly values more after her run-ins with the child welfare system.

To this day, she still ponders the contrast between her own entanglements with the system and her childhood. Despite her mother's substance overuse, child welfare never intervened. Part of the reason was the commitment to collective care: "It was everyone looking out for everyone. ... I didn't know of any child welfare involvement... We just took care of everyone." Sandra believes firmly that knowledge about how to address poverty resides with the people themselves and that the community wraparound from her childhood could be a model for moving forward: "You think that because we are living under poverty in most cases, that we have no wherewithal about what we need, what it would take, how we need to support each other. We know. We absolutely know."[10] Sandra's story is evidence of communal care that was less than structured than the Nollie Jenkins Family Center but nevertheless provided the support her family needed. Her mother's small public assistance grant was crucial but not enough, so the mechanisms of communal care kicked in to ensure the family's well-being. These are both examples of a "care infrastructure" outside a market- and profit-driven system.

Care collectives also emerged in the early 2000s among disabled people and their allies in response to the inadequacy of public health care. These collectives were founded on an ethic of interdependence: everyone gives and receives care, even as it is acknowledged that some people have more needs than others. This

dynamic creates a form of what gender and women's studies professor Akemi Nishida calls "messy dependency," where mutuality
is not reciprocal but based on desire, ability, and agency. It can be
unruly and, according to neoliberal metrics, unequal. Mutual dependence in this context means that people contribute what they
can, rather than equally. Controlled by the disabled people, these
"care webs," as disability justice activist Leah Lakshmi Piepzna-Samarasinha calls them, are a way to build community power.
The disability justice group Sins Invalid, relies on the "rich and
unique" wisdom—"crip wisdom"—of the disability community
to redefine dependency from its stigmatized and disempowered
connotations to a term that reflects deep and valuable communal
relations.[11]

Another example is mutual aid, which legal scholar and activist
Dean Spade defines as the "collective coordination to meet each
other's needs, usually from an awareness that the systems we have
in place are not going to meet them."[12] No More Deaths, a volunteer organization, offers direct aid to people trying to cross the
US–Mexico border. The US border patrol has either failed to provide life-saving assistance or, more frequently, has systematically
targeted and meted out violence to migrants. Based in Tucson,
Arizona, No More Deaths provides first aid, food, water, blankets,
and other necessities for survival. According to China Medel: "In
the practice of care, desert aid workers prefiguratively build a world
in which hierarchies of human value are abolished, where migration is an expression of life making, and where food, shelter, medical, and emotional care are available to all, regardless of notions
of deservedness."[13] The organizing and material aid are an "abolitionist gesture" that "builds alternative forms of recognition and
inclusion against the logic of criminalization and the production of
valueless life functioning to 'protect' the United States."[14] Mutual
aid, then, is not premised on paternalistic notions of charity but on

solidarity as a democratic and collaborative process that can undermine capitalist logics.

Communal care may not be explicitly anticapitalist, but it may nevertheless lead to political engagement. Sandra's early experiences with communal care and the failure of state support when she became a single mother propelled her into activism. People may begin to understand their own agency and nurture radical ideas about the kind of world they want to live in. In that way, communal care "can radically remake worlds that exceed those offered by the neoliberal or postneoliberal state, which has proved inadequate in its dispensation of care" write Hi'ilei Julia Kawehipuaakahaopulani Hobart and Tamara Kneese, the editors of an important collection of essays on radical care in *Social Text*.[15] Examples of communal care are, perhaps, "rehearsals for living," as Robyn Maynard and Leanne Simpson describe it, in which people are finding new ways of being and developing new visions for the future.[16]

The Care Manifesto was published in 2017 by the Care Collective, which started as a London-based reading group and has become an important text for reimagining care. It calls for social transformation premised on a universal ethic of care that is not tied to the market economy and rejects hierarchical decision-making and unequal valuation of life:

> Universal care means that we are all collectively responsible for hands-on care work as well as the work necessary for the maintenance of communities and the planet. ... It translates into reclaiming forms of genuinely communal life—from schools to public space to lending libraries. It means shortening the working week so that caring for children, for example, can be more easily shared. It involves reversing the corporate marketisation of care

and caring infrastructures, both by "insourcing" and by extending democratic alternatives to capitalist markets, which have never aligned well with the work of caring. It also means restoring and radically deepening our welfare states, both centrally and locally, through progressive forms of municipalism and strengthening or introducing universal basic services.[17]

This is a powerful vision. The Care Collective calls for reimagining democratic society premised on what they call a feminist, antiracist, eco-socialist, queer political vision of care, a commitment to helping and caring for others as an alternative to both individualism and marketization.[18] In this reading, care is a feminist politics that promises to transform a neoliberal, individualistic, profit-oriented, extraction-based economic system.

This articulation of radical care pushes the conversation about how we can practice care in promising directions because it is collective, people centered, and an egalitarian form of social organization. However, the Care Collective seems to aim its criticism specifically at the neoliberal and postneoliberal state rather than the capitalist state more broadly. Neoliberalism's diminishing support for care and collective well-being has resulted in economic inequality, people without basic resources and services, social isolation, health crises, and ecological destruction. The Care Collective argues, correctly, that there is an "irreconcilability of care with market logics," and it wants to restore and radically "deepen our welfare state."[19] It sees moving care needs from the market to the state as part of the solution. It is possible that the liberal welfare state can offer some supports for care: we cannot discount the state completely. But what my research has shown is that the state and the market are and always have been intertwined. The state has always been implicated in extracting profit from social reproduction, and a "care agenda" is increasingly being embraced by the private for-profit sector with the cooperation of government officials. Given the interpenetration of the state and the nonprofit and for-profit sectors, it is not clear that the kind of care the collective hopes for can be achieved by expanding the current state.

One of the key arguments of this book is that the care economy and extraction of profit from social reproduction are not products of neoliberalism but of capitalism. As we've seen in the histories recounted in earlier chapters, even the liberal welfare state of the mid-twentieth century—which is celebrated for its support of social reproduction—further institutionalized hierarchy and inequality. We cannot, then, uncritically embrace an expansion of the welfare state or invest hope in government programs without weighing community need and asking tough questions about how programs are run and who truly benefits.

Although the pandemic, neoliberalism, and the escalating number of environmental disasters due to climate change have led to a proliferation of mutual aid and radical care practices, collective care predates all of these. Capitalism has always wreaked havoc on people's ability to care for one another, and people have responded by banding together to create systems of support. For Black and Brown people, historically, there has been little distinction between the production of profit and the production of life. They have always struggled to provide care and support because the state and capitalism have almost always failed them. Reddy's abolitionist politics, for example, tackles the long history of racism that has plagued the Delta. Even under the most trying, horrific, and dehumanizing conditions, from settler colonialism to slavery to indentured servitude to incarceration to displacement to capitalist logics of ability and productivity, people carve out spaces of humanity, sociality, and community. Identifying the problem as tied to capitalism rather than neoliberalism enables us to develop long-term, structural—rather than patchwork—solutions. Although some people have faith that a robust care agenda can remake capitalism, history shows us that care will not remake capitalism. Remaking care requires abolishing capitalism.

Some radical care practices, as demonstrated by the Black Panther Party and Young Lords, are tied to social movements. The Damayan Migrant Workers Association, for instance, is a self-proclaimed anti-imperialist, antisexist, antiracist, and anticapitalist organization. It attributes the exploitation and political disposability of Filipino migrant workers to both neoliberal economic change and the long history of US imperialism. But it is also committed to support and care, an ethic embedded in the organization's history. In Tagalog, the word *damayan* means mutual aid. In addition to running a cooperative, Damayan cares for, organizes, and educates its mostly low-wage membership. Damayan members embrace an ethic of care in their daily lives, which the organization understands as inextricably connected to grassroots organizing.

Filipino migrants organize "communities of care" horizontally, "*from* migrants *to* other migrants," explains sociologist Valerie Francisco-Menchavez. Sharing resources and collective aid is part of how these workers survive. They help one another apply for passports and visas and offer assistance and information if they learn that someone is trapped in an abusive situation and needs an escape route. During the pandemic, Damayan's network of support for domestic workers in New York City was activated. It delivered care packages, distributed financial assistance that it received from the National Domestic Workers Alliance, advised people about navigating state assistance programs, and offered shelter. This work was particularly important because undocumented members didn't qualify for state aid and had nowhere to turn. As Damayan co-founder Linda Oalican says: "Being a Filipino, you will always share what you have, you know, with your *kababayans*, roommates, in the apartment."[20]

Street medics who volunteer assistance to people during political protests are another example. This eclectic group includes nurses, doctors, veterinarians, medical students, emergency medical service workers, and home health-care aides. They go where needed. They were present during the Standing Rock protests in 2016, when tens of thousands of people peacefully protested the construction of the Dakota Access oil pipeline through the Standing Rock Sioux Reservation that threatened sacred land and would have contaminated the water source. Street medics provided care as police and private security shot rubber bullets, used sound cannons, and turned water hoses on the protestors in freezing weather.

Medics were also highly visible in the nationwide 2020 protests of racist police violence. As in Standing Rock, police relied on rubber bullets, tear gas, pepper balls, pepper spray, and stun grenades. Street medics set up first-aid stations and provided CPR, antibiotics, and bandages to injured protesters as well as water and food to anyone who needed it. They established transportation networks to take seriously injured people to the hospital. Although most medics underwent training for both administering medical assistance and steering clear of street actions, they were often targeted by police, who sometimes destroyed medic stations.

These medics—people with skills who self-organized—are an important alternative to for-profit hierarchical care. They respond collectively to an urgent situation. According to one medic who got their training during the Occupy protests of 2011: "Medicing is not just physical care. The quiet emotional work matters just as much… The anti-authoritarian nature of street medicing is at the nexus of our practice and knowledge… Effectively responding to authoritarianism requires a form of care that is informed by the past to build a radical future."[21] Street medics provide care, support organizing, and build community and connection. As with Damayan, their goal extends beyond care: they aim to contribute to social transformation.

Audre Lorde articulated the critical connection between radical care and social movements in her essay "A Burst of Light." Although she has become an icon for the self-care movement, for her, self-care was necessary because of decades of collective political struggle, including battles with the US and South African apartheid governments. Shortly after being diagnosed with cancer in 1988, Lorde wrote: "Caring for myself is not self-indulgence, it is self-preservation, and that is an act of political warfare."[22] She was always committed to fundamental social transformation and saw self-care tied to movement building.

The insights of grassroots activists remind us that it is possible, and even *necessary*, to think long term and short term, to consider how to meet people's needs now while also working toward social transformation. Angela Davis, Gina Dent, Erica Meiners, and Beth Richie, in their powerful book, *Abolition. Feminism. Now.*, draw on the insights of grassroots activists to discuss abolition feminism as a method and a practice that embraces "the space between necessary responses to immediate needs and collective and radical demands for structural and ultimately revolutionary change."[23]

> For us, abolition feminism is political work that embraces this both/and perspective, moving beyond binary either/or logic and the shallowness of reforms. We recognize the relationality of state and individual violence and thus frame our resistance accordingly: supporting survivors and holding perpetrators accountable, working locally and internationally, building communities while responding to immediate needs. We work alongside

people who are incarcerated while we demand their release. We mobilize in outrage against the rape of another woman and reject increased policing as the response. We support and build sustainable and long-term cultural and political shifts to end ableism and transphobia, while proliferating different "in the moment" responses when harm does happen.[24]

Some of the most promising practices for rethinking care and disentangling it from the care economy come from the abolitionist movement: prison abolitionists; parent organizers, whom Dorothy Roberts calls "the new abolitionists"; and organizers in the Movement for Black Lives, who have centered collective care and healing justice. The prison abolition movement imagines a world without policing, prisons, and surveillance. In addition to dismantling the carceral state, abolitionists argue that there must be a process of rebuilding. Critical Resistance, one of the earliest prison abolitionist organizations, works to "dismantle, change, and build."[25]

The abolitionist movement has also fostered a model of what it calls "abolitionist care"—that is, imagining a different kind of society with new social and political relationalities and non-hierarchical care practices. So, what does abolitionist care look like, and what do abolitionists mean by "reimagining" care? For organizer Mariame Kaba, building and sustaining relationships work in tandem with prison abolition. She has spearheaded a defense campaign to support incarcerated people, which she argues can be an "ethic and a practice of abolitionist care."[26] The campaign is not only about the release of incarcerated individuals, although that is one intended goal, but also about building a movement and cultivating solidarity. The defense campaign, Kaba explains, "marries community service with political education and political activism that's actually focused on challenging power and oppressive systems."[27] Kaba argues,

> Effective defense campaigns provide thousands of people with opportunities to demonstrate care for criminalized individuals through various tactics (including letter writing, financial support, prison visits, and more). They connect people in a heartfelt, direct way that teaches specific lessons about the brutality of prisons. And this can change minds and hearts, helping people to (hopefully) develop more radical politics.[28]

Abolition politics also informs campaigns to end the child welfare system's policing, surveillance, and family separation. In New York City, Joyce McMillan, a parent advocate who had her children taken from her by the state, calls for "Miranda rights," so parents are informed of their rights and get access to legal representation. McMillan started an organization called JMacForFamilies and has led a movement to abolish the New York City Administration for Children's Services.[29] McMillan and countless other advocates around the country are calling for the abolition of child services because, as Dorothy Roberts puts it, reforms are futile "when the system's very design is antithetical to care."[30]

Roberts calls for both immediate assistance and support for families and children as well as the long-term transformation of child welfare. As she writes, "We need to build a safer society by reimagining the very meaning of child welfare and protection and by creating caring ways of supporting families and meeting children's needs."[31] Roberts points out that, during the pandemic, when children's and other New York City services shut down, thousands of mutual aid groups organized and offered material assistance and services to "generate more caring and effective ways to support families."[32] In combination with state aid, such as the

Child Tax Credit and the extension of unemployment benefits, these families did just fine without the city's Administration for Children's Services.

The Black food justice movement is a Black feminist–led movement that works to empower Black farmers, advocate for policy reforms, and create alternative models of stewarding the land. It, too, offers a vision for collective care and social transformation. As organizers Dara Cooper and Ashanté Reese write in their beautifully titled article, "Making Spaces Something Like Freedom," Black food justice looks beyond "carceral and destructive food systems to new imaginaries of freedom, nourishment, sustainability, and affirmations of Black dignity and humanity."[33] Cooper has deep roots in environmental justice and community organizing across the US, with a particular focus on the Black farmers in the South who are leading the regenerative agriculture movement. She is a cofounder of and strategic advisor with the National Black Food and Justice Alliance, working toward both Black food sovereignty and land justice. She is also a cofounder of Health Environment Agriculture and Labor (HEAL) Food Alliance, a multiracial, multisectoral alliance that addresses workers' rights, land, and the intersections of the prison-industrial complex and the food system. For Cooper, food sovereignty is tied to intersectional movement building and is anticorporate, collective, sustainable, and self-determining. The Black food justice movement has distributed money, offered support to Black food and land projects around the country, and initiated experiments in collective, community-controlled models of land stewardship. "Self-determining food economies" can be realized, Cooper and Reese believe, through democratic decision-making, resource-sharing, kinship care, and care for the Earth.

The Movement for Black Lives is a broad, umbrella organization comprising numerous grassroots organizations, including the

#BlackLivesMatter Global Network, Black Youth Project 100, Assata's Daughters, the BlackOUT Collective, Project South, Southerners on New Ground, and Blackbird, as well as Kaba's Project Nia and Cooper's National Black Food and Justice Alliance. These organizations have foregrounded an intersectional radical Black feminist politics. As scholar-activist Barbara Ransby, drawing on both personal experience and analytical insight, explains: "Black feminist politics and sensibilities have been the intellectual lifeblood of this movement and its practices."[34]

Although most recognized for its work around police violence, the Movement for Black Lives has crafted an expansive platform that calls for a right to education, housing, land, and health care. Members have implemented collective care practices, and advocate for democratically run institutions and adequate resources to ensure that people are cared for. Radical care in the Movement for Black Lives, argues political scientist Deva Woodly, aims to unmake racial capitalism, cisheteropatriarchy, the carceral state, and the colonial present.[35]

My goal is not to provide a comprehensive overview of this rich and nuanced work—there is clearly a great deal that I have not addressed in this brief discussion. Instead, I want to consider the usefulness of an abolitionist framework for the care economy. These snapshots of abolitionist thinking and practice contribute to our imagining more just futures. Is the abolitionist framework transferable to the care economy? To argue for the abolition of the carceral state, the primary purpose of which is to contain and control, is one thing. But can we—should we—argue for the abolition of public assistance, child welfare services, the health and hospital industry, and the school system?

There are undoubtedly components of the care economy that must be abolished. Child welfare seems to be one of those. As Dorothy Roberts has persuasively argued, this "family policing system" has many links with the carceral state and doesn't just fail families but destroys them. But the effects of other programs are not so clear-cut. TANF stigmatizes, surveils, and disciplines single parents—yet, it also provides a much needed although meager stipend for some families. MLICCI fights to expand welfare and childcare assistance for families across Mississippi, despite the obvious problems with the program. We need to be strategic about which programs are worth keeping and which are not. The answer to that question may change over time and from location to location, and depends upon people's needs. Abolitionist care requires simultaneously providing care for people now, developing a long-term inclusive and egalitarian vision for an ethic of care, and dismantling the profit-oriented care economy.

Dismantling the care economy may mean reverting some care needs to community spaces, as was the case with the communal care discussed above and the disability justice models. But collective care has limitations, particularly when care needs are extensive. It is unlikely that individuals can provide sustained care without some structural supports—equipment, supplies, and state resources. Although the exhaustion experienced by caregivers is often framed as "burnout," women's, gender, and sexuality studies professor Hil Malatino argues that the language of burnout transfers the source of stress and fatigue from resource deprivation to the person in need of care and, in the process, erases the ethic of interdependency.[36] So, institutional and material support are vital.

In addition, other care practices cannot be easily transferred to the community. Taking care of a neighbor's child is one thing; performing surgery is another. This raises the question of whether communal care can fully meet our needs. Do we still need a state to prepare people in care practices that require extensive background knowledge and specific training? Although we want to take profit-making out of the production of pharmaceuticals, should we have an agency of people dedicated to developing life-saving medications? These specialized needs require us to think strategically about how some care will get done and by whom, and how governance structures will play a role in that.

We should continue to demand state resources, because failing to do so is to abandon the people who are the most vulnerable. Both the welfare rights movement and the domestic workers' rights movement, for example, sought either state protection or resources. For JMacForFamilies, state aid was critical for the community to carry out the work of caring for families and children. Damayan counted on cash assistance to distribute to members during the pandemic. The people in Ellen Reddy's community, some of whom are living on the economic margins, do not have the luxury of saying no to state resources. So, making use of whatever resources are available now—*and*, even better, leveraging the state for no-strings-attached resources (like a guaranteed income)—will allow us to care for one another and organize. Failing to hold the state accountable makes our jobs harder and may mean ceding those resources to someone else.

Although we can and must be deeply critical of the state and capital's role in the care economy and strategic about our engagement, we cannot reject all forms of governance. Ensuring that everyone is cared for requires a decision-making structure. Cooperatives and collective ownership offer one governance model for antihierarchical care. Cooperation Jackson, for instance, is a celebrated experiment in economic democracy in the heart of Jackson, Mississippi. Founded by Kali Akuno, Cooperation Jackson is building a solidarity economy by putting into practice sustainable and equitable production and agricultural cooperatives that are collectively owned and democratically managed—working together for the good of the community. Cooperation Jackson promises to redefine economic relations in the heart of the Deep South in order to work toward a just transition to a socialist society. [37]

We can also look to an "anti-capitalist commons" that is collectively owned, sits outside the for-profit market economy, and requires obligations as well as entitlements, write George Caffentzis and Silvia Federici. [38] The commons, they argue, is "not the end point of a struggle…but its means" to create an alternative to capitalism [39]: "Anti-capitalist commons, then, should be conceived as both autonomous spaces from which to reclaim control over the conditions of our reproduction, and as bases from which to counter the processes of enclosure and increasingly disentangle our lives from the market and the state." [40] As with so much of radical organizing, Caffentzis and Federici recognize the need to meet people's immediate needs, develop alternative models, and work toward fundamental transformation. Collective production, collective ownership, allocation of resources, and organization of care require a governing structure to ensure everyone has the support structure and care that they need.

These examples of radical care demonstrate the simultaneous undoing of the present and the construction of the future. Political theorist Christopher Paul Harris argues that models of radical care are in part about "extracting ourselves and each other from the ideas, values, and institutions of Western modernity." [41] It illustrates how care is a process rather than an act, and how each of these examples are contributing to a larger collective movement as well as a vision for how to transform care.

But how does that happen? How do these local efforts contribute to a larger collective movement? What difference will this kind of community organizing make in the long run? Can grassroots organizing lead to larger structural change? Does it need to be scaled up in order to effectively confront the power of the care economy and the current state that supports it? And what would be the impact of scaling up? Davis, Dent, Meiners, and Richie argue that "scaling up can foreclose transformation."[42] Over the past two decades some social movements have scaled up and become nationally established and institutionalized. Increasingly dependent on nonprofit funding, they are beholden to people who pay their salaries and maintain their operations and in the process their commitment to transformation and organizing has waned. Spade argues that mutual aid organizations should remain locally run and operated. Scaling up, in this case, means more rather than larger mutual aid groups.[43] In addition to more grassroots initiatives, we also need to consider how to connect them.

Historian Barbara Ransby calls on us to build solidarity among organizations and make connections among issues—a process she calls "political quilting," whereby movements are able to coordinate, develop a coherent analysis, and provide support for one another. Such "quilting"—where the goal is to step outside of one's personal interests and consider broader collective goals—multiplies the impact of any single organization.[44] Political quilting will provide a forum to address tensions and identify points of connection. Local initiatives and constituencies sometimes have competing agendas. Is it possible, for example, to reconcile Indigenous demands for "land back" with the rights of refugees to enter and stay in the United States? How might the need to build medical equipment that relies on the extraction of natural resources sit with the imperative to protect the Earth? How do we balance individual understandings of care with collective interests?

Grappling with the inevitable tensions and cultivating political solidarities are parts of a necessary process in order to build a transformative movement. The goal is not a strategic alliance that involves trade-offs or collapsing struggles but finding common ground and understanding movements as battling the same

state and global power—what gender and women's studies professor Nadine Naber calls "conjoined forces"—and then engaging
in conversation and debate.[45] "Care is about a set of relational arrangements," argues anthropologist Miriam Ticktin, "not moral
dispositions."[46] What care looks like up close, how it gets done,
emerges out of practice, identifying individual and collective
needs.[47] Radical care, then, is part of a collective process leading
to social transformation. The authors of *Abolition. Feminism. Now.*
similarly point to the importance of collective engagement: "Key
to this abolition feminist ecosystem are networks, organizations,
and collectives. This work is never a solo project. Individuals tire,
fade. Movements deepen and continue."[48]

For generations, Indigenous communities have practiced radical care grounded in connection to the land, natural resources,
and community, where the boundary between human and non-
human care is not clearly delineated. For professor of Native
studies Kim TallBear, caretaking, which is central to Indigenous
kinship practices, is about "obligations of our human kin with
our other kin." Indeed, human well-being is inextricably connected to the other forms of life around us—plants and animals,
as well as the health of our waterways, soil, and air. We are not
an independent species but part of an ecosystem. For groups like
Seeding Sovereignty, an Indigenous-led collective; Pueblo Action
Alliance; and the Land Back and Water Back movements, practicing that broad vision of radical care is inseparable from dismantling settler colonialism and heteropatriarchal racial capitalism.[49]

Red Nation is a grassroots Native-led organization that is
committed to the liberation of Native peoples from colonialism
and capitalism. One of its principles of unity reads: "We are anti-capitalist and anti-colonial. We are Indigenous feminists who
believe in radical relationality. We do not seek a milder form of
capitalism or colonialism—we demand an entirely new system

premised on peace, cooperation, and justice. For our Earth and relatives to live, capitalism and colonialism must die."[50] Red Nation addresses issues of inadequate housing, health, shelter, and violence in border (or white-dominated) towns adjacent to Native reservations. Their No Dead Natives mutual aid campaign has gathered clothing, toiletries, and other necessities for houseless people in Albuquerque, according to Red Nation member Jennifer Marley, and is evidence that "caretaking can come in the form of security."[51] So, for Marley, meeting people's basic needs was bound up with creating a different kind of society: "In these moments when we can make kin, when we can feed and eat together, this is how we're envisioning the world. These are spaces of freedom where we get to live, for a second, in the world that we want to see. Indigenous communities have practiced kinship in deep and radical ways that directly oppose the capitalist-imperial machine that is the US empire."[52]

Red Nation's radical care politics comes out of Indigenous feminist queer practices. It calls for not expanded state care but a transformational politics:

> The communist world we build will come not only from street revolts and guerilla actions against the settler state, but the previously obscured work that women, queers, and trans people of all genders have done in the realms of care. This is the labor of sustaining us, our basic needs whether these be for food, shelter, or pleasure. Care encompasses a set of practices for recreating the world and reimagining our relationship to all our relatives. We have already seen and experienced this under global pandemic with the rise of widespread mutual aid networks that have the potential to become caretaking infrastructures. The economies of our capitalist present are premised on abuse.

The economies of our socialist transition and communist future will be premised on care.[53]

Red Nation's work of "radical relationality" offers a new way of caring that is distinct from "relations of extraction," as Melanie Yazzie and Cutcha Risling Baldy describe it. Radically reimagining the relationship between land, water, and people, they argue, is crucial to resistance and decolonization.[54]

What connects these diverse radical care practices is a commitment to social transformation, community empowerment, relationship building, and care that is nonhierarchical, antimarket, antistate, and collective. Groups practicing radical care aim to care for people in their community and to consider how their practices can alter power relations. Alternative caring practices, which have a long history in marginalized communities of color—from other-mothering to trans collectives to communal Indigenous healing practices—have found renewed urgency under neoliberalism. They have become a means for surviving the precarity of the moment and a strategy to counter systemic inequality for people under siege. Such practices build communities and relationships that lay the groundwork for transformative politics by providing a vision of what we want and pointing to how to get there.

Reimagining care also means reimagining work. Capital has encroached upon and turned social reproduction into a site of profit. Yet, care work—the feeding, nurturing, educating, nursing labor— is a critical part of a radical future. How do we understand the role of work and its connection to care in our radical future? What will be our relationship to care work as individuals and as a collective? What are our individual and collective rights and responsibilities?

For many people, a radical future is linked to personal freedom and individual autonomy so they can develop their capacities and be their best selves. Feminist philosopher Kathi Weeks, for example, advocates a post-work radical future, where people are able to pursue creative interests, to follow their hearts, and to find joy. She argues, in her book *The Problem with Work*, that because work has come to dominate life, we are expected to work more and harder. Even progressive proposals for change, she points out, are about dignified work, better pay, and more jobs. Instead, she urges us to refuse work so we can live and carve out time for leisure and love. Weeks's argument is compelling. Discussions of joy, leisure, and pleasure are too often missing from conversations about radical politics, and the preoccupation with work fails to account for people who cannot work or who engage in labor that is valued differently. Everyone should have the time, space, and resources to pursue personal interests—to "live," as Weeks understands it.[55]

The question animating Weeks's book is why work dominates life. A parallel question is why capital dominates work—even the work we do out of love and care. In addition to thinking about how we can work less, we might consider how we can work for ourselves and our communities to create the kind of world we aspire to: How can work can also bring us joy? More important, how can we think about pleasure, joy, and work collectively rather than individually? A truly caring radical future will require a commitment to a collective, not just individual, freedom.

I imagine that work will underpin any radical future. Thus, how we define work matters.[56] Work is a broad category. Not all work is the same. Weeks and other post-work theorists are referring to paid work in the capitalist marketplace. In a radical future, exploitative paid work, as well as coerced paid and unpaid labor, must be reimagined or abolished. Yet, collective needs will demand work that we may not always want to do. That is also an essential component of any radical future and stands in contrast to a vision of individual freedom. As much as we need to construct spaces of leisure, we cannot refuse some kinds of work—and perhaps we don't want to.

Care is a fundamental ethic and praxis in households, families, communities, and social movements. Since the dawn of human history, people have cared for and about one another. With the dismantling of the social safety net and diminished state support for the poor, this critical labor has been performed by friends, family, and community. The unpaid labor that so many of us engage in is often not accounted for. This labor may not involve direct care of another human. It could consist of mowing a lawn or washing dishes. It can be emotionally and physically taxing. Yet, the ethic of caring that prompts friends to help a disabled friend, children to care for elderly parents, and neighbors to offer assistance is central to human survival and the essence of what makes us social beings. It is a building block for a different kind of society, gesturing to an abolitionist future in which care is not defined by capitalist profit-making or racial and gendered norms but by an equally distributed commitment to the well-being of others.

Disabled queer and trans people of color who are part of the disability justice movement are engaged in a "radical rewriting of what care means," as Piepzna-Samarasinha describes in *Care Work: Dreaming Disability Justice,* in which care moves from an individual chore to a collective responsibility. The hope, as they put it, is that we can reimagine care as "a site of pleasure, joy, [and] community building."[57] Labor to sustain families and communities, to care for people around us, is essential to creating a truly caring society. We can strive to make that work loving rather than coercive. We must de-gender and de-racialize it. But it must be done.

We do not operate as autonomous beings. Radical social movements have been unequivocal about the need to work together to ensure our collective well-being. Uplifting the way activists care for one another in social movements suggests that a liberated future will require collective work. Any freedom agenda must address desire as well as how we live, how we care for one another and ourselves, how we feed and sustain our communities, and how we care for the Earth.

A few years ago, I had an especially illuminating experience about the importance of thinking collectively rather than individually. I was teaching a course called Mississippi Semester, in partnership with the MLICCI. My students were constructing an index of women's economic security to assist the organization in its efforts to lobby the state to expand childcare and welfare assistance. We interviewed people across the state to get their input about what variables to include in the index. One of our first interviews was with a job training program, Women in Construction (WinC), run by the nonprofit Moore Community House in Biloxi. Initiated during Hurricane Katrina, which devastated the Mississippi Gulf Coast, the program enabled poor women on public assistance to access higher-paying construction trades to make a dent in the gender-pay gap. It did so by giving participants practical skills, a stipend, and childcare. About twenty of us were sitting in a circle at Moore Community House—fifteen trainees and five of us from Barnard College. The trainees were mostly African American, with some Latinx and white women.

The previous night, the eight students, the course assistant, and I crammed into my Best Western hotel room to review our list of questions. We decided that getting a handle on women's economic security meant not only thinking about insecurity—what people lacked—but also understanding what security meant. How would one's life be transformed with economic security? What would individuals do that they are unable to do now? Economic security seems to translate into more leisure time and self-gratification. The translation is not intuitive, however. The alleged correlation of economic security with personal fulfillment is a product of neoliberal ideas of individualism circulated in popular culture. Marketing agencies have instilled in us aspirations for a life of travel, relaxation, hobbies, and walks along the beach. Economic security and happiness, we are told, means finally doing the things we have always wanted to do.

We predicted that, for our interviewees, economic security would mean quality time with their children or engaging in self-care. It might mean that day-to-day life would be less stressful and most certainly not be centered on crisis management. Or it might mean a full night's sleep—a luxury for single parents who sometimes have to work two jobs or travel long distances for work. We had several predictions about what having an economically secure life would mean for women in Mississippi.

We did not anticipate the response articulated by most women at the meeting. Their sense of communal responsibility was surprising and inspiring. Our interviewees didn't have steady work, were sometimes separated from their children, had been on welfare, and/or had poor health, and many of them were in debt. Despite these multiple challenges, their long-term goals and their visions for a better life were about collective well-being, not individual advancement or personal leisure. Rather than seeking personal fulfillment, they said they would choose to give back to the community and help others. Interviewees hoped, for example, to create a recreational space for young people in the neighborhood. They wanted to ensure that the less fortunate were cared for. Our meeting at Moore Community House revealed how ordinary people, hidden from public view, are creating alternative models of collective well-being and social justice in response to state abandonment.

Although there should always be space for individual pursuits and personal joys, I don't believe that any radical future premised on individualism will survive. As Ashanté Reese and Dara Cooper write about the Black food justice movement: "A Black feminist approach to food justice seeks to rejoin or heal these fractures through care-based practices that recognize multiple layers of interconnectedness: between past, present, and futures; between the spiritual and physical realms of the human experience; and between us and the Land."[58] We must see the connections to the land, to each other, and to our temporalities. We will never have a society that does not need care. We are social beings with different needs and multiple forms of mutual dependencies. Anyone who considers themselves independent and self-sufficient will someday need care from others. For that reason, we must consider how we can contribute to one another's well-being at all phases of our lives, every day. Care is not only something to incorporate into our future but is also part of our present. Hopefully, our solutions will be collective processes that are fulfilling rather than extractive.

In her essay "The Master's Tools," Audre Lorde wrote presciently:

> For women, the need and desire to nurture each other is not pathological but redemptive, and it is within that knowledge that our real power is rediscovered.... Only within that interdependency of different strengths, acknowledged and equal, can the power to seek new ways of being in the world generate, as well as the courage and sustenance to act where there are no charters.[59]

No charters, indeed. There is no map to guide us. Nothing is foretold. In 2019, none of us would have predicted that a pandemic would shut things down and take as many lives as it did. The pandemic transformed both how people understood care and the scope of possibilities they could imagine. Although the move toward alternative and oppositional caring practices was in play long before the pandemic, those initiatives went into high gear as people realized that we have little choice but to care for ourselves. The various ways that people came together, offered aid, and looked out for one another were nothing short of astonishing. Some of these were "wild experiments," to borrow Piepzna-Samarasinha's phrase, in which people were using the limited tools at their disposal to create new communal care practices. But it is experimentation, courage, and imagination that will take us to new places and generate models for how to create a better, more caring world.

Acknowledgments

I t is hard to account for all the people who contributed to the making of this book.

My heartfelt gratitude to the community advocates, organizers, and grassroots activists (including people in the archive) whom I have encountered and learned from over the past three decades. Their words and wisdom are woven throughout this book. Thanks very much to everyone who took the time to meet with me, read portions of the manuscript, and respond to email queries.

In particular, I want to acknowledge the amazing organizers at the Mississippi Low-Income Child Care Initiative: Roberta Avila, Carol Burnett, Jearlean Osborne, Ellen Reddy, and Matt Williams. They traveled around the state with me and my students. We learned about their advocacy work and relationship-building and witnessed the practice of radical care. The grassroots organizing in Mississippi has been deeply influential for me. I am grateful to Cassandra Welchin for approaching me at the Ms. Foundation grantees gathering in Washington D.C. in 2016, and inviting me to attend the Women's Economic Security Summit in Jackson. Thanks also to the amazing staff and members of Damayan, who, I have collaborated with for the past fifteen years, especially Linda Oalican, Riya Ortiz, and Lydia Catina Amaya. I am helping Linda write her autobiography because her story, from frontline battles against martial law in the Philippines in the 1970s to becoming a national labor leader in the US, must be told. Members of Damayan, many of whom are labor trafficking survivors, courageously shared stories with me and my students. I will not name them because some have politically sensitive cases. Christine Lewis, one of the leaders of Domestic Workers United, continues to inspire me with her cultural and political work, and her unwavering commitment to worker-led organizing. I am lucky to have had the opportunity to be in conversation for many years with Silvia Federici, one of the founders of the Wages for Housework movement. Rosa Navarro generously offered her insight about domestic worker organizing in Chicago. I am grateful that Sandra Killett shared her deeply moving story about her encounter with child welfare. I appreciate reporter Anna Wolfe taking the time to assist me even as she was knee-deep in unearthing the story about misuse of welfare funds in Mississippi.

The Haymarket team has exceeded my expectations throughout this process. Many, many thanks to Anthony Arnove, Maria Isabelle Carlos, Caroline Luft, Katy O'Donnell, and Jameka Williams, especially for their patience as I made more revisions than they anticipated and missed a few deadlines. Their thoughtful, meticulous, and politically incisive suggestions made this book much better. Thanks also to Alyea Canada and Alex Gargialiano for their editorial assistance. I had a stellar group of research assistants: Sharmie Azurel, Pagona Kytzidis, Kaili Meier, and Onnie Woods. Pagona, in particular, was with this project from the beginning and was as much a thought partner as a research assistant. I am grateful for her insight and honest critique.

A number of people read all or a portion of this manuscript or earlier writing that laid the foundation for my thinking about care. I cannot thank them enough for taking the time to offer invaluable feedback, given their demanding schedules: Claire Dunning, Hester Eisenstein, Nicole Fleetwood, Sandy Grande, Mara Green, Sarah Jaffe, Priya Kandeswamy, Robin D. G. Kelly,

Rosa Navarro, Celia Naylor, Akemi Nishida, Barbara Ransby, Shana Redmond, Mary Romero, Robyn Spencer, Emma Teitleman, Miriam Ticktin, Sarah Tobias, and Joan Tronto. Other people who are part of my intellectual community and have been critical for my thinking about care include Katherine Acey, Halah Ahmad, Aren Aizura, Emma Amador, Swapna Bannerjee, Eileen Boris, Tamara Mose Brown, Linda Burnham, Grace Chang, Marisa Chappell, Narbada Chhetri, Kathleen Coll, Dara Cooper, Angela Davis, Dana-Aín Davis, Bonnie Thorton Dill, Johanna Fernandez, Jennifer Fish, Gwendolyn Fowler, Valerie Francisco-Menchavez, Jennifer Guglielmo, Beverly Guy-Sheftall, Sarah Haley, Victoria Haskins, Tera Hunter, Allison Julien, Mariame Kaba, Cindi Katz, Jennifer Klein, Alice Kessler-Harris, Lisa Levenstein, Vanessa May, Robyn Maynard, Gay McDougall, Jennifer Mittelstadt, Alice O'Connor, Annelise Orleck, Cara Page, Ai-Jen Poo, Dorothy Roberts, Destiny Julia Spruill, Kirsten Swinth, Keeanga-Yamahtta Taylor, Andrew Urban, Nilita Vachani, Lara Vapnek, Linta Varghese, Melody Webb, and Rhonda Williams. This is just a partial listing. There are many other people (including the very large NWSA community) whom I did not or could not name, but have had conversations or engaged with in some way. I also extend my thanks to them.

My analysis about care has evolved over years. I owe a debt of gratitude to the brilliant scholars who deepened my thinking and on whose shoulders this work stands, many of whom are referenced in the text or footnotes. I wrote critically about care in *Household Workers Unite*, but the first paper I gave on care as a conceptual category was at the Rutgers Institute for Research on Women in 2016, organized by Nicole Fleetwood and Sarah Tobias. Ideas in this book were shared in a number of seminars and lectures over the past several years, including the University at Buffalo Gender Institute, Strathclyde Feminist Research Network, Fordham University School of Law Faculty Colloquium on Race and Ethnicity, Fordham University Care and Capitalism Conference, The Society of Fellows and Heyman Center for the Humanities at Columbia University, Rutgers Center for Historical Analysis, Rutgers Institute for Research on Women, the Wolf Humanities Center at the University of Pennsylvania, and Université Paris-Est Créteil.

Barnard College has been a wonderful place to teach and think and learn. In addition to my research and activism, I was prompted to work on this book because of community-engaged teaching: "Mississippi Semester," "COVID-19 and Care Work: An Oral History," and "Pandemic Tales: Curated Conversations with Migrant Workers." The Barnard Engages program enabled me to develop a three-year curricular partnership with Damayan. These courses were also an entrée into working with a phenomenal group of students, many of whom I am still in touch with. I am grateful to the college and provost Linda Bell for her unfailing support of innovative teaching and her willingness to listen to faculty ideas. Barnard College also funded the research for this book and gave me a sabbatical leave in 2021–2022. Thanks to Lisa Tiersten for her support as my department chair. I am lucky to have a superb group of dedicated and supportive colleagues in the history department and the college more widely.

The Barnard Center for Research on Women is, in many ways, my home now. My codirector, Janet Jakobsen, is a model of leadership, integrity, and generosity. Thanks to the amazing staff that has helped make BCRW a rich intellectual space and site of cutting-edge social justice organizing: Avi Cummings, Hope Dector, Sophie Kreitzerg, Miriam Neptune, and Pam Phillips. The Transnational Black Feminisms working group was an important source of support during the depths of COVID: Vanessa Agard-Jones, Yvette Christiansë, Dana Davis, Abosede George, Natasha Lightfoot, Manijeh Moradian, Celia Naylor, Tami Navarro, Keisha-Khan Perry, Robyn Spencer, Keeanga-Yamahtta Taylor.

While I was in South Africa in 2022, I had uninterrupted time to write and think. Many thanks to the staff at the Johannesburg Institute for Advanced Study and the fellows: Yolande Bouka, Siya Khumalo, Sue Nyathi, Srila Roy, Nafisa Sheik, Tendayi Sithole, and Maria Suriano. In addition, my extended family in Johannesburg, Durban, and Cape Town fed and cared for me. For that, I will be forever grateful. Thanks to Saroj Moodley, Tracy and Marshall Naicker, George and Rubi Naidoo, Anthony and Rajes Moodley, Deysie and Leo Naiker, Mala Chetty, Percy Reddy, Ben Padayachee, Aunty Thunga, Aunty Devi, as well as cousins Priscilla, Kamen, Nimalen, Praven, Lionel, Kumarie, and adopted cousin Siveshni.

I'm grateful to have a supportive family (and chosen family), some who provided care for me during rough patches over the past two years. Jeff and Carol Nadasen and their children Shay and Grey, Kasie and Sheila Padayachee, Renita and Nicole, Denise Nadasen and Tom Reynolds and their children Clay and Jeremy, Nicole and Dave Martin, Jacinth Hyman, Robyn Spencer, Dana Davis, Barbara Ransby, Celia Naylor, Anu Rao, John Johnson, Luciano Dos Santos, Jeffrey Palichuck, and David Fletcher. My children, Tyler and Indira, never cease to amaze me with their thoughtfulness and independent spirits. Moving into adulthood, they have adopted a healthy skepticism about the rules of the game and seek nontraditional educational and occupational choices. I am so grateful to Indira for carefully reading the manuscript and offering the sharp and unfiltered insight of a nineteen-year-old who has immersed herself in the world of care work. Billy, always a source of support, continues to bring light into my life with his sense of humor and insistence that I occasionally stop and have fun. My father, at eighty-six, still has his wits about him, even though his pace has slowed. Over the course of his life, he endured many hardships, which made him stronger, more resilient, and even more deeply committed to justice. No one taught me more about care and compassion than my mother. Although she is no longer with us physically, I carry her lessons close to my heart.

Notes

Introduction

1. Timothy J. McClimon, "Doing Well and Doing Good," *Forbes*, April 20, 2020, https://www.forbes.com/sites/timothyjmcclimon/2020/04/20/doing-well-and-doing-good/?sh=1c7dbf8b3da0.
2. IAC News, "IAC Announces Close of $500 Million Care.com Acquisition," *PR Newswire*, February 11, 2020, https://www.prnewswire.com/news-releases/iac-announces-close-of-500-million-carecom-acquisition-301002873.html.
3. Will Feure, "Quest Says High Demand for Covid Testing Drove Record Revenues, Increases Dividend," *CNBC*, February 4, 2021, https://www.cnbc.com/2021/02/04/quest-says-high-demand-for-covid-testing-drove-record-revenues-increases-dividend.html.
4. Chris Isidore, "Pfizer Revenue and Profits Soar on Its Covid Vaccine Business," *CNN Business*, November 2, 2021, https://www.cnn.com/2021/11/02/business/pfizer-earnings.
5. Naomi Klein, *Shock Doctrine* (New York: Henry Holt, 2008).
6. Lise Vogel, *Marxism and the Oppression of Women: Toward a Unitary Theory* (New Brunswick: Rutgers University Press, 1983); Nancy Fraser, "Contradictions of Capitalism and Care," *New Left Review* 100 (2016): 99–117; Susan Ferguson, *Women and Work: Feminism, Labour, and Social Reproduction* (London: Pluto Press, 2020); Tithi Bhattacharya, *Social Reproduction Theory Remapping Class, Recentering Oppression* (London: Pluto Press, 2017).
7. Fraser, "Contradictions of Capitalism and Care."
8. Mae Ngai, *The Chinese Question: The Gold Rushes and Global Politics* (New York: W.W. Norton & Company, Inc., 2021).
9. Elizabeth Hinton, *From the War on Poverty to the War on Crime: The Making of Mass Incarceration in America* (Cambridge: Harvard University Press, 2016).

10. Keeanga-Yamahtta Taylor, *Race for Profit: How Banks and the Real Estate Industry Undermined Black Homeownership* (Chapel Hill: University of North Carolina Press, 2019).

11. Claudia Jones, "An End to the Neglect of the Problems of the Negro Woman!," *Political Affairs*, June 1949, reprint, National Women's Commission, CPUSA. For more on this see: Dayo F. Gore, *Radicalism at the Crossroads: African American Women Activists in the Cold War* (New York: New York University Press, 2011); Carole Boyce Davies, *Left of Karl Marx: The Political Life of Black Communist Claudia Jones* (Durham, NC: Duke University Press, 2008); Erik McDuffie, *Sojourning for Freedom: Black Women, American Communism, and the Making of Black Left Feminism* (Durham, NC: Duke University Press, 2011); Denise Lynn, "Socialist Feminism and Triple Oppression: Claudia Jones and African American Women in American Communism," *Journal for the Study of Radicalism* 8 (2)(Fall 2014): 1-20; Linda Burnham, "The Wellspring of Black Feminist Theory," *Southern University Law Review* 28 (2001): 265–270.

12. The Combahee River Collective, *The Combahee River Collective Statement: Black Feminist Organizing in the Seventies and Eighties* (Latham, NY: Kitchen Table, Women of Color Press, 1986).

13. Barbara Laslett and Johanna Brenner, "Gender and Social Reproduction: Historical Perspectives," *Annual Review of Sociology* 15 (1989): 381–404; Vogel, *Marxism and the Oppression of Women*; Maria Mies, *Patriarchy and Accumulation on a World Scale* (London: Zed Books Ltd, 1986).

14. Emily Kos, Nan DasGupta, Gabrielle Novacek, Rohan Sajdeh, "To Fix the Labor Shortage, Solve the Care Crisis," Boston Consulting Group, May 19, 2022, https://www.bcg.com/publications/2022/address-care-crisis-to-fix-labor-shortage.

Chapter 1

1. Vivian Gornick, "There Once Was a Union Maid/Who Never Was Afraid," *Village Voice*, November 29, 1976, *Ms.* magazine records, series 7, box 39, folder 12, Sophia Smith Collection, Smith College.

2. Carolyn Reed, quoted in Hazel Garland, "Early Morning TV Can Be Very Informative," *Pittsburgh Courier*, February 9, 1980.

3. Geraldine Roberts, interview by Donna Van Raaphorst, March

30–June 29, 1977, Cleveland, Ohio, Program on Women and
Work, Institute of Labor and Industrial Relations, University of
Michigan, Walter P. Reuther Library, Wayne State University, 70.

4. Arlie Russell Hochschild, *The Managed Heart: Commercialization of
Human Feeling* (Berkeley: University of California Press, 1983).

5. There is a voluminous scholarship on care and care work as
well as a growing critique. Nancy Folbre, *For Love or Money: Care
Provision in the United States* (Russell Sage Foundation, 2012). For a
critique of white, middle-class, gendered logic of care, see Martin
F. Manalansan, "Queer Intersections: Sexuality and Gender in
Migration Studies," *International Migration Review* 40, no. 1 (2006):
224-49; Michelle Murphy, "Unsettling Care: Troubling Transnational Itineraries of Care in Feminist Health Practices," *Social
Studies of Science* 45, no. 5 (October 2015): 717–737, asks us to "un-
settle" the "fraught histories of feminist mobilizations of care."

6. National Domestic Workers Alliance, "Domestic Workers Bills
of Rights", last modified 2021, https://www.domesticworkers.
org/programs-and-campaigns/developing-policy-solutions/
bill-of-rights/#:~:text=Domestic%20workers%20do%20the%20
work,rights%20and%20dignity%20they%20deserve.

7. Marilyn Waring, *If Women Counted: A New Feminist Economics*
(San Francisco: Harper Collins, 1988); Julie Nelson, *Feminism,
Objectivity, and Economics* (New York: Routledge, 1996); Theresa
L. Amott and Julie Matthaei, *Race, Gender, and Work: A Multi-cul-
tural Economic History of Women in the United States* (Boston: South
End Press, 1996).

8. Joan Tronto, *Moral Boundaries A Political Argument for an Ethic of
Care* (New York: Routledge, 1993).

9. Barbara Ehrenreich and Arlie Russell Hochschild, "Love and
Gold," in *Global Woman: Nannies, Maids, and Sex Workers in the
New Economy* (New York: Metropolitan Books, 2003), 15–30.

10. Laura Briggs, *How All Politics Became Reproductive Politics: From
Welfare Reform to Foreclosure to Trump* (Oakland: University of Cal-
ifornia Press, 2017), 11. Mimi Abramovitz also writes about this
as a crisis of social reproduction. See Mimi Abramovitz, "From
Welfare State to Carceral State: Whither Social Reproduction?,"
in *Democracy and the Welfare State: The Two Wests in the Age of
Austerity*, ed. Alice Kessler-Harris and Maurizio Vaudagna, (New
York: Columbia University Press, 2017), 195–226.

11. Mona Harrington, *Care and Equality: Inventing a New Family*

Politics (New York: Routledge, 2000); Anne-Marie Slaughter, *Unfinished Business* (London: Oneworld, 2015); Joan Tronto, *Moral Boundaries A Political Argument for an Ethic of Care* (New York: Routledge, 1993).

12. Mary Romero and Nancy Pérez, "Conceptualizing the Foundation of Inequalities in Care Work," *American Behavioral Scientist* 60, no. 2 (2015): 172–88. Quote on page 185.

13. For a critique, see Manalansan, "Queer Intersections: Sexuality and Gender in Migration Studies"; Rachel Brown, "Re-examining the Transnational Nanny: Migrant Carework Beyond the Chain," *International Feminist Journal of Politics* 18, no. 2 (2016): 210–229.

14. Ehrenreich and Hochschild, *Global Woman: Nannies, Maids, and Sex Workers in the New Economy.*

15. Evelyn Nakano Glenn, "From Servitude to Service Work: Historical Continuities in the Racial Division of Paid Reproductive Labor," *Signs* 18, no. 1 (1992):1-43; Evelyn Nakano Glenn, *Forced to Care: Coercion and Caregiving in America* (Cambridge: Harvard University Press, 2010); Dorothy E. Roberts, "Spiritual and Menial Housework," *Yale Journal of Law & Feminism* 9, no.1 (1997): 51–80; Mignon Duffy, "Reproducing Labor Inequalities: Challenges for Feminists Conceptualizing Care at the Intersections of Gender, Race, and Class," *Gender & Society* Vol. 19, no. 1 (2005): 66–82. D. K. Barker and S. F. Feiner, "Affect, Race, and Class: An Interpretive Reading of Caring Labor," *Frontiers: A Journal of Women Studies* 30, no. 1 (2009): 41–54.

16. Dana Ain Davis, "Manufacturing Mammies: The Burdens of Service Work and Welfare Reform among Battered Black Women," *Anthropologica* 46, no. 2 (2004): 273–88.

17. Andrew Urban, *Brokering Servitude: Migration and the Politics of Domestic Labor During the Long 19th Century* (New York: New York University Press, 2017); Manalansan, "Queer Intersections." See also, for example, Robyn Pariser, "Masculinity and Organized Resistance in Domestic Service in Colonial Dar es Salaam, 1919–1961," *International Labor and Working-Class History* 88, (2015): 109–29. And the special issue of *Men and Masculinities* 13, no. 1 (2010). For a critique of gendered assumptions of the labor see Speranta Dumitru, "From 'Brain Drain' to 'Care Drain': Women's Labor, Migration, and Methodological Sexism," *Women's Studies International Forum* 47 (November–December 2014): 203–212.

18. Mignon Duffy, *Making Care Count: A Century of Gender, Race, and*

Paid Care Work (New Brunswick: Rutgers University Press, 2011), 117.

19. Duffy, *Making Care Count*, 126.
20. Anne-Marie Slaughter, *Unfinished Business* (London: Oneworld, 2015).
21. Shengwei Sun, "National Snapshot: Poverty Among Women and Families," National Women's Law Center, January 2023. https://nwlc.org/wp-content/uploads/2023/02/2023_nwlc_PovertySnapshot-converted.pdf.
22. Joan Tronto attempted to disrupt this association decades ago by arguing that care is not specifically a woman's issue but is central to human relationships. Tronto, *Moral Boundaries*; Manalansan, "Queer Intersections."
23. Arlie Russell Hochschild, "Global Care Chains and Emotional Surplus Value," in *On The Edge: Living with Global Capitalism*, eds. Will Hutton and Anthony Giddens (London: Jonathan Cape, 2000), 131. For a critique, see Manalansan, "Queer Intersections" and Brown, "Re-examining the Transnational Nanny."
24. Hochschild, "Love and Gold," 39.
25. Cameron Lynne Macdonald, *Shadow Mothers: Nannies, Au Pairs and the Micropolitics of Mother* (Berkeley: University of California Press, 2011).
26. Folbre, *For Love or Money*.
27. Thavolia Glymph, *Out of the House of Bondage: The Transformation of the Plantation House* (Cambridge: Cambridge University Press, 2003); Grace Elizabeth Hale, *Making Whiteness: The Culture of Segregation in the South, 1890–1940* (New York: Vintage, 1999); K. Sue Jewell, *From Mammy to Miss America and Beyond: Cultural Images and the Shaping of US Social Policy* (New York: Routledge, 1992); Kimberly Wallace-Sanders, *Mammy: A Century of Race, Gender, and Southern Memory* (Ann Arbor: The University of Michigan Press, 2008).
28. Peggi R. Smith, "Regulating Paid Household Work: Class, Gender, Race and Agendas of Reform," *American University Law Review* 48 (1999).
29. Anna Romina Guevarra, *Marketing Dreams, Manufacturing Heroes: The Transnational Labor Brokering of Filipino Workers* (New Brunswick: Rutgers University Press, 2010); Anna Romina Guevarra, "Supermaids: The Racial Branding of Filipino Care Labour" in *Migration and Care Labour: Theory, Policy and Politics*, eds. Bridget

Anderson and Isabel Shutes, (Houndmills, Basingstoke, Hampshire: Palgrave Macmillan, 2014), 130–150.

30. Valerie Francisco-Menchavez, *The Labor of Care: Filipina Migrants and Transnational Families in the Digital Age* (Urbana: University of Illinois Press, 2018). Aren Aizura uses the term "communization of care." Aren Aizura, "Communizing Care in Left Hand of Darkness," *Ada: A Journal of Gender, New Media, and Technology*, no. 12. https://adanewmedia.org/2017/10/issue12-aizura/. See also Tamara Mose Brown, *Raising Brooklyn: Nannies, Childcare and Caribbeans Creating Community* (New York: New York University Press, 2011). Brown writes about how Caribbean domestic workers, some of whom are migrant workers, forge community and solidarity.

31. Manalansan, "Queer Intersections."

32. Joan Tronto distinguishes between care for, caring about, caring with, caregiving, and care receiving. See Joan Tronto, *Caring Democracy*.

33. Heather Berg, "An Honest Day's Wage for a Dishonest Day's Work: (Re)Productivism and Refusal," *Women's Studies Quarterly* 42, no. ½ (2014): 161–177.

34. Premilla Nadasen, "Power, Intimacy, and Contestation: Dorothy Bolden and Domestic Worker Organizing in Atlanta in the 1960s," in *Intimate Labors: Culture, Technologies, and the Politics of Care*, ed. Eileen Boris and Rhacel Parreñas (Stanford University Press, 2010).

35. Anne T. Winston, Maids' Honor Day Nomination for Rosie Lee Powell, May 1972, box 1627, folder 87, NDWU Records.

36. Elizabeth Runyan to National Domestic Workers of America, May 25, 1976, box 1628, folder 90, NDWU Records; Flo Anne Menzler to National Domestic Workers of America, May 24, 1976, box 1628, folder 90, NDWU Records; Evelyn and Alton Reeves to National Domestic Workers of America, May 24, 1976, box 1628, folder 90, NDWU Records.

37. Reminiscences of Carolyn Reed, as interviewed by Martha Sandlin, April 15, 1980, transcript, 32, Columbia Center for Oral History, Butler Library, Columbia University, New York.

38. Edith Sloan, "Keynote Address" in *NCHE News* 2, no. 7 (July 1971), Schlesinger Library, Radcliffe Institute.

39. Paul Laurence Dunbar, "We Wear the Mask," in *The Complete Poems of Paul Laurence Dunbar* (New York: Dodd, Mead and Com-

pany, 1922), 71; Darlene Clark Hine, "Rape and the Inner Lives of
Black Women in the Middle West," *Signs* 14, no. 4 (1989): 912–20.

40. Rosa Navarro, email interview with author, December 1, 2020.

41. Linda Oalican, email interview with author, July 4, 2021.

42. Sarah Jaffe, *Work Won't Love You Back: How Devotion to Our Jobs
Keeps Us Exploited, Exhausted, and Alone* (New York: Bold Type
Books, 2021).

43. Miriam Ticktin, *Casualties of Care: Immigration and the Politics of
Humanitarianism in France* (Berkeley: University of California
Press, 2011); See also Lisa Marie Cacho, *Social Death: Racialized
Rightlessness and the Criminalization of the Unprotected* (New York:
New York University Press, 2012).

44. Hart Research Associates, "Parents' and Teachers' Views on Re-
opening School: Key Findings from Nationwide Surveys Among
US Parents and Teachers," August/September 2020, https://web.
williams.edu/Mathematics/sjmiller/public_html/119/talks/sur-
vey_school-reopening_augsept2020.pdf.

45. Linda Oalican, interview by Narizza Saladino, March 2, 2021.

Chapter 2

1. Sherna Berger Gluck, interview #3 with Johnnie Tillmon, 1991,
The Virtual Oral/Aural History Archive, University of South-
ern California; Premilla Nadasen, *Welfare Warriors: The Welfare
Rights Movement in the United States* (New York: Routledge, 2005);
Gwendolyn Fowler, "'Maybe We Poor Welfare Women Will
Really Liberate Women in this Country': Tracing an Intellectual
History of Mrs. Johnnie Tillmon-Blackston" (MA thesis, Sarah
Lawrence College, May 2017).

2. Jennifer Mittelstadt, *From Welfare to Workfare: The Unintended Con-
sequences of Liberal Reform, 1945–1965* (Chapel Hill: University of
North Carolina Press, 2005); Lisa Levenstein, *A Movement Without
Marches: African American Women and the Politics of Poverty in Postwar
Philadelphia* (Chapel Hill: University of North Carolina Press,
2009); Premilla Nadasen, Jennifer Mittelstadt, Marisa Chappell,
Welfare in the United States: A History With Documents, 1935–1996
(New York: Routledge 2009).

3. Barbara Laslett and Johanna Brenner, "Gender and Social Reproduction: Historical Perspectives," *Annual Review of Sociology* 15
(1989): 381–404; Lise Vogel, *Marxism and the Oppression of Women:*

Toward a Unitary Theory (New Brunswick: Rutgers University Press, 1983); Maria Mies, *Patriarchy and Accumulation on a World Scale* (London: Zed Books Ltd, 1986).

4. Cindi Katz, "Vagabond Capitalism and the Necessity of Social Reproduction," *Antipode* 33, no.4 (2001): 709–728; Mariarosa Dalla Costa and Selma James, *The Power of Women and the Subversion of the Community* (Bristol: Falling Wall Press Ltd), 1975; Angela Y. Davis, *Women, Race and Class* (New York: First Vintage Books Edition, 1983); Lise Vogel, *Marxism and the Oppression of Women: Toward a Unitary Theory* (New Brunswick: Rutgers University Press, 1983); Margaret Lowe Benston, "The Political Economy of Women's Liberation," *Monthly Review 21* (1969): 13–27; Barbara Laslett and Johanna Brenner, "Gender and Social Reproduction: Historical Perspectives," *Annual Review of Sociology* 15 (1989): 381–404; Kate Bezanson and Meg Luxton, eds, *Social Reproduction: Feminist Political Economy Challenges to Neo-Liberalism* (Montreal: McGill-Queens University Press, 2006); Lise Vogel, *Marxism and the Oppression of Women: Toward a Unitary Theory* (New Brunswick: Rutgers University Press, 1983); Silvia Federici, *Revolution at Point Zero* (Oakland: PM Press, 2012).

5. Barbara Laslett and Johanna Brenner, "Gender and Social Reproduction: Historical Perspectives," *Annual Review of Sociology* 15 (1989); Costa and James, *The Power of Women and the Subversion of the Community;* Silvia Federici, *Wages Against Housework* (London: Power of Women Collective, 1975).

6. Jeanne Boydston calls this the "pastoralization of housework." See Jeanne Boydston, *Home and Work: Housework, Wages and the Ideology of Labor in the Early Republic* (New York: Oxford University Press, 1990).

7. Phyllis Palmer, *Domesticity and Dirt: Housewives and Domestic Servants in the United States, 1920–1945* (Philadelphia: Temple University Press, 1989).

8. Diana Paton argues that slavery enabled plantation owners to externalize the costs of social reproduction of enslaved people by exploiting the reproductive labor of African women. See Diana Paton, "Gender History, Global History and Atlantic Slavery," *American Historical Review* 127, no. 2 (June 2022): 726–754.

9. Jennifer Morgan, *Reckoning with Slavery: Gender, Kinship, and Capitalism in the Early Black Atlantic* (Durham: Duke University Press, 2021); Eric Williams, *Capitalism and Slavery* (Chapel Hill: The

University of North Carolina Press, 1944).

10. Jennifer Morgan, "Partus Sequitur Ventrem: Law, Race, and Reproduction in Colonial Slavery," *Small Axe* 22, no. 1 (March 2018): 1–17; Jennifer Morgan, *Laboring Women: Reproduction and Gender in New World Slavery* (Philadelphia: University of Pennsylvania, 2004).

11. Sarah Haley, *No Mercy Here: Gender, Punishment, and the Making of Jim Crow Modernity* (Chapel Hill: The University of North Carolina Press, 2016), 159.

12. Manu Karuka, *Empire's Tracks: Indigenous Nations, Chinese Workers and the Transcontinental Railroad* (Berkeley: University of California, 2019).

13. Mae Ngai, *The Chinese Question: The Gold Rushes and Global Politics* (New York: W.W. Norton & Company, Inc., 2021).

14. Katz, "Vagabond Capitalism,"; Bhattacharya, *Social Reproduction Theory*.

15. W. E. B. DuBois, *Black Reconstruction* (Millwood: Kraus-Thomson Organization Ltd., 1976); Steven Hahn, *A Nation under our Feet: Black Political Struggles in the Rural South from Slavery to the Great Migration* (Cambridge: Belknap Press of Harvard University Press, 2003).

16. Tera W. Hunter, *To 'Joy My Freedom: Southern Black Women's Lives and Labors After the Civil War* (Cambridge: Harvard University Press, 1998); Jacqueline Jones, *Labor of Love, Labor of Sorrow: Black Women, Work, and the Family from Slavery to the Present* (New York: Basic Books, 1985).

17. Alice Kessler-Harris, *In Pursuit of Equity: Women, Men, and the Quest for Economic Citizenship in 20th Century America* (Oxford: Oxford University Press, 2001).

18. Elizabeth D. Esch, *The Color Line and the Assembly Line: Managing Race in the Ford Empire* (Oakland: University of California Press, 2018).

19. David M. Kennedy, *Freedom from Fear: The American People in Depression and War, 1929–1945* (New York: Oxford University Press, 1999); Jefferson Cowie, *The Great Exception: The New Deal & the Limits of American Politics* (Princeton: Princeton University Press, 2016).

20. Eileen Boris, "The Racialized Gendered State: Constructions of Citizenship in the United States," *Social Politics: International Studies in Gender, State and Society* 2, no. 2 (Summer 1995): 160–80.

21. Alice Kessler-Harris, *In Pursuit of Equity: Men, Women, and the Quest for Economic Citizenship in 20th Century America* (New York: Oxford University Press, 2001); Linda Gordon, *Pitied But Not Entitled*; Frances Fox Piven and Richard A. Cloward, *Regulating the Poor: The Functions of Public Welfare* (New York: Random House, Inc., 1993); Mimi Abramovitz, *Regulating the Lives of Women: Social Welfare Policy From Colonial Times to the Present* (Boston: South End Press, 1988); Gwendolyn Mink, *The Wages of Motherhood: Inequality in the Welfare State, 1917–1942* (Ithaca: Cornell University Press, 1995).

22. Winifred Bell, *Aid to Dependent Children* (New York: Columbia University Press, 1965).

23. Cotten Seiler, "Origins of White Care," *Social Text* 38, no. 1 (March 2020).

24. Shatema Threadcraft, *Intimate Justice: The Black Female Body and the Body Politic* (New York: Oxford University Press, 2018); Kevin Begos, Danielle Deaver, John Railey, Scott Sexton, Paul Lombardo, *Against Their Will: North Carolina's Sterilization Program and the Campaign for Reparations* (Bangalore, Karnataka, India: Gray Oak Books, 2012); Laura Briggs, *Reproducing Empire: Race, Sex, Science, and U.S. Imperialism in Puerto Rico* (Berkeley: University of California Press, 2002); Nancy Ordover, *American Eugenics: Race, Queer Anatomy, and the Science of Nationalism* (Minneapolis: University of Minnesota Press, 2003). Angela Saini, *Superior: The Return of Race Science* (Boston: Beacon Press, 2019).

25. See also Dorothy Roberts, *Killing the Black Body: Race, Reproduction, and the Meaning of Liberty* (New York: Pantheon, 1997).

26. "AFDC Caseload Data" Office of Family Assistance, Administration for Children and Families, Department of Health and Human Services, December 2004. https://www.acf.hhs.gov/ofa/data/afdc-caseload-data-1970.

27. Lisa Duggan, *The Twilight of Equality?: Neoliberalism, Cultural Politics, and the Attack on Democracy* (Boston: Beacon Press, 2004); Nancy MacLean, *Democracy in Chains: The Deep History of the Radical Right's Stealth Plan for America* (New York: Viking, 2017).

28. Pew Research Center, "The Rise in Dual Income Households," June 18, 2015, https://www.pewresearch.org/ft_dual-income-households-1960-2012-2/.

29. Barbara Ehrenreich and Arlie Russell Hochschild, *Global Woman: Nannies, Maids, and Sex Workers in the New Economy* (New York:

Metropolitan Books, 2003); Nancy Folbre, *For Love or Money*; Madonna Harrington Meyer, *Care Work: Gender, Labor and the Welfare State* (New York: Routledge, 2000); Rhacel Salazar Parreñas, *Servants of Globalization: Women, Migration, and Domestic Work* (Stanford: Stanford University Press, 2001).

30. "Employment by Detailed Occupation," Bureau of Labor Statistics, 2021, https://www.bls.gov/emp/tables/emp-by-detailed-occupation.htm.

31. "Employment by Major Industry Sector," Bureau of Labor Statistics, 2021, https://www.bls.gov/emp/tables/employment-by-major-industry-sector.htm.

32. Evelyn Nakano Glenn, "From Servitude to Service Work: Historical Continuities in the Racial Division of Paid Reproductive Labor," *Signs* 18, no. 1 (1992): 1–43; Dorothy E. Roberts, "Spiritual and Menial Housework," *Yale Journal of Law & Feminism* 9, no. 1 (1997): 51–80.

33. Gabriel Winant, *The Next Shift: The Fall of Industry and the Rise of Health Care in Rust Belt America* (Cambridge: Harvard University Press, 2021).

34. Tanja Aho, "Neoliberalism, Racial Capitalism, and Liberal Democracy: Challenging an Emergent Critical Analytic," *Lateral* 6.1 (2017).

35. Laura Briggs, *How All Politics Became Reproductive Politics: From Welfare Reform to Foreclosure to Trump* (Oakland, University of California Press, 2017), 11. The same is true for the Global South. Alessandra Mezzadri, Susan Newman & Sara Stevano, "Feminist Global Political Economies of Work and Social Reproduction," *Review of International Political Economy* (2021): 1–21; see Newman Mezzadri and Alessandra Stevano Mezzadri, "Social Reproduction and Pandemic Neoliberalism: Planetary Crises and the Reorganisation of Life, Work and Death," *Organization* 29, no. 3 (May 2022): 379–400.

36. Susan Ferguson, *Women and Work: Feminism, Labour, and Social Reproduction* (London: Pluto Press, 2020); Nancy Fraser, "Contradictions of Capitalism and Care," *New Left Review* 100 (2016): 99–117; *Social Reproduction Theory: Remapping Class, Recentering Oppression*, ed. by Tithi Bhattacharya (London: Pluto Press, 2017). Salar Mohandesi and Emma Teitelman have suggested moving away from production to social reproduction as a starting point for our analysis. See Salar Mohandesi, Emma Teitelman, and Lise Vogel,

"Without Reserves," in *Social Reproduction Theory: Remapping Class, Recentering Oppression*, ed. by Tithi Bhattacharya (London: Pluto Press, 2017), 37–67.

37. Fraser, "Contradictions of Capitalism and Care," 99.

38. Fraser, "Contradictions of Capitalism and Care," 117.

39. Eric Eustace Williams, *Capitalism and Slavery* (London: A. Deutsch, 1944); Robin Blackburn, *The Making of New World Slavery: From the Baroque to the Modern, 1492–1800* (London: Verso, 1997); Walter Johnson, *Soul by Soul: Life Inside the Antebellum Market* (Cambridge: Harvard University Press, 1999); Sharon Ann Murphy, "Securing Human Property: Slavery, Life Insurance and Industrialization in the Upper South," *The Journal of the Early Republic* 25, no. 4 (2005): 615–652.

40. This assumption underlies the work of Nancy Fraser in particular. See Fraser, "Contradictions of Capitalism and Care."

41. Nichola De Genova, "The Legal Production of Mexican/Migrant 'Illegality'," *Latino Studies* 2, no. 2 (2004): 160–185; see also Paloma E. Villegas, "Interlocking Migrant Illegalization With Other Markers of Social Location: The Experiences of Mexican Migrants Moving and Working in Toronto," *Women's Studies International Forum* 48, (2015): 185–193.

42. Ruth Wilson Gilmore, *Golden Gulag: Prisons, Surplus, Crisis, and Opposition in Globalization in California* (Berkeley: University of California Press, 2007).

43. Caroline Isaacs, "Treatment Industrial Complex: How For-Profit Prison Corporations are Undermining Efforts to Treat and Rehabilitate Prisoners for Corporate Gain," published by the American Friends Service Committee, November 2014.

44. Fraser, "Contradictions of Capitalism and Care."

Chapter 3

1. Asha Banerjee, Katherine deCourcy, Kyle K. Moore, and Julia Wolfe, "Domestic Workers Chartbook," Economic Policy Institute, November 22, 2022, https://www.epi.org/publication/domestic-workers-chartbook-2022.

2. Bridget Anderson, *Doing the Dirty Work? The Global Politics of Domestic Labour* (London: Zed Books, 2000); Grace Chang, *Disposal Domestics: Immigrant Women Workers in the Global Economy* (Boston: South End Press, 2000); Angela Davis, *Women, Race, and Class*

(New York: Vintage Books, 1981); Bonnie Thornton Dill, *Across the Boundaries of Race and Class: An Exploration of Work and Family Among Black Female Domestic Servants* (New York: Garland, 1994); Keona Ervin, *Gateway to Equality: Black Women and the Struggle for Economic Justice in St. Louis* (Lexington: University Press of Kentucky, 2017); Palmer, *Domesticity and Dirt*; Thavolia Glymph, *Out of the House of Bondage: The Transformation of the Plantation Household* (Cambridge: Cambridge University Press, 2003); Terry Repak, *Waiting on Washington: Central American Workers in the Nation's Capital* (Philadelphia: Temple University Press, 1995); Victoria K. Haskins, *Matrons and Maids: Regulating Indian Domestic Service in Tucson, 1914–1934* (Tucson: University of Arizona Press, 2012); Rachel Salazar Parrenas, *Servants of Globalization: Women, Migration and Domestic Work* (Stanford University Press, 2001); Pierrette Hondagneu-Sotelo, *Doméstica: Immigrant Workers Cleaning and Caring in the Shadows of Affluence* (Los Angeles: University of California Press, 2001); Tera Hunter, *To 'Joy My Freedom: Southern Black Women's Lives and Labors after the Civil War* (Cambridge: Harvard University Press, 1998); Danielle T. Phillips-Cunningham, *Putting Their Hands on Race: Irish Immigrant and Southern Black Domestic Workers* (New Brunswick: Rutgers University Press, 2020); Peggie R Smith, "Regulating Paid Household Work: Class, Gender, Race and Agendas of Reform," *American University Law Review* 48, no. 4 (1999): 851–923; Andrew Urban, *Brokering Servitude: Migration and the Politics of Domestic Labor During the Long Nineteenth Century* (New York: New York University Press, 2017).

3. Victoria Haskins, *Matrons and Maids: Regulating Domestic Service in Tucson, 1914-1934* (Tucson: University of Arizona Press, 2012); Victoria Haskins and Claire Lowrie, *Colonization and Domestic Service: Historical and Contemporary Perspectives* (New York: Routledge, 2015); Margaret D. Jacobs, *White Mother to a Dark Race: Settler Colonialism, Maternalism, and the Removal of Indigenous Children in the American West, 1880–1940* (Lincoln: University of Nebraska Press, 2009).

4. Leonard C. Lewin, notarized statement, December 20, 1946, section 4, Presidente del Senado, series 2, Gobierno Ensular, subseries 9B, Employment and Migration Bureau, folder 277, document 17, Archivo Histórico Fundación Luis Muñoz Marín, San Juan, Puerto Rico.

5. Carmen Isales, draft, "Report on the Cases of Puerto Rican

Laborers Brought to Chicago to Work as Domestics and Foundry Workers Under Contract with Castle, Barton and Associates," March 22, 1947, section 4, Presidente del Senado, series 2, Gobierno Ensular, subseries 9B, Employment and Migration Bureau, folder 277, document 16, Archivo Histórico Fundación Luis Muñoz Marín.

6. Emma Amador, "Linked Histories of Welfare, Labor and Puerto Rican Migration," *Modern American History* 2 (2019): 165–168. For more on Puerto Rican domestic worker migration, see Nicolas De Genova and Ana Y. Ramos-Zayas, "Latino Rehearsals: Racialization and the Politics of Citizenship Between Mexicans and Puerto Ricans in Chicago," *Journal of Latin American Anthropology* 8, no. 2 (June 2003): 18–57; Edwin Maldonado, "Contract Labor and the Origins of Puerto Rican Communities in the United States," *International Migration Review* 13, no. 1 (Spring 1979): 103–21; Lilia Fernandez, "Of Immigrants and Migrants: Mexican and Puerto Rican Labor Migration in Comparative Perspective, 1942–1964," *Journal of American Ethnic History* 29, no. 3 (Spring 2010); Maura I. Toro-Morn, "A Historical Overview of the Work Experiences of Puerto Rican Women in Chicago," *Centro Journal* 13, no. 2 (Fall 2001): 24–43.

7. Jennifer Morgan, *Laboring Women: Reproduction and Gender in New World Slavery* (Philadelphia: University of Pennsylvania Press, 2004); Deborah Gray White, *Ar'n't I a Woman? Female Slaves in the Plantation South* (New York: W.W. Norton & Company, 1999); Thavolia Glymph, *Out of the House of Bondage: The Transformation of the Plantation Household* (Cambridge: Cambridge University Press, 2003).

8. Priya Kandaswamy, *Domestic Contradictions: Gendered Citizenship from Reconstruction to Welfare Reform* (Durham: Duke University Press, 2021).

9. Kandaswamy, *Domestic Contradictions*, 129.

10. Sarah Haley, *No Mercy Here: Gender, Punishment, and the Making of Jim Crow Modernity* (Chapel Hill: University of North Carolina Press, 2016), chapter 4.

11. Haley, *No Mercy Here*, 158.

12. Haley, *No Mercy Here*, 177.

13. Hannah Enobong Branch and Melissa E. Wooten, "Suited for Service: Racialized Rationalizations for the Ideal Domestic Servant from the Nineteenth to the Early Twentieth Century," *Social*

Science History 36, no. 2 (2012): 169–89.

14. Danielle T. Phillips-Cunningham, *Putting Their Hands on Race: Irish Immigrant and Southern Black Domestic Workers* (New Brunswick: Rutgers University Press, 2020).

15. David Roediger, *The Wages of Whiteness: Race and the Making of the American Working Class* (London: Verso, 1991); Noel Ignatiev, *How the Irish Became White* (New York: Routledge, 1995).

16. Andrew Urban, *Brokering Servitude: Migration and the Politics of Domestic Servitude: Migration and the Politics of Domestic Labor During the Long Nineteenth Century* (New York: New York University Press, 2018).

17. Margaret Lynch-Brennan, Margaret, *The Irish Bridget: Irish Immigrant Women in Domestic Service in America, 1840–1930* (Syracuse: Syracuse University Press, 2009).

18. "Occupation of the Experienced Civilian Labor Force and the Labor Reserve," 1960 Census of Population, Supplementary Reports, US Census Bureau. December 31, 1962. https://www2.census.gov/library/publications/decennial/1960/pc-s1-supplementary-reports/pc-s1-40.pdf; National Academies of Sciences, Engineering, and Medicine, *America Becoming: Racial Trends and Their Consequences: Volume II* (Washington, DC: National Academies Press, 2001), 127. https://nap.nationalacademies.org/read/9719/chapter/7#127.

19. Evelyn Nakano Glenn, "From Servitude to Service Work: Historical Continuities in the Racial Division of Paid Reproductive Labor," *Signs: Journal of Women in Culture and Society* 18, no. 1 (Autumn 1992): 1–43.

20. Ella Baker and Marvel Cooke, "The Slave Market," *The Crisis* 42 (1935).

21. Geraldine Roberts, interview by Donna Van Raaphorst, Cleveland, OH, March 30–June 29, 1977, p. 71, Program on Women and Work, Institute of Labor and Industrial Relations, University of Michigan, Reuther Library, Wayne State University, Detroit, MI.

22. Sarah Haley, *No Mercy Here: Gender, Punishment, and the Making of Jim Crow Modernity* (Chapel Hill: University of North Carolina, 2016); Evelyn Nakano Glenn, "From Servitude to Service Work: Historical Continuities in the Racial Division of Paid Reproductive Labor," *Signs: Journal of Women in Culture and Society* 18, no. 1 (Autumn 1992): 1–43; Andrew Urban, *Brokering Servitude: Migration and the Politics of Domestic Labor During the Long Nineteenth*

Century (New York: New York University Press, 2018).

23. Asha Banerjee, Katherine DeCourcy, Kyle K. Moore, and Julia Wolfe "Domestic Workers Chartbook, 2022" Economic Policy Institute, November 22, 2022. https://www.epi.org/publication/domestic-workers-chartbook-2022/.

24. Cati Coe, *The New American Servitude: Political Belonging among African American Immigrant Home Care Workers* (New York: New York University Press, 2019), 45. Sociologist Judith Rollins relies on Nietzsche's concept of *ressentiment*, to describe domestic workers' "long-term, seething, deep-rooted negative feeling toward those whom one feels unjustly have power or an advantage over one's life." See Judith Rollins, *Between Women: Domestics and Their Employers* (Philadelphia: Temple University Press, 1985), 227.

25. Coe, *The New American Servitude.*

26. Urban, *Brokering Servitude.*

27. Robyn M. Rodriguez, *Migrants for Export.*

28. Commission on Filipinos Overseas, "Philippine Migration at a Glance," Office of the President of the Philippines, https://cfo.gov.ph/statistics-2/.

29. 2021 Overseas Filipino Workers, Philippine Statistics Authority, December 2, 2022. https://psa.gov.ph/statistics/survey/labor-and-employment/survey-overseas-filipinos.

30. Robyn M. Rodriguez, *Migrants for Export;* Valerie Francisco-Menchavez, *The Labor of Care*; Parreñas, *Servants of Globalization*; Neferti Xina M. Tadiar, *Things Fall Away: Philippine Historical Experience and the Makings of Globalization* (Durham: Duke University Press, 2009); Nicole Constable, *Made to Order in Hong Kong: Stories of Migrant Workers* (Cornell University Press, 1997).

31. Fruhlein Chrys Econar, "For Generations, Filipino Nurses Have Been on America's Front Lines," *CNN,* October 8, 2021, https://www.cnn.com/interactive/2021/10/health/filipino-nurses-cnn-photos.

32. Daniel Costa, "As the H-2B Visa Program Grows, the Need for Reforms That Protect Workers Is Greater Than Ever," Economic Policy Institute, August 18, 2022, https://www.epi.org/publication/h-2b-industries-and-wage-theft/.

33. Grace Chang, *Disposal Domestics: Immigrant Women Workers in the Global Economy* (Boston: South End Press, 2000).

34. During the first decades of the twentieth century, when the border between the US and Mexico was open, Mexicans easily trav-

eled back and forth. They were welcomed into the US as laborers, especially after the passage of the restrictive 1924 immigration law, which did not apply to the Western Hemisphere. During the Great Depression when demand for labor waned, the Border Patrol rounded up what some estimate to be 2 million Mexicans and Mexicans Americans (who were US citizens) and sent them to Mexico. When there was another labor shortage during World War II, the Bracero Program, a formal labor migration agreement between the US and Mexico, arranged for Mexican workers to labor on a temporary basis. Between 1942 and 1964, 4.6 million contract workers, mostly men doing agricultural work, entered the US.

35. "Number of US Contingent Workers Totals 51.5 Million; Temps Assigned by Staffing Firms at 8.5 Million: SIA Report," August 25, 2021. https://www2.staffingindustry.com/Editorial/Daily-News/Number-of-US-contingent-workers-totals-51.5-million-temps-assigned-by-staffing-firms-at-8.5-million-SIA-report-58836.

36. Glenn, *Forced to Care*.

37. Glenn, *Forced to Care*.

38. Elain Tyler May, *Homeward Bound: American Families in the Cold War Era* (New York: Basic Books, 1988).

39. Aditya Aladangady and Akila Forde, "Wealth Inequality and the Racial Gap," *Fed Notes*, Board of Governors of the Federal Reserve System, October 22, 2021. https://www.federalreserve.gov/econres/notes/feds-notes/wealth-inequality-and-the-racial-wealth-gap-20211022.html#:~:text=In%20the%20United%20States%2C%20the,percent%20as%20much%20net%20wealth.

Chapter 4

1.   Katharyne Mitchell, Sallie A. Marston, and Cindi Katz, *Life's Work: Geographies of Social Reproduction* (Chichester: Blackwell Publishing Inc., 2004. For examples of nontraditional labor struggles, see Chana Kai Lee, *For Freedom's Sake: The Life of Fannie Lou Hamer* (Urbana: University of Illinois, 1999); Ronald Lawson and Mark Naison, *Tenant Movement in New York City, 1904–1984* (New Brunswick: Rutgers University Press, 1986); Lana Dee Povitz, *How Activist New Yorkers Ignited a Movement for Food Justice* (Chapel Hill: University of North Carolina Press, 2019); Emily E.

LB. Twarog, *Politics of the Pantry: Housewives, Food, and Consumer Protest in Twentieth Century America* (New York: Oxford University Press, 2017); Dana Frank, *Purchasing Power: Consumer Organizing, Gender, and the Seattle Labor Movement, 1919–1929* (Cambridge: Cambridge University Press, 1994); Dorothy Sue Cobble, *The Other Women's Movement* (Princeton: Princeton University Press, 2004).

2. See for example: Cinzia Arruzza, Tithi Bhattacharya, and Nancy Fraser, *Feminism for the 99%: A Manifesto* (New York: Verso Books, 2019); Salar Mohandesi, Emma Teitelman, and Lise Vogel, "Without Reserves," in *Social Reproduction Theory: Remapping Class, Recentering Oppression*, ed. Tithi Bhattacharya (London: Pluto Press, 2017): 37–67; Susan Ferguson, *Women and Work: Feminism, Labour, and Social Reproduction* (London: Pluto, 2020); Fraser, "Contradictions of Capitalism and Care"; Bhattacharya, *Social Reproduction Theory*.

3. Louise Thompson Patterson, "Toward a Brighter Dawn," *Woman Today* (April 1936); Esther V. Cooper, "The Negro Woman Domestic Worker in Relation to Trade Unionism," masters thesis, Fisk University, 1940; Claudia Jones, "An End to the Neglect of the Problems of the Negro Woman!," *Political Affairs* (June 1949), reprint, National Women's Commission, CPUSA.

4. For examples of this new labor organizing, see Sarah Jaffe, *Necessary Trouble: Americans in Revolt* (New York: Bold Type Books, 2016); Annelise Orleck, *We Are All Fast-Food Workers Now: The Global Uprising Against Poverty Wages* (Boston: Beacon Press, 2018); Jennifer Gordon, *Suburban Sweatshops: The Fight for Immigrant Rights* (Cambridge, MA: Belknap Press, 2005): Ruth Milkman, *L.A. Story: Immigrant Workers and the Future of the U.S. Labor Movement* (New York: Russell Sage, 2006); Vanessa Tait, *Poor Workers' Unions: Rebuilding Labor From Below* (Cambridge, MA: South End Press, 2005).

5. Robin D. G. Kelley, *Hammer and Hoe: Alabama Communists during the Great Depression* (Chapel Hill: the University of North Carolina Press, 2015); Robin D. G. Kelley, *Race Rebels: Culture, Politics, and the Black Working Class* (New York: Simon & Schuster, 1996); Robin D. G. Kelley, *Yo' Mama's Disfunctional: Fighting the Culture Wars in Urban America* (Boston: Beacon Press, 1998).

6. Robin D. G. Kelley, *Race Rebels: Culture, Politics, and the Black Working Class* (New York: Simon & Schuster, 1996); Tera Hunter, *To 'Joy My Freedom: Southern Black Women's Lives and Labors after the*

Civil War (Cambridge, MA: Harvard University Press, 1998); Elizabeth Clark-Lewis, *Living In, Living Out: African American Domestics and the Great Migration* (New York: Kodansha America, 1996); Emma Amador, "Organizing Puerto Rican Domestics: Resistance and Household Labor Reform in the Puerto Rican Diaspora after 1930," *International Labor and Working-Class History* 8 (Fall 2015): 67–86; Brown, Raising Brooklyn; Bonnie Thornton Dill, *Across the Boundaries of Race and Class: An Exploration of Work and Family Among Black Female Domestic Servants* (New York: Garland, 1994); Premilla Nadasen, *Household Workers Unite: the Untold Story of African-American Women Who Built a Movement* (Boston: Beacon Press, 2015); Eileen Boris and Premilla Nadasen, "Domestic Workers Organize!" *Working USA: The Journal of Labor and Society*, vol. 11 (December 2008): 413–437; Vanessa May, *Unprotected Labor: Household Workers, Politics, and Middle-Class Reform in New York City, 1870–1940* (Chapel Hill: University of North Carolina Press, 2011); Donna L. Van Raaphorst, *Union Maids Not Wanted: Organizing Domestic Workers, 1870–1940* (New York: Praeger, 1988); Mary Romero, *Maid in the U.S.A.* (New York: Routledge, 1992); Keona K. Ervin, *Gateway to Equality: Black Women and the Struggle for Economic Justice in St. Louis* (University Press of Kentucky, 2017); Peggie Smith, "Organizing the Unorganizable: Private Paid Household Workers and Approaches to Employee Representation," *North Carolina Law Review* 79 (2000): 45–110; Esther V. Cooper, "The Negro Woman Domestic Worker in Relation to Trade Unionism"(MA thesis, Fisk University, 1940).

7.   Hunter, *To 'Joy My Freedom.*
8.   Elizabeth Clark-Lewis, Living In, Living Out: African American Domestics and the Great Migration (New York: Kodansha America, 1996).
9.   Cooper, "The Negro Woman Domestic Worker in Relation to Trade Unionism"; Vanessa May, *Unprotected Labor: Household Workers, Politics, and Middle-Class Reform in New York City, 1870–1940* (Chapel Hill: University of North Carolina Press, 2011).
10. Romero, *Maid in the U.S.A.*
11. Nadasen, *Household Workers Unite.*
12. Premilla Nadasen, "Power, Intimacy, and Contestation: Dorothy Bolden and Domestic Worker Organizing in Atlanta in the 1960s," in *Intimate Labors: Cultures, Technologies, and the Politics of Care*, ed. Eileen Boris and Rhacel Salazar Parreñas (Stanford:

Stanford Social Sciences, 2010), 204–16; Premilla Nadasen, "Citizenship Rights, Domestic Work, and the Fair Labor Standards Act," *Journal of Policy History* 24, no. 1 (January 2012): 74–94; Nadasen, *Household Workers Unite.*

13. Peggie R. Smith, "Regulating Paid Household Work: Class, Gender, Race, and Agendas of Reform," *American University Law Review* 48, no. 4: 851–923; Nadasen, "Citizenship Rights, Domestic Work, and the Fair Labor Standards Act"; Phyllis Palmer, "Outside the Law: Agricultural and Domestic Workers Under the Fair Labor Standards Act," *Journal of Policy History* 7, no. 4 (1995): 416–40. Mary Poole, *The Segregated Origins of Social Security: African Americans and the Welfare State* (Chapel Hill: University of North Carolina Press, 2006); Ira Katznelson, *Fear Itself: The New Deal and the Origins of Our Time* (New York: Liveright, 2013); Eileen Boris, "The Racialized Gendered State: Constructions of Citizenship in the United States," *Social Politics: International Studies in Gender, State and Society* 2, no. 2 (Summer 1995): 160–80.

14. Statement of Mrs. Edith Barksdale Sloan, executive director, and Mrs. Josephine Hulett, field officer, National Committee on Household Employment (NCHE), *Hearings Before the General Subcommittee on Labor, Committee on Education and Labor, on HR 10948,* August 13, 1970, p. 3, NCHE Records, series 003, subseries 01, box 11, folder 06, National Archives for Black Women's History, Mary McLeod Bethune Council House National Historic Site, Landover, MD.

15. Ron Chernow, "All in a Day's Work," *Mother Jones,* August 1976, 11.

16. NCHE, "Minimum Wage Coverage for Domestics: At Last!!!," press release, April 8, 1974, NCHE Records, Series 003, Subseries 01, box 11, folder 7.

17. Josephine Hulett, interview by Janet Dewart, "Household Help Wanted: Female," *Ms.,* February 1973, 46.

18. Christine Lewis, "A Little Tattle-Tale Around the Nannying Gig," in *Alien Nation: 36 True Tales of Immigration,* ed. Sofija Stefanovic, (New York: HarperVia Publisher, 2021), 100–109. Quote on p.103.

19. Christine Lewis, interview by author via Zoom, February 21, 2022.

20. Christine Lewis, interview by author via Zoom, February 21, 2022.

21. Lewis, *Alien Nation,* 104.

22. Lewis, *Alien Nation,* 108.

23. Christine Lewis, interview by author via Zoom, February 21, 2022.

24. Christine Lewis, interview by author via Zoom, February 21, 2022.
25. Christine Lewis, interview by author via Zoom, February 21, 2022.
26. Linda Oalican, interview by Isabel Terracciano, November 1, 2018.
27. Linda Oalican, interview by Isabel Terracciano, November 1, 2018.
28. Premilla Nadasen, "Sista Friends and Other Allies: Domestic Workers United and Coalition Politics" in *New Social Movements in the African Diaspora: Challenging Global Apartheid,* ed. Leith Mullings (New York: Palgrave Macmillan, 2009).
29. Ai-Jen Poo, interview by author, September 28, 2007.
30. Erline Browne, interview by author, New York City, April 1, 2008.
31. C189-Domestic Workers Convention, 2011, International Labour Organization, https://www.ilo.org/dyn/normlex/en/f?p=NORMLEXPUB:12100:0::NO::P12100_ILO_CODE:C189.
32. Jennifer Natalie Fish, *Domestic Workers of the World Unite: A Global Movement for Dignity and Human Rights* (New York: New York University Press, 2017).
33. Nadasen, *Household Workers Unite*; Pierrette Hondagneu-Sotelo, *Domestica: Immigrant Workers Cleaning and Caring in the Shadows of Influence* (Berkeley: University of California Press, 2001); Grace Chang, *Disposable Domestics: Immigrant Women Workers in the Global Economy* (Cambridge: South End Press, 2000); Vanessa Tait, *Poor Workers Union: Rebuilding Labor From Below* (Cambridge: South End Press, 2005); Monisha Das Gupta, *Unruly Immigrants: Rights, Activism, and Transnational South Asian Politics in the United States* (Durham: Duke University Press, 2006); Premilla Nadasen, "Sista Friends and Other Allies: Domestic Workers United and Coalition Politics," in *New Social Movements in the African Diaspora: Challenging Global Apartheid*, ed. Leith Mullings (New York, Palgrave Macmillan, 2009), 285–298.
34. Jennifer Gordon, *Suburban Sweatshops* (Cambridge: Harvard University Press, 2005); Janice Fine, *Worker Centers: Organizing Communities at the Edge of the Dream* (Ithaca: Cornell University Press, 2006).
35. Cobble, *The Other Women's Movement*; Joshua Freeman, *Working-Class New York: Life and Labor Since World War II* (New York: New Press, 2001); Karen Brodkin, *Caring by the Hour: Women, Work and Organizing at Duke Medical Center* (Urbana: University of Illinois Press, 1987).
36. Eileen Boris and Jennifer Klein, *Home Health Workers in the Shad-*

ow of the Welfare State (Oxford: Oxford University Press, 2012).

37. For an excellent discussion of the CTU in the context of neoliberalism, see Rose M. Brewer, "21st-Century Capitalism, Austerity, and Black Economic Dispossession," *Souls: A Critical Journal of Black Politics, Culture, and Society*, vol. 14, no. 3–4 (2012): 227–239.

38. Saru Jayaraman, *Behind the Kitchen Door* (Ithaca: ILR Press, 2013); Vanessa Tait, *Poor Workers Union: Rebuilding Labor From Below* (Cambridge: South End Press, 2005).

39. Cinzia Arruzza, Tithi Bhattacharya, and Nancy Fraser, *Feminism for the 99%: A Manifesto* (New York: Verso Books, 2019). Maud Perrier uses the framework of "maternal worker" to make an argument about potential cross race and class solidarity among paid and unpaid childcare workers. See Maud Perrier, *Childcare Struggles, Maternal Workers, and Social Reproduction* (Bristol: Bristol University Press, 2022).

40. Annelise Orleck, *We Are All Fast Food Workers Now: The Global Uprising Against Poverty Wages* (Boston: Beacon Press, 2018).

41. Louise Toupin, *Wages for Housework: A History of an International Feminist Movement, 1972–77* (London: Pluto Press, 2018).

42. Silvia Federici, *Wages Against Housework*; Mariarosa Dalla Costa and Selma James, *The Power of Women and the Subversion of the Community* (Bristol: Falling Wall Press, 1972). Power of Women was originally published as a pamphlet in 1972.

43. Costa and James, *The Power of Women and the Subversion of the Community*.

44. Federici, *Wages Against Housework*, 3.

45. Federici, *Wages Against Housework*, 4

46. Federici, *Wages Against Housework*, 6.

47. Costa and James, *The Power of Women and the Subversion of the Community*, 36.

48. For a critique of the Wages for Housework movement, see Angela Davis, *Women, Race and Class* (New York: Penguin Random House, 1981).

49. Nadasen, *Welfare Warriors*, Annelise Orleck, *Storming Caesar's Palace: How Black Mothers Fought Their Own War on Poverty* (Boston: Beacon Press, 2005); Mary Eleanor Triece, *Tell It Like It Is: Women in the National Welfare Rights Movement* (Columbia SC: University of South Carolina Press, 2013). Rosie C. Bermudez, "Recovering Histories: Alicia Escalante and the Chicana Welfare Rights Organization, 1967–1974" (PhD dissertation, California

State University, 2010); Wilson Sherwin, "'Nothing but Joy': The Welfare Rights Movement's Antiwork Freedom Dream," *Souls: A Critical Journal of Black Politics, Culture and Society* 22, no. 2–4 (2020): 185–212; Frances Fox Piven and Richard Cloward, *Poor People's Movements: Why They Succeed, How They Fail* (New York: Vintage, 1978). Guida West, *The National Welfare Rights Movement: The Social Protest of Poor Women* (New York: Praeger, 1981); Martha F. Davis, *Brutal Need: Lawyers and the Welfare Rights Movement, 1960–1973*, new ed. (New Haven, CT: Yale University Press, 1995); Jacqueline Pope, *Biting the Hand That Feeds Them: Organizing Women on Welfare at the Grass Roots Level* (New York: Praeger, 1989); Felicia Ann Kornbluh, *The Battle for Welfare Rights: Politics and Poverty in Modern America* (Philadelphia: University of Pennsylvania Press, 2007); Lawrence Neil Bailis, *Bread or Justice: Grassroots Organizing in the Welfare Rights Movement* (Lexington, MA: Lexington Books, 1974).

50. Johnnie Tillmon, "Welfare is a Woman's Issue," *Ms.* 1 (Spring 1972): 111–116.

51. Nadasen, *Welfare Warriors*, chapter 7; Marisa Chappell, *The War on Welfare: Family, Poverty, and Politics in Modern America* (Philadelphia: University of Pennsylvania Press, 2012); Bermudez, "Recovering Histories"; Sherwin, "'Nothing But Joy.'"

52. For examples of universal basic income, see Annie Lowrey, *Give People Money: How a Universal Basic Income Would End Poverty, Revolutionize Work, and Remake the World* (New York: Crown, 2018); Andy Stern, *Raising the Floor, How a Universal Basic Income Can Renew Our Economy and Rebuild the American Dream* (New York: Public Affairs, 2016).

53. Melody Webb, "Building a Guaranteed Income to End the 'Child Welfare' System," *Columbia Journal of Race and Law* 12, no. 1 (July 2022): 668–687; Halah Ahmad, Stephen Nuñez, with Saru Jayaraman, "The Political Economy of Guaranteed Income: Where Do We Go From Here?" Jain Family Institute, August 2022.

54. Almaz Zelleke, "Feminist Political Theory and the Argument for an Unconditional Basic Income," *Policy and Politics* 39 (2011): 27–42.

55. Rhonda Y. Williams, *The Politics of Public Housing: Black Women's Struggles Against Urban Inequality* (Oxford: Oxford University Press, 2004).

56. Orleck, *Storming Caesar's Palace.*

57. George Caffentzis and Silvia Federici, "Commons against and beyond capitalism," *Community Development Journal* 49, suppl. 1 (January 2014): 101.

58. Silvia Federici, *Wages Against Housework*, 7.

Chapter 5

1. Sandra Killett, interview by author via Zoom, February 13, 2022.

2. Care for All Agenda 2021, H.R. 1, 117th Congress (March 1, 2021).

3. U.S. Congress, House Ways and Means Committee, Background Material and Data on Programs within the Jurisdiction of the Committee on Ways and Means, 1986 Edition (Washington, DC: Government Printing Office, 1986), 392.

4. "The Mystery of Rising Relief Costs," *U.S. News and World Report*, March 8, 1965.

5. Ange-Marie Hancock, *The Politics of Disgust: The Public Identity of the Welfare Queen* (New York: New York University Press, 2004).

6. Lisa Levenstein, *A Movement Without Marches: African American Women and the Politics of Poverty in Postwar Philadelphia* (Chapel Hill: University of North Carolina Press, 2009); Jennifer Mittelstadt, Marisa Chappell, *Welfare in the United States: A History With Documents, 1935–1996* (New York: Routledge 2009).

7. Roger A. Freeman, "Wayward Ambitions of the Welfare State," *New York Times*, December 4, 1971; see Chappell, *The War on Welfare*; Levenstein, *A Movement Without Marches*.

8. For broader historical context of this shift, see Mittelstadt, *Welfare to Workfare*.

9. Diana Azevedo-Mccaffrey and Ali Safawi, "To Promote Basic Equity, States Should Invest More TANF Dollars in Basic Assistance," Center on Budget and Policy Priorities, January 12, 2022, https://www.cbpp.org/research/family-income-support/to-promote-equity-states-should-invest-more-tanf-dollars-in-basic-0.

10. For an overview of policies see Maggie McCarty, Randy Alison Aussenberg, and Gene Falk, "Drug Testing and Crime-Related Restrictions in TANF, SNAP, and Housing Assistance," Congressional Research Service, July 2013; LaDonna Pavetti, "TANF Studies Show Work Requirement Proposals for Other Programs Would Harm Millions, Do Little to Increase Work," Center on Budget and Policy Priorities, November 2018; Jess Mador, "Geor-

gia Lawmakers to Consider Full Medicaid Expansion During the Legislative Session," WABE, January 13, 2023; "Understanding Georgia's New Medicaid Work Requirement Program," Early County News, December 27, 2022. https://www.earlycountynews.com/articles/understanding-georgias-new-medicaid-work-requirement-program/.

11. Loic Wacquant, *Punishing the Poor: The Neoliberal Government of Social Insecurity* (Durham: Duke University Press, 2009); Julilly Kohler-Hausmann, *Getting Tough: Welfare and Imprisonment in 1970s America* (Princeton, NJ: Princeton University Press, 2017); Genevieve LeBaron and Adrienne Roberts, "Confining Social Insecurity: Neoliberalism and the Rise of the 21st Century Debtors' Prison," *Politics and Gender* 8, no. 1 (March 2012); Dorothy E. Roberts, *Shattered Bonds: The Color of Child Welfare* (New York: Basic Books, 2001); Kaaryn S. Gustafson, *Cheating Welfare: Public Assistance and the Criminalization of Poverty* (New York: NYU Press, 2011).

12. "Caseload Data 1995 (AFDC Total)," Office of Family Assistance, Administration for Children and Families, Department of Health and Human Services, December 19, 2004, https://www.acf.hhs.gov/ofa/data/caseload-data-1995-afdc-total.

13. Elizabeth Hinton, *From the War on Poverty to the War on Crime: The Making of Mass Incarceration in America* (Cambridge: Harvard University Press, 2016); Ruth Wilson Gilmore, *Golden Gulag: Prisons, Surplus, Crisis, and Opposition in Globalization in California* (Berkeley: University of California Press, 2007); Michelle Alexander, *The New Jim Crow: Mass Incarceration in the Age of Colorblindness* (New York, The New Press, 2012).

14. Dorothy Roberts, *Torn Apart: How the Child Welfare System Destroys Black Families—and How Abolition Can Build a Safer World* (New York: Basic Books, 2022), 39.

15. Emily Putnam-Hornstein, et al., "Cumulative Rates of Child Protection Involvement and Terminations of Parental Rights in a California Birth Cohort, 1999–2017," *American Journal of Public Health* 111 (2021): 1157–1163.

16. Dorothy E. Roberts, "Child Protection as Surveillance of African American Families," *Journal of Social Welfare and Family Law* 36, no. 4 (November 2014): 426–437.

17. Dorothy E. Roberts, "Prison, Foster Care, and the Systemic Punishment of Black Mothers," *UCLA Law Review* 59 (2012):

1474-1502.

18. US Department of Labor, *Employee and Worksite Perspectives of the Family and Medical Leave Act: Results from the 2018 Surveys* (Rockville: ABT Associates, July 2020), https://www.dol.gov/sites/dolgov/files/OASP/evaluation/pdf/WHD_FMLA2018SurveyResults_FinalReport_Aug2020.pdf.

19. Kalee Burns and Liana E. Fox, "The Impact of the 2021 Expanded Child Tax Credit on Child Poverty," Social, Economic, and Housing Statistics Division, US Census Bureau, https://www.census.gov/library/working-papers/2022/demo/SEHSD-wp2022-24.html#:~:text=This%20paper%20examines%20the%20impact,lifted%20above%20the%20poverty%20line.

20. Elaine Maag, "Options to Improve the Child Tax Credit for Low-Income Families" Tax Policy Center, December 14, 2022, https://www.taxpolicycenter.org/taxvox/options-improve-child-tax-credit-low-income-families.

21. Kirsten Swinth, *Feminism's Forgotten Fight: The Unfinished Struggle for Work and Family* (Cambridge: Harvard University Press, 2018). Anna Danziger examines why organizations such as NOW did not advocate a comprehensive vision of childcare that prioritized the needs of poor women; see Anna Klein Danziger Halperin, "An Unrequited Labor of Love: Child Care and Feminism," *Signs* 45, no. 4 (Summer 2020): 1011–1034.

22. Simon Black, *Social Reproduction and the City: Welfare Reform, Child Care, and Resistance in Neoliberal New York* (University of Georgia Press, 2020) tells the story of the struggle for quality day care and decent pay for childcare providers in New York City in the wake of welfare reform.

23. Anne Branigin, "Some Child-care Workers at Google Live up to 50 Miles Away. The Company Is Calling Them Back with No Transportation Plans," *The Lily*, May 20, 2021, https://www.thelily.com/some-child-care-workers-at-google-live-up-to-50-miles-away-the-company-is-calling-them-back-with-no-transportation-plans/; "Living Wage Calculator," Massachusetts Institute of Technology, https://livingwage.mit.edu/; Amy K. Glasmeier and the Massachusetts Institute of Technology, "Living Wage Calculation for Santa Clara County, California," 2022, https://livingwage.mit.edu/counties/06085.

24. Branigin, "Some Child-care Workers at Google Live up to 50 Miles Away."

25. Sheryl Sandberg, *Lean In: Women, Work, and the Will to Lead* (London: W. H. Allen, 2015).

26. Anne Marie Slaughter, *Unfinished Business: Women, Men, Work, Family* (New York: Random House, 2016). For a critique of what Hester Eisenstein calls hegemonic feminism, see Hester Eisenstein, *Feminism Seduced: How Global Elites Use Women's Labor and Ideas to Exploit the World* (New York: Routledge, 2010). There is a rich history of how feminists, including some of the socialist-feminists I discuss, sought to provide support for working women. See Swinth, *Feminism's Forgotten Fight*.

27. Avery Hartmans, "Free Childcare, Flexible Schedules, and Months Off: How Silicon Valley Is Switching Up Lavish In-office Perks to Benefit Parents Working from Home," *Business Insider*, October 1, 2020, https://www.businessinsider.com/silicon-valley-parenting-perks-benefits-coronavirus-pandemic-google-facebook-amazon-2020-10.

28. Billy Perrigo, "Inside Facebook's African Sweatshop," *Time*, February 14, 2022, https://time.com/6147458/facebook-africa-content-moderation-employee-treatment/.

29. Julia Carrie Wong, "Revealed: Google Illegally Underpaid Thousands of Workers Across Dozens of Counties," *Guardian*, September 10, 2021, https://www.theguardian.com/technology/2021/sep/10/google-underpaid-workers-illegal-pay-disparity-documents.

30. The Official Poverty Measure remains the primary way poverty is measure. But, in 2010, the Census Bureau developed a Supplemental Poverty Measure that takes into account expenditures on food, clothing, shelter and utilities, different household composition, and non-cash income. It is a more realistic assessment of need but relies on the same model of material deprivation. For a discussion, see Premilla Nadasen, Fatima Koli, Alisa Rod, David Weiman, "Mississippi Semester: A New Social Justice Approach to Teaching Empirical Reasoning in Context," *Numeracy: Advanced Education in Quantitative Literacy* 12, no. 1 (2018), and Mark Robert Rank, "Poverty in 2021 Looks Different Than in 1964 – but the US Hasn't Changed How It Measures Who's Poor Since LBJ Began His War," *The Conversation*, July 12, 2021, https://theconversation.com/poverty-in-2021-looks-different-than-in-1964-but-the-us-hasnt-changed-how-it-measures-whos-poor-since-lbj-began-his-war-163626.

31. "Living Wage Calculator," Massachusetts Institute of Technology.

32. Amartya Sen, *Development as Freedom* (New York: Oxford University Press, 1999).

33. US Census Bureau, "National Poverty in America Awareness Month: January 2023," January 2023, https://www.census.gov/newsroom/stories/poverty-awareness-month.html#:~:text=Official%20Poverty%20Measure,and%20Table%20A%2D1).

34. Premilla Nadasen, "Extreme Poverty Returns to America," *Washington Post*, December 21, 2017, https://www.washingtonpost.com/news/made-by-history/wp/2017/12/21/extreme-poverty-returns-to-america/.

35. Philip Alston, "The Parlous State of Poverty Eradication," Report of the Special Rapporteur on Extreme Poverty and Human Rights, UN Human Rights Council, 2020, https://chrgj.org/wp-content/uploads/2020/07/Alston-Poverty-Report-FINAL.pdf.

36. United Nations, "American Dream is Rapidly Becoming American Illusion,' Warns UN Rights Expert on Poverty," press release, December 15, 2017, https://www.ohchr.org/en/press-releases/2017/12/american-dream-rapidly-becoming-american-illusion-warns-un-rights-expert?LangID=E&NewsID=22546.

37. Emmanuel Saez, "Income and Wealth Inequality: Evidence and Policy Implications" in *United States Income, Wealth, Consumption, and Inequality,* ed. Diana Furchtgott-Roth (Oxford: Oxford University Press, 2020), 47–48.

38. "US Poverty Rate of Hispanic Families with a Single Mother, 1990–2021," Statista Research Department, US Census Bureau, August 2022. https://www.statista.com/statistics/205195/percentage-of-poor-hispanic-families-with-a-female-householder-in-the-us/ "U.S. Poverty Rate of Black Single Mothers 1990-2021," Statista Research Department, US Census Bureau, August 2022. https://www.statista.com/statistics/205114/percentage-of-poor-black-families-with-a-female-householder-in-the-us/ "U.S. Poverty Rate of White, non-Hispanic Single Mother Households 1990-2021" Statista Research Department, US Census Bureau, August 2022, https://www.statista.com/statistics/205049/percentage-of-poor-white-families-with-a-female-householder-in-the-us/.

39. Shengwei Sun, "National Snapshot: Poverty Among Women and Families," National Women's Law Center, January 2023, https://nwlc.org/wp-content/uploads/2023/02/2023_nwlc_PovertySnapshot-converted.pdf.

40. The Federal Reserve, "Disparities in Wealth by Race and Eth-

nicity in the 2019 Survey of Consumer Finances," Neil Bhutta, et al, September 28, 2020, https://www.federalreserve.gov/econres/notes/feds-notes/disparities-in-wealth-by-race-and-ethnicity-in-the-2019-survey-of-consumer-finances-20200928.htm.

41. Meizhu Lui, Bárbara Robles, Betsy Leondar-Wright, Rose Brewer, Rebecca Adamson, *The Color of Wealth: The Story Behind the U.S. Racial Wealth Divide* (New York: New Press, 2006).

42. Julie Pagaduan, "Millions of Americans are Housing Insecure: Rent Relief and Eviction Assistance Continue to be Critical," National Alliance to End Homelessness, November 9, 2021. https://endhomelessness.org/resource/housing-insecurity-rent-relief-eviction-assistance/.

43. Household Debt and Credit Report, Center for Microeconomic Data, Federal Reserve of New York, 2022, https://www.newyorkfed.org/microeconomics/hhdc; "Total Household Debt Reaches $16.51 Trillion in Q3 2022; Mortgage and Auto Loan Originations Decline," press release, Federal Reserve Bank of New York, November 15, 2022, https://www.newyorkfed.org/newsevents/news/research/2022/20221115.

44. Adrienne Roberts, "Financing Social Reproduction: The Gendered Relations of Debt and Mortgage Finance in Twenty-First Century America," *New Political Economy* 18, no. 1 (April 2012): 21–42.

45. https://debtcollective.org/

46. US Census Bureau, Poverty Status in the Past 12 Months, S1701, American Community Survey, Feb. 12, 2023, https://data.census.gov/table?t=Official+Poverty+Measure&g=0100000US,$0400000&tid=ACSST5Y2020.S1701.

47. The American Families Plan included assistance for pre-K, government subsidized paid family and medical leave, an extension of the pandemic child tax credit, and money for families paying for childcare.

Chapter 6

1. See reporting by Anna Wolfe in *Mississippi Today*, five-part series, April 2022, https://mississippitoday.org/author/awolfe/.

2. "Fortune 500," *Fortune*, 2022, https://fortune.com/ranking/fortune500/.

3. NHE Fact Sheet, 2021. Centers for Medicare and Medicaid Services, https://www.cms.gov/research-statistics-data-and-sys-

tems/statistics-trends-and-reports/nationalhealthexpenddata/
nhe-fact-sheet#:~:text=NHE%20grew%202.7%25%20to%20
%244.3,17%20percent%20of%20total%20NHE.

4. Key Elements of the US Tax System, Tax Policy Center Briefing Book, May 2020, https://www.taxpolicycenter.org/briefing-book/how-much-does-federal-government-spend-health-care.

5. Centers for Medicare and Medicaid Services, "CMS Office of the Actuary Releases 2019 National Health Expenditures," press release, December 16, 2020, https://www.cms.gov/newsroom/press-releases/cms-office-actuary-releases-2019-national-health-expenditures.

6. Chiara Cordelli, *The Privatized State* (Princeton: Princeton University Press, 2020). Mimi Abramovitz, "The Privatization of the Welfare State: A Review," *Social Work*, July-August 1986, 31(4): 257–264.

7. Caitlin Henry, "Time and the Social Reproduction of American Health Care," *Women's Studies International Forum* 48 (2015): 165–173.

8. "Household Health Spending Calculator," Kaiser Family Foundation, Health System Tracker. https://www.healthsystemtracker.org/household-health-spending-calculator/?_sft_hhsc_insurance=average&_sft_hhsc_size=average&_sft_hhsc_income=average&_sft_hhsc_health=average-health See also "State Trends in Employer Premiums and Deductibles: 2010-2020," The Commonwealth Fund, January 12, 2022. https://www.commonwealthfund.org/publications/fund-reports/2022/jan/state-trends-employer-premiums-deductibles-2010-2020.

9. Wendi C. Thomas, "Nonprofit Hospital Almost Never Gave Discounts to Poor Patients During Collections, Documents Show," *ProPublica,* December 4, 2020, https://www.propublica.org/article/nonprofit-hospital-almost-never-gave-discounts-to-poor-patients-during-collections-documents-show.

10. Lunna Lopes, Audrey Kearney, Alex Montero, Liz Hamel, and Mollyann Brodie, "Health Care Debt in the US: the Broad Consequences of Medical and Dental Bills," Kaiser Family Foundation, June 16, 2022, https://www.kff.org/report-section/kff-health-care-debt-survey-main-findings/.

11. Krysten Crawford, "America's Medical Debt is Much Worse Than We Think," *Stanford Institute for Economic Policy Research,* July 20, 2021, https://siepr.stanford.edu/news/americas-medical-debt-much-worse-we-think.

12. Matthew Rae, Gary Claxton, Krutika Amin, Emma Wager, Jared Ortaliza, and Cynthia Cox, "The Burden of Medical Debt in the United States," Kaiser Family Foundation Health Tracker System, March 20, 2022. https://www.healthsystemtracker.org/brief/the-burden-of-medical-debt-in-the-united-states/.

13. Serap Saritas Oran, "Pensions and Social Reproduction," in *Social Reproduction Theory: Remapping Class, Recentering Oppression*, ed. Tithi Bhattacharya (London: Pluto Press, 2017).

14. PRA Group, 2021 Annual Report, https://view.ceros.com/pra-group/2021-annual-report-1-1/p/1.

15. Encore Capital Group, 2021 Annual Report. https://encorecapital.com/sec-filings/annual-reports/.

16. Genevieve LeBaron and Adrienne Roberts, "Confining Social Insecurity: Neoliberalism and the Rise of the 21st Century Debtors' Prison, *Politics and Gender* 8 (2012): 25–49.

17. Alec MacGillis, "Jared Kushner's Other Real Estate Empire in Baltimore," *New York Times*, May 23, 2017, https://www.nytimes.com/2017/05/23/magazine/jared-kushners-other-real-estate-empire.html?smid=fb-share.

18. Tithi Bhattacharya, "Turning a Profit from Death: On Modi's Pandemic Response in Neoliberal India," *Spectre Journal,* May 3, 2021, https://spectrejournal.com/turning-a-profit-from-death/. See also John Nichols, *Coronavirus Criminals and Pandemic Profiteers: Accountability for Those Who Caused the Crisis* (New York: Verso Books, 2022).

19. Regeneron Pharmaceuticals Inc., "Regeneron Announces Manufacturing and Supply Agreement for Barda and U.S. Department of Defense for Regn-COV2 Anti-Viral Antibody Cocktail," *PR Newswire*, July 7, 2020, https://investor.regeneron.com/news-releases/news-release-details/regeneron-announces-manufacturing-and-supply-agreement-barda-and; Jacob Jarvis, "Fact Check: Regeneron Monoclonal Antibody Costs Government $2,100 Per Dose," *Newsweek*, October 12, 2021, https://www.newsweek.com/fact-check-regeneron-regen-cov-covid-monoclonal-antibody-cost-1637526.

20. Regeneron, Regeneron 2022 Proxy Statement and Notice of Annual Shareholder Meeting, June 10, 2022, https://investor.regeneron.com/static-files/872c0727-055f-4df9-9ba9-dec6a565d711. Information is on page 82.

21. US Securities and Exchange Commission, Form 10-K, Annual

Report Pursuant to Section 13 or 15(d) of the Securities Exchange Act of 1934, for the Fiscal Year Ended December 31, 2021,
UnitedHealth Group Incorporated, https://www.investor.jnj.
com/annual-meeting-materials/2022-proxy-statement; https://
www.unitedhealthgroup.com/content/dam/UHG/PDF/inves-
tors/2021/UNH-Q4-2021-Form-10-K.pdf; https://s2.q4cdn.
com/447711729/files/doc_financials/2021/ar/CVS2021_Annu-
al-Report.pdf; https://s27.q4cdn.com/742843823/files/doc_fi-
nancials/2021/q4/ccfa22e8-0ba7-4f44-b01e-0b441829769b.pdf.

22. "Agency Profile: Department of Health and Human Services,"
USASpending.gov, August 30, 2022, https://www.usaspending.
gov/agency/department-of-health-and-human-services?fy=2022.

23. "Audit of DHS Reveals Millions Wasted," Mississippi Office of
the State Auditor, May 4, 2020. https://www2.osa.ms.gov/news/
audit-of-dhs-reveals-millions-wasted/.

24. Center on Budget and Policy Priorities, "Mississippi Raises
TANF Benefits But More Improvements Needed, Especially
in South," May 4, 2021, https://www.cbpp.org/blog/mississip-
pi-raises-tanf-benefits-but-more-improvements-needed-especial-
ly-in-south.

25. *Human Services Stories: 2021 Annual Report*, Mississippi Department of Human Services, https://www.mdhs.ms.gov/annual-re-
ports/. See Anna Wolfe, "Report: Fewer Mississippians Received
Cash Assistance, Even During the Pandemic," *Clarion-Ledger*,
November 14, 2020, https://www.clarionledger.com/story/
news/politics/2020/11/14/tanf-report-fewer-mississippi-resi-
dents-got-cash-assistance-2020/6286660002/.

26. Anna Wolfe, "Deep Dive: Mississippi Not the Only State Turning Away Most Welfare Applicants," *Mississippi Today*, October
5, 2022, https://mississippitoday.org/2022/10/05/mississippi-re-
ject-most-welfare-applicants/; *Human Services Stories: 2021 Annual
Report*, Mississippi Department of Human Services, https://www.
mdhs.ms.gov/annual-reports/.

27. "State-Imposed Child Care Policies Prevent Parents from Working: Results from a Survey of Child Care Payment Program
(CCPP) Child Care Providers," Mississippi Low-Income Child
Care Initiative, September 2021, https://www.mschildcare.org/
reports-policy-analysis/. Author interview via Zoom with Roberta Avila, Jearlean Osborne, Matt Williams, Carol Burnett, Ellen
Reddy, November 2, 2021.

28. Anna Wolfe, "Deep Dive: Mississippi Not the Only State Turning Away Most Welfare Applicants," *Mississippi Today*, October 5, 2022, https://mississippitoday.org/2022/10/05/mississippi-reject-most-welfare-applicants/.

29. Carol Burnett, "Mississippi Democratic Caucus Public Hearing Testimony," May 19, 2022, Jackson, MS. The state requires the childcare centers to spend the grants in six months, but the centers are not getting the necessary information, support, and approvals in a timely manner, resulting in a lag time.

30. Mississippi Low-Income Child Care Initiative, "State-Imposed Child Care Policies Prevent Parents from Working: Results from a Survey of Child Care Payment Program (CCPP) Child Care Providers," September 2021, 2.

31. Josefa Velasquez, "Meet the Company Reaping Big Bucks From N.Y.'s Budget-Busting Medicaid Surge," *The City*, February 24, 2020, https://www.thecity.nyc/health/2020/2/24/21210512/meet-the-company-reaping-big-bucks-from-n-y-s-budget-busting-medicaid-surge.

32. Tracie McMillan, "How One Company is Making Millions Off Trump's War on the Poor," *Mother Jones*, January-February 2019, https://www.motherjones.com/politics/2018/12/how-one-company-is-making-millions-off-trumps-war-on-the-poor/.

33. Hatcher, *The Poverty Industry*, 83.

34. Hatcher, *The Poverty Industry*, 46.

35. Hatcher, *The Poverty Industry*, 68.

36. Maximus, FY2021 Form 10-K for the fiscal year ended September 30, 2021 (filed November 19, 2020), https://investor.maximus.com/sec-filings/all-sec-filings/content/0001628280-21-023790/0001628280-21-023790.pdf.

37. Sarah Jones, "A Distinctly American Irony," *New York*, February 3, 2020, https://nymag.com/intelligencer/2020/02/for-maximus-inequality-is-big-business.html.

38. Jones, "A Distinctly American Irony."

39. Hatcher, *The Poverty Industry*, 1.

40. Maximus, Form 10-K.

41. Maximus, Form 10-K.

42. Hatcher, *The Poverty Industry*, 1.

43. Daniel L. Hatcher, *The Poverty Industry: The Exploitation of America's Most Vulnerable Citizens* (New York: NYU Press, 2016), 38.

44. Julia Conley, "For-Profit Child Care Chains Showered Manchin

in Cash After he Blocked Universal Care," December 16, 2022, https://www.commondreams.org/news/2022/12/16/profit-child-care-chains-showered-manchin-cash-after-he-blocked-universal-care.

45. Hatcher, *The Poverty Industry: The Exploitation of America's Most Vulnerable Citizens*, 28.

46. Rachel Aviv, "How the Elderly Lose Their Rights," *New Yorker*, October 9, 2017, https://www.newyorker.com/magazine/2017/10/09/how-the-elderly-lose-their-rights.

47. Jean Callahan, Raquel Malina Romanick, and Angela Ghesquiere, "Guardianship Proceedings in New York State: Findings and Recommendations," *Bifocal: A Journal of the Commission on Law and Aging* 37, no. 4 (March–April 2016): 83–89; Nina Bernstein, "To Collect Debts, Nursing Homes Are Seizing Control Over Patients," *New York Times*, January 25, 2015, https://www.nytimes.com/2015/01/26/nyregion/to-collect-debts-nursing-home-seizing-control-over-patients.

48. Government Accounting Office, "Cases of Financial Exploitation, Neglect, and Abuse of Seniors," Report to the Chairman, Special Committee on Aging, September 2010.

49. Official statistics about guardianship are not available. See Brenda K. Uekert and Richard Van Duizend, "Adult Guardianships: A 'Best Guess' National Estimate and the Momentum for Reform," *Future Trends in State Courts*, 2011. https://www.eldersandcourts.org/__data/assets/pdf_file/0017/5435/adultguardianships.pdf.

50. Claire Dunning, "New Careers for the Poor: Human Services and the Post-Industrial City," *Journal of Urban History* 44, no. 4 (August 2017): 669–690. Claire Dunning, *Nonprofit Neighborhoods: An Urban History of Inequality and the American State* (Chicago: University of Chicago Press, 2022).

51. Mark Hrywna, "NPT Top 100 (2019): An In-Depth Study of America's Largest Nonprofits," *Nonprofit Times*, November 4, 2019, https://www.thenonprofittimes.com/report/npt-top-100-2019-an-in-depth-study-of-americas-largest-nonprofits/.

52. Theresa Funiciello, *Tyranny of Kindness: Dismantling the Welfare System to End Poverty in America* (New York: Grove Atlantic, 1993), 139. See also Janet Poppendieck, *Sweet Charity: Emergency Food and End of Entitlement* (New York: Penguin, 1999), who writes about the emergency food program serves everyone except the hungry and contributes to the failure to address deeper structural problems

of economic inequality and the dismantling of welfare.

53. Funiciello, *Tyranny of Kindness*, 178–179.

54. Funiciello, *Tyranny of Kindness*, 188–189.

55. Feeding America, website, "About Us," https://www.feedingamerica.org/about-us/financials/990-forms https://www.feedingamerica.org/sites/default/files/2022-03/Feeding%20America%20Form%202020%20fiscal%20year%202021%20-%20Public%20Disclosure.PDF.

56. Steven Rathgeb Smith and Michael Lipsky, *Nonprofits for Hire: The Welfare State in the Age of Contracting Cambridge* (Cambridge: Harvard University Press, 1993), 19.

57. Velasquez, "Meet the Company Reaping Big Bucks From N.Y.'s Budget-Busting Medicaid Surge." This quote was slightly edited after the author's communication with the assemblymember.

58. AIG Retirement Services, *Nonprofit Impact Matters*.

59. Jonathan Levy, "From Fiscal Triangle to Passing Through: Rise of the Nonprofit Corporation," in *Corporations and American Democracy* (Cambridge: Harvard University Press, 2017).

60. US Bureau of Labor Statistics, "Nonprofits account for 12.3 million jobs, 10.2 percent of private sector employment, in 2016," *TED: The Economics Daily*, August 31, 2018, https://www.bls.gov/opub/ted/2018/nonprofits-account-for-12-3-million-jobs-10-2-percent-of-private-sector-employment-in-2016.htm.

61. Lester M. Salamon, "Nonprofits: America's Third Largest Workforce," *Nonprofit Employment Bulletin* 46 (April 2018), http://ccss.jhu.edu/wp-content/uploads/downloads/2018/04/NED-46_National-2015_4.2018.pdf.

62. Independent Sector, "Health of the U.S. Nonprofit Sector: A Quarterly Review," 2022, https://independentsector.org/wp-content/uploads/2022/08/Quarterly-Health-Report-March-2022.pdf.

63. For a critique of nonprofits, see special issue: Navigating Neoliberalism in the Academy, Nonprofits, and Beyond, ed. Soniya Munshi and Craig Willse, *Scholar and Feminist Online* 13, no. 2 (Spring 2016); Dean Spade and Hope Dector, "Queer Dreams and Nonprofit Blues: Understanding the NonProfit Industrial Complex," February 28, 2016, http://www.deanspade.net/2016/02/28/queer-dreams-and-nonprofit-blues/.

64. Linda Oalican, interview by Isabel Terracciano, November 1, 2018.

65. Jonathan Levy, "From Fiscal Triangle to Passing Through: Rise

of the Nonprofit Corporation," in *Corporations and American Democracy* (Cambridge, Harvard University Press, 2017).

66. Oalican interview, November 1, 2018.
67. https://www.investin.care/.
68. Kos, et al., "To Fix the Labor Shortage."

Chapter 7

1. Robyn C. Spencer, *The Revolution Has Come: Power, Gender, and the Black Panther Party in Oakland* (Durham: Duke University Press, 2016); Alondra Nelson, *Body and Soul: The Black Panther Party and the Fight Against Medical Discrimination* (Minneapolis: University of Minnesota Press, 2013); Tracye A. Matthews, "No One Ever Asks What A Man's Role in the Revolution Is: Gender Politics and Leadership in the Black Panther Party 1966–71," in *Sisters in the Struggle*, ed. Bettye Collier-Thomas and V. P. Franklin (New York: New York University Press, 2001).

2. Barker and Feiner, "Affect, Race, and Class"; Alondra Nelson, *Body and Soul: The Black Panther Party and the Fight Against Medical Discrimination* (Minneapolis: University of Minnesota Press, 2011).

3. "One of the Biggest, Baddest Things We Did: Black Panthers' Free Breakfast, 50 Years On," *Guardian*, October 18, 2019, https://www.theguardian.com/us-news/2019/oct/17/black-panther-party-oakland-free-breakfast-50th-anniversary.

4. Johanna Fernández, *The Young Lords: A Radical History* (Chapel Hill, The University of North Carolina Press, February 2020), 111.

5. Pablo "Yoruba" Guzmán, "One Year of Struggle," *Palante*, July 12, 1970, 12. Quoted in Fernandez, *The Young Lords*, 108.

6. Amy Marvin, "Groundwork for Transfeminist Care Ethics: Sara Ruddick, Trans Children, and Solidarity in Dependency," *Hypatia* 34, no. 1 (2019): 101–120; Hil Malatino, *Trans Care* (Minneapolis: University of Minnesota Press, 2020).

7. Cara Page and Erica Woodland, eds., *Healing Justice Lineages: Dreaming at the Crossroads of Liberation, Collective Care, and Safety* (Berkeley: North Atlantic Books, 2023).

8. Harsha Walia, *Undoing Border Imperialism* (Oakland, CA: AK Press), 19.

9. Audio recording, group meeting with Ellen Reddy and NJFC Youth, March 2018, Jackson, MS; Audio recording, group meeting with Ellen Reddy and NJFC Staff, March 2019, Durant, MS;

Premilla Nadasen, "Pedagogy and the Politics of Organizing in Mississippi," *Radical Teacher* 118 (Fall 2020): 64–70.

10. Sandra Killett, Interview with author via Zoom, February 13, 2022.

11. Akemi Nishida, *Just Care: Messy Entanglements of Disability, Dependency, and Desire* (Philadelphia: Temple University Press, 2022); Leah Lakshmi Piepzna-Samarasinha, *Care Work: Dreaming Disability Justice* (Vancouver: Arsenal Pulp Press, 2018).

12. Dean Spade, *Mutual Aid: Building Solidarity During this Crisis (and the Next)* (London: Verso, 2020), 7.

13. China Medel, "Abolitionist Care in the Militarized Borderlands," *South Atlantic Quarterly* 116, no. 4 (October 2017): 874.

14. Medel, "Abolitionist Care in the Militarized Borderlands," 874.

15. Hi'ilei Julia Kawehipuaakahaopulani Hobart and Tamara Kneese, "Radical Care: Survival Strategies for Uncertain Times," *Social Text* 38, no. 1 (2020): 3.

16. Robyn Maynard and Leanne Betasamosake Simpson, *Rehearsals for Living* (Chicago: Haymarket Books, 2022).

17. Andreas Chatzidakis, Jamie Hakim, Jo Littler, Catherine Rottenberg, and Lynne Segal, "From Carewashing to Radical Care: The Discursive Explosions of Care During Covid-19," *Feminist Media Studies* 20, no. 6 (2020): 889–895, quote on 893. For a further discussion, see *The Care Collective, The Care Manifesto: The Politics of Interdependence* (London: Verso, 2020).

18. *The Care Manifesto*, 96.

19. *The Care Manifesto*, 78.

20. Linda Oalican, interview by Narizza Saladino, March 2, 2021.

21. Riley Clare Valentine, "Radicalizing Care: Street Medics and Solidarity," *The Activist History Review*, June 2, 2020.

22. Audre Lorde, "A Burst of Light: Living With Cancer," *A Burst of Light: and Other Essays* (Ithaca: Firebrand Books, 1988), 130.

23. Angela Davis, Gina Dent, Erica R. Meiners, and Beth E. Richie, *Abolition. Feminism. Now.* (Chicago: Haymarket Books, 2022), 5.

24. Davis, et. al, *Abolition. Feminism. Now.*, 3.

25. Mariame Kaba, *We Do This 'Til We Free Us: Abolitionist Organizing and Transforming Justice* (Chicago: Haymarket Books, 2021); Derecka Purnell, *Becoming Abolitionists: Police, Protest, and the Pursuit of Freedom* (New York: Astra House, 2021); Davis, et al., *Abolition. Feminism. Now.*; Ruth Wilson Gilmore, *Abolition Geography: Essays Toward Liberation* (London: Verso, 2022).

26. Mariame Kaba, "Free Us All: Participatory Defense Camaigns as Abolitionist Organizing," New Inquiry, May 8, 2017, https://thenewinquiry.com/free-us-all/; Kaba, *We Do This 'Til We Free Us.*

27. Sarah Alkhafaji, "Activist Mariame Kaba Calls Mutual Aid Key to Ending Prison Industrial Complex at BARS Event," *Daily Pennsylvanian*, February 2, 2022, https://www.thedp.com/article/2021/02/penn-bars-conference-mariame-kaba.

28. Kaba, "Free Us All."

29. "Why a Child Welfare 'Miranda Rights' Law is Essential: A Q&A with Advocate and Organizer Joyce McMillan," The New School Center for New York City Affairs, June 2, 2021. http://www.centernyc.org/urban-matters-2/2021/6/2/why-a-child-welfare-miranda-rights-law-is-essential-a-qampa-with-advocate-and-organizer-joyce-mcmillan; Eileen Grench, "NYC Child Welfare Officials Helped Get Her Fired Over Social Media Posts. Activism Got Her Back on the Job," *The City,* February 11, 2021, https://www.thecity.nyc/work/2021/2/11/22277355/nyc-child-welfare-acs-fired-over-social-media-posts.

30. Roberts, *Torn Apart*, 282.

31. Roberts, *Torn Apart,* 284.

32. Roberts, *Torn Apart,* 291.

33. Ashanté M. Reese and Dara Cooper, "Making Spaces Something Like Freedom: Black Feminist Praxis in the Re/Imagining of Just Food System," *ACME: International Journal for Critical Geographies* 20, no. 4 (2021): 456.

34. Barbara Ransby, *Making All Black Lives Matter: Reimagining Freedom in the Twenty-First Century* (Oakland: University of California Press, 2018), 3.

35. Deva Woodly et. al, "The Politics of Care," *Contemporary Political Theory* 20, no. 4 (2021): 890–925; Deva R. Woodly, *Reckoning: Black Lives Matter and the Democratic Necessity of Social Movements* (Cambridge: Oxford University Press, 2021).

36. Hil Malatino, *Trans Care* (Minneapolis: University of Minnesota Press), 25.

37. See, for example, Jessica Gordon Nembhard, *Collective Courage: A History of African American Cooperative Economic Thought and Practice* (University Park, PA: Pennsylvania State University Press, 2014). Also see Irvin J. Hunt, "Planned Failure: George Schuyler, Ella Baker, and the Young Negroes Cooperative League," *American Quarterly* 72, no. 4 (December 2020).

38. George Caffentzis and Silvia Federici, "Commons Against and Beyond Capitalism," *Upping the Anti: a Journal of Theory and Action* 15 (September 2013): 83–97.
39. Caffentzis and Federici, "Commons against and beyond Capitalism," 103.
40. Caffentzis and Federici, "Commons against and beyond Capitalism," 101.
41. Christopher Paul Harris, "(Caring For) The World That Must be Undone," in *The Politics of Care*, ed. Deva Woodly, et al., 905.
42. Davis, et. al, *Abolition. Feminism. Now.*, 129.
43. Spade, *Mutual Aid*.
44. Barbara Ransby, *Making All Black Lives Matter*, see chapter 8.
45. Nadine Naber, "'The U.S. and Israel Make the Connections for Us': Anti-Imperialism and Black-Palestinian Solidarity," *Critical Ethnic Studies* 3, no. 2 (2017): 17.
46. Miriam Ticktin, "Care and the Commons," quoted in Deva Woodly, et. al., *The Politics of Care*, 918. See also Malatino, *Trans Care*.
47. María Puig de la Bellacasa, *Matters of Care: Speculative Ethics in More Than Human Worlds* (Minneapolis: University of Minnesota Press, 2017).
48. Davis, et. al, *Abolition. Feminism. Now.*, 13.
49. Kim Tallbear, "Making Love and Relations Beyond Settler Sexualities," https://www.youtube.com/watch?v=zfdo2ujRUv8; de la Bellacasa, *Matters of Care*.
50. The Red Nation, "About," http://therednation.org/about/.
51. Alyosha Goldstein with Julia Bernal, Reyes DeVore, Jennifer Marley, and Justine Teba, "For Living Otherwise," *Social Text* 149 (December 2021): 38-45, quote on 42.
52. Goldstein et.al, "For Living Otherwise," 44.
53. Red Nation, "Communism is the Horizon, Queer Indigenous Feminism is the Way," September 21, 2020, https://therednation. org/communism-is-the-horizon-queer-indigenous-feminism-is-the-way/.
54. Melanie K. Yazzie and Cutcha Risling Baldy,"Introduction: Indigenous Peoples and the Politics of Water," *Decolonization: Indigeneity, Education & Society* 7, no. 1 (2018): 1–18.
55. Kathi Weeks, *The Problem with Work: Feminism, Marxism, Antiwork Politics, and Postwork Imaginaries* (Durham: Duke University Press, 2011).

56. For a distinction between work and labor, see Isabella Bakker and Stephen Gill, "Ontology, Method, and Hypotheses" in *Power, Production and Social Reproduction: Human In/security in the Global Political Economy*, ed. Isabella Bakker and Stephen Gill (London: London: Palgrave Macmillan, 2003), 17–41.

57. Piepzna-Samarasinha, *Care Work*, 28.

58. Ashanté Reese and Dara Cooper, "Making Spaces Something Like Freedom," *ACME: An International Journal for Critical Geographies* 20, no. 4 (2021): 454.

59. Audre Lorde, "The Master's Tools Will Never Dismantle the Master's House," in *Audre Lorde, Sister Outsider: Essays and Speeches* (Trumansburg: Crossing Press, 1984), 112.

Index

About Haymarket Books

Haymarket Books is a radical, independent, nonprofit book publisher based in Chicago. Our mission is to publish books that contribute to struggles for social and economic justice. We strive to make our books a vibrant and organic part of social movements and the education and development of a critical, engaged, and internationalist Left.

We take inspiration and courage from our namesakes, the Haymarket Martyrs, who gave their lives fighting for a better world. Their 1886 struggle for the eight-hour day—which gave us May Day, the international workers' holiday—reminds workers around the world that ordinary people can organize and struggle for their own liberation. These struggles—against oppression, exploitation, environmental devastation, and war—continue today across the globe.

Since our founding in 2001, Haymarket has published more than nine hundred titles. Radically independent, we seek to drive a wedge into the risk-averse world of corporate book publishing. Our authors include Angela Y. Davis, Arundhati Roy, Keeanga-Yamahtta Taylor, Eve L. Ewing, Aja Monet, Mariame Kaba, Naomi Klein, Rebecca Solnit, Olúfẹ́mi O. Táíwò, Mohammed El-Kurd, José Olivarez, Noam Chomsky, Winona LaDuke, Robyn Maynard, Leanne Betasamosake Simpson, Howard Zinn, Mike Davis, Marc Lamont Hill, Dave Zirin, Astra Taylor, and Amy Goodman, among many other leading writers of our time. We are also the trade publishers of the acclaimed Historical Materialism Book Series.

Haymarket also manages a vibrant community organizing and event space in Chicago, Haymarket House, the popular Haymarket Books Live event series and podcast, and the annual Socialism Conference.

Also Available from Haymarket Books

Abolition. Feminism. Now.
Angela Y. Davis, Gina Dent, Erica R. Meiners, and Beth E. Richie

Abolition Feminisms Vol. 2
Feminist Ruptures against the Carceral State
Edited by Alisa Bierria, Jakeya Caruthers, and Brooke Lober

The Billboard
Natalie Y. Moore, Foreword by Imani Perry

Black Women Writers at Work
Edited by Claudia Tate, Foreword by Tillie Olsen

Let This Radicalize You:
Organizing and the Revolution of Reciprocal Care
Kelly Hayes and Mariame Kaba
Foreword by Maya Schenwar, Afterword by Harsha Walia

Organizing for Power
Building a 21st Century Labor Movement in Boston
Aviva Chomsky and Steve Striffler

So We Can Know
Writers of Color on Pregnancy, Loss, Abortion, and Birth
Edited by Aracelis Girmay

Waiting in the Wings: Portrait of a Queer Motherhood
Cherríe Moraga

About the Author

© Matt Harvey

Premilla Nadasen is a professor of history at Barnard College, Columbia University. She served as president of the National Women's Studies Association (2018–2020) and is currently codirector of the Barnard Center for Research on Women. Born in South Africa, Nadasen has been involved in social justice organizing for many decades and published extensively on the multiple meanings of feminism, alternative labor movements, and grassroots community organizing. Among her many awards and fellowships are the Fulbright Visiting Professorship, the Marguerite Casey Foundation Freedom Scholar Award, the John Hope Franklin Prize, and the inaugural Ann Snitow Prize for feminist intellectual and social justice activism. Her books include *Welfare Warriors: The Welfare Rights Movement in the United States* and *Household Workers Unite: The Untold Story of African American Women Who Built a Movement.*